The Economy of Kerala
Yesterday, Today and Tomorrow

The Economy of Kerala

Yesterday, Today and Tomorrow

Edited by

B. N. Ghosh

PhD. (India), PhD. (Australia), M.CIM (UK), GFCR (Harvard)
Professor of Economics, Eastern Mediterranean University, Cyprus, and Director (Hon.), Centre for the Study of Human Development, Leeds (UK)

&

Padmaja D. Namboodiri

M.A., M. Phil., PhD. (Kerala)
Head, Department of Economics, S.D. College, Alleppey (Kerala)

SERIALS PUBLICATIONS
NEW DELHI (INDIA)

First Published - 2009

ISBN: 978-81-8387-297-3

Published by

SERIALS PUBLICATIONS
4830/24, Prahlad Street, Ansari Road
Darya Ganj, New Delhi-110002 (India)
Phone : 23245225 Fax : 91-11-23272135
E-mail: serials@satyam.net.in

CONTENTS

PART–THREE
Dimensions of Human Development

PART–FOUR
The Influential Externalities

PREFACE

Kerala, a small state in south India, appears to have a big appeal to development theorists and policy-makers. In spite of its low per capita income and moderate economic growth rate, Kerala has been able to provide a human development index (0.80) which is the best in India, and perhaps also among many developing countries. The Kerala model of human development and social reproduction has been a howling success. The development experiment in Kerala has established the fact that for developing countries in general, the proper emphasis should not be on quantitative economic growth but on human development and improvement of the quality of human life. Development, in fact, does not mean that one has to have more but that one should be more. As exemplified by Kerala, the quality of life does not necessarily depend so much on the absolute level of income as on the pattern of income distribution, social capital and health education and knowledge.

While analysing the story of economic development in Kerala, a plethora of questions flashes across the mind of a development economist. How has Kerala been able to achieve almost cent per cent literacy rate? Why is the life expectancy in Kerala (73 years) the highest in India? Why does Kerala have the lowest fertility rate in India? There are many other similar achievements of Kerala in the area of anthropic development that astonish economists and policy-makers alike.

Unfortunately, many academicians, researchers and students of development economics are still ignoramus about the Kerala model of development. Somehow, the exciting drama of Kerala's development experience is monastically flung apart from the rest of the world. Our first objective to edit this book on the *Economy of Kerala* is to spread the message of its spectacular achievement to the people outside Kerala. Kerala's development experience is not confined merely to public health and education but is pervasively present in all the sectors of the economy of Kerala. Hence, the need for a book on the economy of Kerala to explain this point of view. The sprawling economy of Kerala is not simply to be read about, but deserves a meticulous study. With this aim in mind, we have edited a comprehensive book consisting of two volumes.

In the preparation of this book, we have incurred intellectual indebtedness to many a person; their names are too numerous to make an individual acknowledgement. We have spared no time to discuss various aspects of this book with the faculty members of the Department of Economics, S. D. College, Alleppey. We are thankful to all of them for providing us with many positive externalities and sane suggestions for the improvement of the book.

Our special thanks are due to the valuable contributors who have stolen away some precious time from their busy schedule on our request to write for this book. Their labour of love is immensely appreciated by us. We are also thankful to our publisher, Mr. Vijay Kumar of Serials Publications, New Delhi, who has taken the trouble of publishing it within a very short period of time.

We have tried our best to introduce a bit of product differentiations by making the volume balanced, comprehensive, up-to-date and not-too-technical. A note of caveat is in order: no one involved in this project is implicated for the possible lapses and mistakes that might have remained. The editors are the duopolists of all such shortcomings.

November 23, 2008

B. N. Ghosh
Padmaja Namboodiri

LIST OF CONTRIBUTORS

Anitha S. Ramachandran, M. A., PhD. Reader, P.G Department of Economics N.S.S. College for Women, Trivandrum.

Balju K. C., M.A, M.Phil, Ph. D. Reader and Guide P.G. Department of Economics Institute for Management in Kerala, Trivandrum.

Ghosh, B. N., Ph.D. (India), Ph.D. (Australia), M.CIM (UK), GFCR (Harvard), Professor of Economics, Eastern Mediterranean University, Cyprus, and Director (Hon.), Centre for the Study of Human Development, Leeds (UK).

G. Gopikuttan, M.A Ph.D. Former Head of the Department of Economics, N.S.S. College, Pandalam. At present with Project on Human Development Report at Centre for Development Studies, Trivandrum.

Jose J. Naduthotty, M.A, M.Phil, Ph.D. Reader and Guide, P.G. Department of Economics . St. Dominic College, Kajirappally.

Kumari Latha Devi, M.A, M.Phil. Ph.D., Selection Grade Lecturer, P.G. Department of Economics N.S.S. College for Women, Trivandrum.

K. Gangadharan, M.A. Ph.D. Reader and Head, School of Development Studies, Department of Applied Economics, Kannur University.

Lathika M., M.A., M.Phil, Ph.D., Selection Grade Lecturer, P.G. Department of Economics N.S.S. College for Women, Trivandrum.

N. Madhava Menon, M.A, M.Phil, Ph.D., Reader, P.G. Department of Economics N.S.S. College , Cherthala.

Padmaja D. Namboodiri, M.A., M. Phil., PhD., Head, Department of Economics, S.D. College, Alleppey.

P. Krishna Kumar, M.A. Ph.D., Reader, P.G. Department of Economics, M.G. College Trivandrum.

P. Rajendran Nair, M.A, M.Phil. Ph.D., Selection Grade Lecturer, P.G Department of Economics N.S.S. CollegePandalam.

Usha L. R., M.A, M.Phil, Ph.D., Selection Grade Lecturer P.G. Department of Economics, Fathima Matha National College, Kollam.

AN INTRODUCTION TO THE ECONOMY OF KERALA: A SYNOPTIC VIEW

B. N. Ghosh & Padmaja Namboodiri

It is said that those who can perform, they do, but those who cannot, they teach. Those who cannot teach, do research, and those who cannot do research, edit books. Whilst there is some substratum of truth in this statement, it is not, like all other sayings, completely a gospel truth. Editing a book needs a very special type of knowledge and vast experience on the subject. An editor might not have done substantial research in each and every aspect of the area, but he/she is fully acquainted with the nitty-gritty of the whole subject. A subject like the economy of Kerala encompasses many dimensions, and its development is so expansive and complexifying that it is impossible for one person to be a specialist in the true sense of the term. Hence, editing a book on such a subject becomes imperative. In this volume, we have incorporated the papers from those teachers and researchers who have specialised in a particular area of the Keralian economy.

The economy of Kerala has many ramifications including its growth dynamics, structural changes, labour market problems, social reproduction and so on, and rapid changes have taken place in all these sectors during the last two decades or so.

Padmaja Namboodiri (Chapter one) observes that Kerala's trajectory of development has been marked by social investment, redistribution, reforms by the State, relatively poor growth rates in the commodity producing sectors and high quality of living standards. Despite the fact that there are growth-enhancing effects of social investment, the stagnation of the Kerala economy in the 1970s and 1980s raised serious questions about the viability and sustainability of its developmental trajectory. An overview of the Kerala Economy from 1980-2005 shows that the decade of 1980s was a period of deceleration and positive signs of recovery were seen in the state economy in the 1990s. The potential growth rate of the economy was estimated to be 5.44 per cent. The ratio of actual to potential output was taken as an index of inefficiency. The index of inefficiency calculated for the twenty years showed that six years were marked by high percentage of inefficiency in the 1980s,while only four years were reporting inefficient use of resources in the 1990s. This validated the hypothesis that there are still factors constraining the growth of the Kerala economy.

The sectoral growth accounting established that 39.23 per cent share of the primary sector in Net State Domestic Product in 1980-81 decreased to 28.72 per cent in 1999-2000. The contribution of secondary sector hovered around 22 per cent for the entire 25-year period showing stagnation in that sector. Tertiary sector's share in NSDP was 36 per cent in 1980-81 but increased to 50.64 per cent in 1999-2000. By 2006, the shares were 17.8%, 21.6% and 60.6% respectively. After a detailed of analysis of the various factors affecting the primary sector, the author concluded that the non-availability of extra-land area and large amount of rural unemployment had constrained growth of the primary sector.

The bleak power situation, lack of infrastructure facilities and trade unionism do not provide a climate for industrialisation in the state economy. The on-going reform process which had a positive impact on the whole economy, did not provide a growth-stimulating effect in the industrial sector. The findings of the study also suggest the shyness of capital from within and outside the state to flow into industrial investment. The inadequate capital investment has constrained the pace of modernisation of old units and establishment of new units and products based on modern technology. The growth of the tertiary sector is associated with the growth of social development in Kerala. Tertiary sector has shown good growth rate during the period of analysis.

The study makes it clear that the stagnation in growth rate observed in the eighties is over and a new phase of growth revival has already set in the Kerala economy in the post-reforms period. The study assigns a critical role to technology in accentuating the momentum of growth in Kerala. Private investment becomes necessary as the state coffers are dwindling, and the state no longer can be expected to herald the growth process in the economy. In this context, an investor friendly climate must be brought in at the initiative of the State Government.

B. N. Ghosh asserts that the trajectory of economic development in a country is closely related to its occupation structure, and elaborates on the pattern and implications of the present occupation structure for a developing state like Kerala. A study of Kerala's occupation structure shows that it is much more developed than that of India as a whole, and its occupation structure is better poised for further development. There are a few interesting facts on this issue. First, although the primary sector is shedding labour at the highest rate compared to other sectors, the unemployment rate in the rural sector stands out to be still much higher than that of the urban sector. Second, there exists some scope for the absorption of additional labour in both tertiary and industrial sectors with higher productivity, provided these are modernised with better technology, and capital per worker is adequately augmented. The fact that an increase in capital per worker can significantly improve productivity has been recognised by many economists including Robert Solow. The Solow model of growth (1956) clearly states that output (income) per worker is given by the square root of capital per worker. Thus, a large amount of capital is indeed necessary to bring about some perceptible change in labour productivity. Finally, a sustainable increase in labour productivity is not possible unless human capital and skill endowment of the labour force are significantly improved.

The Keralian economy has not yet attained optimum occupational distribution, for a sectoral reallocation of labour force from agriculture to non-agricultural sector will enhance labour productivity. While this is factually true, it seems to be practically problematic to transfer labour from agriculture unless the primary sector is re-organised, modernised and technologically refurbished, and at the same time, the non-agricultural sector generates sufficient pull factors. But to reorganise the agricultural sector in a slowly-developing state like Kerala will indeed be a heroic undertaking.

In many developing countries, economic infrastructure, particularly electric power is a crucial infrastructure for economic development. N. Madahava Menon's chapter elaborates on the issue in Kerala. The chapter concentrates on the history and growth of power sector, plan-wise achievement of the power sector in Kerala, growth of Kerala's power system in terms of installed capacity generation per annum, per capita consumption of power, import and export of power, growth of transmission and distribution lines, number of consumers and connected load, number of villages electrified; category wise consumers and so on are also reviewed.

It is found from the study that there is a wide gap in the generation and consumption of power in the state. In addition to this, the enormous increase in the demand for power, high transmission and distribution losses add to the power crisis in the state. So an urgent attention needs to be paid not only for increasing the generation but also for reforming the entire T & D system.

But will the decentralised planning model contribute anything substantial to the development of the Keralin economy? The answer is provided by G. Gopikuttan's discussion on the democratic decentralised planning in Kerala. It has been appreciated as a 'model' to be emulated in the rest of the country. The way in which the state has devolved functions, functionaries and finances to the lower levels and the process of decentralised development administration, fiscal decentralisation and local governance has been adjudged the best practice among the Indian states. At present the Local Self Governments (LSGs) have more than a decade of experience in development planning through a democratic and participatory process. *Grama Panchayats* and urban local bodies are mandated to identify the felt needs of the local people and to prepare projects and implement development plans through a participatory process that ensures direct democracy.

Majority of programmes and projects planned under the participatory planning programme were oriented towards the weaker sections of the society, which form only a minority in the local context. The dominant middle class does not see any significant stakes in such activities. This reduced the interest and hence a threat to the lofty ideal of participation expected in plan preparation and implementation. Hence, democratic and participatory discussions and transparent decision-makings became relatively absent in *grama sabha* meetings and *Panchayat* development seminars. These meeting and seminars are held occasionally by the *Panchayat* Board to satisfy constitutional obligations. Since the message of an integrated development agenda has not been percolated down to the grass roots, each ward member began to fight for more schemes and benefits to the ward they represent. Hence, it became difficult to achieve an integrated and balanced development of all regions in the *Panchayat*.

Kerala being a highly politicised State, civil society organisations failed to garner the expected space for democratic dialogues and discussions. They also thought not to invite the ire of the dominant parties. Moreover, voluntarism for regular work such as periodic assessment of the objective realities of the locality, preparation of plans and projects and monitoring of the local development activities would not sustain for long. Cultural attitudes of nucleation with the new media culture of television keep people, especially the young ones away form the public space. Young social workers/volunteers keep high aspirations and expectations about personal gains in terms of positions in institutions or democratically elected bodies. When they find that chances for such gains are bleak in PPC, they started withdrawing from the scene. Like in other parts of the globe, the middle class in Kerala that forms the majority pursue neo-liberal attitude and market approach to development, while the marginalised sections, which form only a minority, look forward to local governments for support to satisfy their basic needs. However, despite these challenges, we hope that with correct and factual database, professional support, clarity of functions and responsibilities and encouraging political and social environment, the democratic decentralisation can definitely be rejuvenated.

Coming to the sectoral development, it is acknowledged that agriculture occupies an important position in the economy of Kerala and it continues to be the same even with the remarkable and commendable strides in the non-agricultural sectors of the state. The story of agriculture is told by M. Lathika. Her chapter seeks primarily to examine the growth performance of agriculture in Kerala over the two distinct phases of the Indian economy, namely, pre- and post-liberalisation periods, and makes an enquiry into the factors that contributed to the current state of affairs in agriculture in the state. Kerala maintains a distinct identity in the agricultural map of India, due not only to its highly productive agro-climatic resource-base but also to its peculiar farming behaviour in terms of its diverse crop pattern with heavy dominance of cash crops, and the higher dependence on international demands. However, the evolution of its economy to its current form, in which agriculture takes a consistently declining role in the economy and the food crops getting increasingly replaced by cash crops, is bound to have disastrous consequences on its food and livelihood security. The process of liberalisation made the economy open and the resultant integration of domestic market with the global economy witnessed a host of problems emerging in the agricultural scene of Kerala - the main one being the price crash of cash crops. Though some crops grew strongly competitive thereafter, others failed to cope with the shocks. These developments have their social sway as well. The new trend of hectic land transfers shot up land prices. The commoditisation of land alienated the peasantry from the land they tilled hitherto. Many of the farmers who ventured new cropping pattern, braving the challenges put up by the newly clamped liberalisation regime, suffered great losses. Some of them finally succumbed to the psychological stress they had undergone, leaving the planners and development experts to find urgent ways to salvage the agricultural sector, especially the food grain agriculture, from the maladies it is currently experiencing. In the context of Kerala's reducing acreage for the purpose of cultivation, one can discuss the situation of land use pattern in Kerala.

The chapter by P. Rajendran Nair analyses land use and cropping pattern in Kerala. He asserts that agriculture in Kerala is passing through a crisis, which has not ever experienced since the formation of the state in 1956. Progressive land reform policies of erstwhile communist government of 1957 placed before Kerala a unique model for social transformation and agricultural development. But none of these steps enabled to uplift Kerala agriculture from the deplorable stage. Massive transformation of agricultural land for non agricultural purposes, conversion of paddy fields for economic crops, reclamation of paddy lands for commercial purposes, massive growth of real estate business and it's profitability, growth of land mafias with political patronage and growing demand for house plots reduce the acreage of net cultivable land. Change in the lifestyle accompanied by attitudinal changes towards agriculture further bleakened the glory of agriculture. Non-profitability of agriculture with soaring costs pulled the farmers to bankruptcy and thus to seek a relief in suicide. Massive suicide of farmers marked a symbol of present agriculture crisis in Kerala. In order to surpass the crisis, now Government of Kerala is introducing a number of steps to promote agriculture through people's participation programs. Financial support is given to NeighbourHood Groups (NHGs) of both men and women to initiate agricultural activities. Kudumbasree has introduced Haritha Sree Programme to cultivate fruits, vegetables and paddy through Lease Land Farming. Last year, Lease Land Farming was done in 57436.28 acres. A total of

3,54,513 families hailing from 35130 Neighbourhood groups were engaged in agricultural activities. Moreover National Rural Employment Guarantee Programme is in implementation in Kerala through which a good support can be given to agricultural promotion. But the sector has a lot of unemployment problem (20%).

P. Kumari Latha Devi dwells on the problem of unemployment in Kerala. Unemployment rate in Kerala, both rural and urban, has been increasing and already reached an alarming level in the beginning of this millennium. On the basis of NSSO survey reports, it was estimated that the rates of both urban and rural unemployment is the highest among the Indian States. It has been noticed that the rise in both rural and urban unemployment rates after 1999-2000 till 2004-05 was much larger than the rise during the period between 1993-94 and 1999-2000. The high incidence of rural unemployment in Kerala may be attributed to the factors such as the existence of small and marginal farmers, uneconomic land holdings, low productivity of major crops, changes in the crop pattern from more labour intensive crop like paddy to less labour intensive commercial crops, decline of traditional labour intensive rural cottage and small-scale industries, occupational shifting of workers from agricultural to non-agricultural activities, rural-urban migration, fall in the prices agricultural commodities, agricultural price instability, distress sales, lack of agricultural research and other institutional factors like poor implementation of land reform measures, agricultural marketing problems and non-availability of cheap credit facilities to the farmers. The incidence of high urban unemployment in Kerala is mainly due to the fact of growing unemployment among the educated and youth. It is also due to the structure of urban labour market which is highly characterized by casual employment. It has been noticed that female unemployment is comparatively higher in Kerala especially in urban areas and it is in the nature of educated unemployment. Female work participation rate is low compared to the national level. It has been already estimated that nearly 50 per cent of the rural female educated labour force and 42 per cent of the female urban labour force are unemployed. The incidence of unemployment among females in the state is higher than among males by two times in the rural areas and by three times in the urban areas. Thus it can be concluded that the problem of unemployment in Kerala is not just one of unemployment among the urban educated youth alone, but the unemployment and under-employment among rural workers in primary sectors like agriculture and household industries and women unemployment are really the major concerns.

Like unemployment, poverty is a serious issue in Kerala, and P. Krishnakumar explains the situation at some length. Past experience of the State of Kerala shows that instead of attempting to alleviate poverty by providing minimum purchasing power/income, we have tried to improve the quality of life of the people. For that objective, the State spent substantial amount on health, education, housing and other basic services, to make it accessible to the poor. Moreover, special attention was given to ensure food security and social security to the poor. But since the late 1970's, we also followed the national policy of direct attack on poverty. It was done by providing assistance to self-employment schemes and wage employment programmes. The decentralised economic planning has to a greater extent enabled the local self government to identify the locally specific problems and tackle them. As a result of all the developmental efforts made after the formation of the State and earlier, Kerala maintains better human development index. Our social development can be compared with that of the advanced nations. But the paradoxical situation is that social development is not reflected in economic performance. Due to high social development, Keralites face a concealed type of poverty, which is remarkably different from that in other parts of India. What we need now is not to under-estimate the intensity of poverty in Kerala. We should formulate appropriate programmes to improve the rural sector to find out viable, workable and sustainable solutions to the problems related to poverty in our state. Rampant poverty and unemployment have compelled people to accept outward-looking attitude and to migrate from the state.

Usha L. R. in her chapter elaborates on various phases of migration from India and Kerala. Following the oil price hike of 1973, Keralites began to emigrate in large numbers to the Middle East countries. This outflow of unskilled, semiskilled and skilled workers continued unabated till 1985. The leading districts of emigrants were Malappuram, Trissur and Thiruvananthapuram. Wayanad and Idukki were the lowest in the list of emigrants. Muslims constituted almost half of the emigrants. Kerala received large amount of remittances and this had its impact on the economy. With economic recession in the Gulf region in the second half of the 1980s, there was a return flow of emigrants to Kerala. The Kuwait war and subsequent wage cut and competition from low-paid workers from other Asian countries resulted in large scale return of migrants in the 1990s. About 16.5 lakh Keralites are now working in the Middle East countries, constituting about 89% of the total emigrants from Kerala. The remittances amounted to Rs 24525 crores in 2007 which was about 21.6% of the Net State Domestic Product. Though there was a large inflow of remittances, it could not be effectively utilized for the development of the state. The industrial backwardness, lack of entrepreneurship, initiatives, absence of industrial infrastructure and shortage of power, etc. acted as constraints in utilizing the skills acquired by the returnee emigrants.

There is often a counter-flow of people, even though for a short period from a country of emigration. Baiju K. C. in this context, elaborates on the history of tourism in Kerala. Tourism in Kerala made tremendous strides since 1950s and this trend is expected to move on higher ladders. History shows that tourism in Kerala had close association with limited areas such as trade, religions and cultural movements, whereas in due course it extended itself towards large spectrums assuming different forms in different situations, locations and time. However, the haphazard development of tourism has created unsavory impacts in many areas such as society, environment and culture. In addition, the basic infrastructure development of the region remains the main bottleneck. Some other national level challenges/issues like terrorism and violence, language barriers, diplomatic relations, lack of awareness, customs, immigration and health are also to be addressed. Too much effective emphasis is required to tap the employment and income potential of local tourism like better human resource management in manpower planning, value addition, job specialization, multi-skill and multi-functioning system, competencies in hospitality industry, off the job training, performance management system etc. Moreover, the regional economy has to make perspective planning in tourism in its employability and income potential at the global level.

The inflow and outflow of people do bring about some interactions at the national and global levels. Education plays a vital role in the migration of people; it empowers people and creates many externalities. It provides exposure and access to new ideas and ways of thinking and triggers a demand for change. Education has had many positive externalities, and it can play an important role in reduction of poverty The basic features of education in Kerala is explained by Anitha S. Ramchandran.

Kerala's remarkable progress in the field of social development and high quality of living are mainly attributed to the educational advancement the state has made over the past so many years. It has the dual distinction of achieving total literacy and quality of life which is comparable to that of the developed countries of the world. This success in spreading education is the natural continuation of a great past which goes back to the first few centuries of the Christian era.

Kerala has several features that distinguish it from the rest of India. Its efforts in improving the quality of life of its population reckoned in terms of life expectancy, sex ratio and literacy are well known. Further, Kerala is far ahead of other states in achieving the goal of universalizing elementary education. The state is ranked first in Educational Development Index (2005-06) and also first among major Indian states in the Human Development Index (HDI) at the three time points of 1981,1991 and 2001. This appears even more dazzling when we observe that these achievements occurred in the absence of high levels of income and economic development.

No doubt, Kerala's achievement in the field of literacy is laudable. We have unlimited scope for the development of human capital, the foundations of which have already been laid through a well developed system of primary and secondary education. But when it comes to higher education, our performance is not up to the mark. After successfully tackling the first generation problems, we are now dealing with the second generation problems. Hence, for a sustained development of the higher education sector, we have to maintain a proper balance between the immediate requirements of the job market and the future needs of the country.

Like education, health is an important part of human capital, and both are intimately connected to each other. We have two chapters on health.

B. N. Ghosh's paper cannibalises on the Kerala model of public health system and traces out its operational trajectory in the pre and post-liberalisation periods, arguing that the so-called Kerala model of development is not so much about development as it is on social reproduction. It resolves the twin paradoxes in the healthcare sector, elaborating on the success of the model in the pre-liberalisation era, and posits that in the post-liberalisation period, a constellation of factors and forces responsible for the conundrum of high morbidity amidst low mortality may lead to the imminent failure of the model. The paper is basically related to the structural transformation in the area of occupations in a small state in India (Kerala). Arguably, the paper posits that structural shift of people from the rural to the urban sector implies that higher income generated in the latter sector can be spent on health and family welfare. Moreover, the urban sector has many more facilities and opportunities for the maintenance of better health. However, with the development of the urban sector and a rapid rate of industrialisation, more and more pressure is generated on the environment of the country.

Another chapter on health dwells on Kerala's health services including their features, problems and policy options. In his chapter, K. Gangadharan finds that though the health status of Kerala is comparatively far better compared to other

Indian states, Kerala still has many lurking problems. First and foremost event is the issue of high morbidity reported both from urban and rural Kerala. Communicable and chronic illness are equally disturbing in the state causing for the hike in morbidity. Lack of basic infrastructural facilities in the interior rural, urban and slum areas are responsible for the hike in illness prevalence rate. In this context, he suggests a number of policy options. Human health is obviously related to environment.

The problems faced in the matter of environment have been elaborated by Jose J. Naduthotty. He affirms that the environmental problems of Kerala are, on the whole, within manageable limits. However there is the absence of an efficient environmental management system. Perhaps, more serious issue is the absence of urgency on the part of the government to deal with environmental issues in a proactive way. There is a dearth of relevant information on many critical aspects. This, perhaps explains why, none of the currently available volumes on Kerala economy, has an exclusive chapter devoted to environment. One may explain away this lacuna by saying that environment is everywhere so that there is no need of a special chapter. But that would amount to repudiating well accepted principles of sustainable development and going against the current trend in Development Economics. When environment is made a mere appendix of production and consumption system, no one will seriously take into account the repercussions of his action on environment. It is very important to place environment at the very centre of all development programmes and planning.

PART–ONE

Economic Growth and Structural Changes

1

KERALA'S TRAJECTORY OF ECONOMIC GROWTH– A MACRO PERSPECTIVE

PADMAJA D. NAMBOODIRI

Economists, right from Adam Smith have always been concerned with the theme of economic growth. This is probably because every society aims at increasing its skills and means to satisfy its needs. Economic, organizational socio-cultural, natural, technical and political conditions prevailing in the society is very vital for achieving this goal. Economic development can be viewed as an interactive process between social, economic and technological factors leading to sustained growth with structural breaks in overall rate of components, pattern, casual elements and their sources.

Empirical and quantitative studies of economic growth have made great advances during the past century. The greater complexity of society and the desire of policy makers and interest groups to influence some of the basic parameters in the economy increased the need for statistical indicators to monitor the economic performance on a more systematic basis than before.

Conventional economic theory argues that high living index is the outcome of high economic growth. In other words

Human Development Indicators like high literacy, public health facilities, social security measures etc. are possible only in a high income society. Against this background of conventional growth theories, the State of Kerala stands out occupying a unique position in the economic, social and political arenas. The unique development trajectory followed by Kerala economy caught the attention of international growth economists when a study sponsored by the United Nations in the early 1970s on the State's economic and social performance was conducted by the experts of the Centre for Development studies under Dr.K.N. Raj. They found the indicators of social development in low levels of birth and death rates, high literacy levels, low infant mortality rates, importance given to girl's education, health care consciousness etc..

"The fact that Kerala is a relatively poor state in India when judged by conventional norms such as per capita income, that the average per capita availability of food is lower in Kerala than in most parts of India; but that nevertheless it has been possible for the state to make fairly impressive advances in the spheres of health and education, and hence bring about improvements that have made a perceptible difference to the quality of life-as also the acquisition of attitudes and skills that could help to accelerate development at the next stage- has certainly some lessons for similar societies seeking social and economic advance". [Centre for Development studies, 1977, p. 153).

Kerala model of development attracted world wide attention. The paradox of high social development *vis-à-vis* economic deceleration in Kerala has already been well documented in economic literature. The growth indices like State Domestic Product, agricultural and industrial production, employment etc. have been showing an uneven trend over the decades. From negative growth rates and virtual stagnation in the 1970's, state income remained stable and oscillating in 1980s.But from 1990s the economy has been indicating definite signs of recovery. A notable feature of the resurgence of economic activity in Kerala is that it coincides with the opening up of the economy.

At the same time the Human Development Indices (HDI) like high literacy levels and female enrolment rates, high life expectancy rate, low infant mortality rates etc. are much above the national average and at par with developed nations. Another notable feature of the state is the uninterrupted international labour migration starting from 1970s. Kerala is also unique in implementing land reforms and decentralised planning in a very effective way. Growth and development issues are now tackled at the Ward/Panchayath/District levels in Kerala.

World Banks' World Development Report 2001 states, "There are also marked differences within India-with the South, particularly the state of Kerala, having sharply better education and health; Kerala has life expectancies greater than those in Washington DC despite vastly lower income levels. The effectiveness of public action in Kerala has been attributed to its strong tradition of political and social mobilisation" (*World Development Report, 2001, 34).*

In this paper an attempt is made to study the growth experience of Kerala economy in recent decades. An identification of the main factors and sources of growth which influenced the economic activity in Kerala over a period of two and a half decades from 1980-81 to 1999-2005 will help to get an overall view of the variables hindering economic growth. An analysis of the state income in the pre and post liberalization periods is followed by a discussion on sectoral changes in the same period culminating in the positives and negatives of Kerala's development trajectory.

GROWTH OF STATE INCOME: KERALA'S PRE LIBERALIZATION SCENARIO (1980-81 TO 1999-2000)

State income is the most important yardstick by which economic growth of an economy is measured. State income is defined as Net State Domestic Product at factor cost (NSDP) and it is the factor income generated within the geographical boundary of a state or it is the sum total of the net value added in the economy in a given period of time. This means that the inflow of remittances from the non resident Keralites are not taken into consideration in the calculation of state income.

An overview of the Kerala economy is undertaken in this section. It is found that the decade of 1980s was a period of deceleration and positive signs of recovery were seen in the state economy in the 1990s.

An accurate measurement of real NSDP has to be undertaken because the long-term nature of the economy's ability to produce goods and services, which the study seeks to analyse, cannot be measured directly, but can be inferred under certain conditions from the measured increase in actual production over a period of time. "The measured increase in real NSDP or actual production is a function of: (a) the growth of economy's potential production that is its ability to produce goods and services and (b) changes in the ratio of actual production to potential production. The former depends on changes in the quantity and quality of the various factors of production and the factors such as the advance of knowledge which raise the average productivity of the available factors of production while the latter is governed by the relationship between aggregate demand and potential production and consequent changes in the intensity of resource utilization". (Dholakia 1974, 15–16).

According to Table 1 Kerala's state income increased by 126.16 per cent over the period 1980-81 to 1999-2000, or at an average annual rate of 4.39 per cent. Like any other average, this average rate obtained for the period as a whole conceals wide differences in the sectoral and temporal patterns of growth.

Table 1 reveals the NSDP in current prices as well as in 1993-94 constant prices and shows yearly growth rates. The trend is that in the decade of 1980s Kerala Economy experienced volatile fluctuations in the growth rates of NSDP. 1981-82, 1983-84 and 1986-87 were years of negative growth rates for the economy. An examination of early years of 1980 shows that 1981-82 and 83-84 were years of drought and lack of monsoon for the economy. A silver lining in this decade is that in 1984-85 the economy was able to recover remarkably well and achieve high level of economic activity. 6.19% growth rate for the year 1984-85 is to be applauded. In the

Table 1
Net State Domestic Product-Kerala State 1980–81: 1999-2000

Year	*In current Prices*	*In Constant Prices 93-94 Series*	*Deflator Value*	*% Growth*	*Index No*
1980-81	382273	1436604	0.27		100.00
1981-82	404973	1418595	0.29	-1.25	98.75
1982-83	471150	1453808	0.32	2.48	101.20
1983-84	552338	1394870	0.40	-4.05	97.09
1984-85	614145	1481268	0.41	6.19	103.11
1985-86	650341	1535677	0.42	3.67	106.90
1986-87	735437	1500581	0.49	-2.29	104.45
1987-88	825756	1565467	0.53	4.32	108.97
1988-89	918172	1722731	0.53	10.05	119.92
1989-90	1066463	1838577	0.58	6.72	127.98
1990-91	1217349	1977617	0.62	7.56	137.66
1991-92	1510165	2016070	0.75	1.94	140.34
1992-93	1717520	2161488	0.79	7.21	150.46
1993-94	1968826	2385107	0.83	10.35	166.02
1994-95	2837516	2690792	1.10	8.62	180.34
1995-96	3446965	2694747	1.28	4.01	187.58
1996-97	3965630	2802645	1.41	4.00	195.09
1997-98	4617801	2863315	1.61	2.16	199.31
1998-99	5355267	3039853	1.76	6.17	211.60
1999 -00	6255675	3249050	1.93	6.88	226.16

Source: Department of Economics and Statistics, Trivandrum, (2000).

years 1988-89 also, the economy had exemplary performance, a commendable growth rate of 10.05 per cent. But the over all growth performance for the decade of 1980-81 to1989-90 was only 2.78 per cent as revealed by Table 2.

Table 2
Decadal Growth Rates of NSDP-Kerala State 1980-81 to 1999-2000

Year	*Annual Compound Growth Rate*
1980-81 to 99-00	4.39
1980-81 to 89-90	2.78
1990-91 to 99-00	5.67

Source: Computed from Table 1.

The decade of 1990 reveals the slow recovery process of the economy. Except for the years 1991-92 and 1997-98, the economy achieved more than 4 per cent annual growth rates in the decade. Among the years 1993-94 was an exciting year with tremendous achievement of 10.35 per cent growth rate. Annual compound growth rate for the decade of 1990 (1990-91 to 99-2000) was 5.67 per cent as shown in Table 2 The over all annual compound growth rate for the whole economy for the period from 1980-81 to 1999-2000 was 4.39 per cent.

As already noted above, this extreme irregularity of changes in real NSDP brings out the dominating part played by the changes in the ratio of actual to potential output in the determination of the short term growth rates.

INDEX OF INEFFICIENCY-RATIO OF ACTUAL TO POTENTIAL NSDP

In this section, an attempt is made to calculate the potential growth rate of Kerala economy. This rate will reflect the ability of the Kerala economy to produce economic goods and services if the full utilisation of all the resources occurs in the economy.

The method adopted to estimate the potential growth rate is taken from Dr. Dholakia's (1974) analysis which necessitates the identification of two prosperous years from among the period of study, and calculating the average compound growth rate between these two years.

The economic performance of the Kerala economy over the period from 1980-81 to 1999-2000 (See Table 1) shows that 1984-85 and 1993-94 stand apart in terms of achievements. The year 1984-85 showed remarkable recovery and 6.19% growth after three years of economic deceleration. In the decade of 1990s, the year 1993-94 recorded 10.35% growth, an achievement unprecedented in the history of Kerala's economic growth. Therefore these two years are chosen for the purpose of calculating potential growth rate. If the economy could achieve 6.19 per cent growth after virtual stagnation and also 10.35 per cent growth rate in a normal year, it is ample proof that in all the other years of study, the economy was not utilising its potential capacity. Therefore, it is necessary to estimate the potential growth rate of the economy, to know the long term sustainability of the economy.

POTENTIAL GROWTH RATE

The potential growth rate for the Kerala economy computed using average compound growth rate between the growth rates of 1984-85 and 1993-94 gives the result as 5.44%. Table 3 gives NSDP both in current prices and constant prices (1993-94 base year) and annual growth rates in both series. Then using the potential growth rate of 5.44%, potential output of Net Domestic Product is estimated. Keeping 1980-81 output as the initial box year, the deviations from previous year's constant value are used to calculate the potential output. (1436604 x 1.0544).

Table 3
Net State Domestic Product-Kerala State 1980-81 to 1999-2000
Actual and Potential Output (in Crores)

			Annual Growth Rate at		
Year	*Current prices*	*Constant prices*	*Current*	*Constant*	*Potential Output*
1980-81	382,273	1,436,604	-	-	1436604
81-82	404,973	1,418,595	5.94	-1.25	1,514,755.26
82-83	471,150	1,453,808	16.34	2.48	1,495,766.57
83-84	552,338	1,394,870	17.23	-4.05	1,532,895.16
84-85	614,145	1,481,268	11.19	6.19	1,470,750.93
85-86	650,341	1,535,677	5.89	3.67	1,561,848.98
86-87	735,437	1,500,581	13.08	-2.29	1,619,217.83
87-88	825,756	1,565,467	12.28	4.32	1,582,212.61
88-89	918,172	1,722,731	11.19	10.05	1,650,628.40
89-90	1,066,463	1,838,577	16.15	6.72	1,816,447.57
90-91	1,217,349	1,977,617	14.15	7.56	1,938,595.59
91-92	1,510,165	2,016,070	24.05	1.94	2,085,199.36
92-93	1,717,520	2,161,488	13.73	7.21	2,125,744.21
93-94	1,968,826	2,385,107	14.63	10.35	2,279,072.95
94-95	2,837,516	2,590,792	44.12	8.62	2,514,856.82
95-96	3,446,965	2,694,747	21.48	4.01	2,731,731.08
96-97	3,965,630	2,802,645	15.05	4.00	2,841,341.24
97-98	4,617,801	2,863,315	16.45	2.16	2,955,108.89
98-99	5,355,267	3,039,853	15.97	6.17	3,019,079.34
1999-2000	6,255,675	3,249,050	16.81	6.88	3,205,221.00

Source: Table 1.

In Table 4 the ratio of actual to potential NSDP is given. Values less than one indicate the extent of deviation of actual output from potential output. This can be taken as a percentage of inefficiency as far as the economy is concerned.

Table 4
Index of Inefficiency-Ratio of Actual to Potential NSDP

Year	*Actual NSDP*	*Potential*	*Actual*	*Inefficiency*
1980-81	1,436,604	1,436,604		-
81-82	1,418,595	1,514,755	0.94	6
82-83	1,453,808	1,495,766	0.97	3
83-84	1,394,870	1,532,895	0.91	9
84-85	1,481,268	1,470,750	1.01	-
85-86	1,535,677	1,561,848	0.98	2
86-87	1,500,581	1,619,217	0.93	7
87-88	1,565,467	1,582,212	0.99	1
88-89	1,722,731	1,650,628	1.04	-
89-90	1,838,577	1,816,447	1.01	-
90-91	1,977,617	1,938,595	1.02	-
91-92	2,016,070	2,085,199	0.97	3
92-93	2,161,488	2,125,744	1.02	-
93-94	2,385,107	2,279,072	1.05	-
94-95	2,590,792	2,514,856	1.03	-
95-96	2,694,747	2,731,731	0.99	1
96-97	2,802,645	2,841,341	0.99	1
97-98	2,863,315	2,955,108	0.97	3
98-99	3,039,853	3,019,079	1.01	-
1999-2000	3,249,050	3,205,221	1.01	-

Source: Table 3.

Table 4 reveals that in the 1980s, the Kerala economy was performing very badly except for 3 years-1984-85, 1988-89 and 1989-90. The index inefficiency was very high in the year 1983-84, a 9 per cent deviation. Within the ten years from 1980-81 to 1989-90 the state economy was able to utilise its resources somewhat reasonably well only in three years. In the 1990s a slight improvement is seen. The index of inefficiency is seen only for 4 years 1991-92, 1995-96, 1996-97 and 1997-98. The notable feature is that the deviation of actual output from potential output has come down to the range of 1 to 3.

This analysis gives a rough idea about the performance of the economy in the last two decades. With all the favourable factors on its side, Kerala was not able to achieve even a very moderate potential growth rate of 5.44 per cent. This highlights the fact that there are constraints facing the economy in achieving its potential growth rate. Against this background, it is interesting and enlightening to compare the growth rate of NSDP over the FiveYear Plan periods.

Table 5
Annual Compound Growth Rates of NSDP and Per Capita Income Kerala 1950-51 to 1996-97(%)

Five Year Plan	*Period*	*NSDP*	*PCI*
First Plan	1951- 56	3.40	1.20
Second Plan	1956- 61	1.80	-0.40
Third Plan	1961 -66	2.50	0.20
Annual Plan	1966 -69	5.60	3.20
Fourth Plan	1969 -74	3.50	3.30
Fifth Plan	1974 -78	1.40	-0.40
Annual Plan	1978 -80	3.90	2.30
Sixth Plan	1980-85	2.90	1.20
Seventh Plan	1985 -90	4.40	3.00
Annual Plan	1990 -92	4.70	3.50
Eighth Plan	1992 -97	6.70	5.30
Nineth Plan (Till 2000)	1997 -2002	5.20	4.30

Note: NSDP at constant prices for 1950-51 to 1973-74 at 1960-61 prices, for 1973-74 to 1984-85 at 1970-71 prices, for 1984-85 to 1996-97 at 1980-81 prices, for 1997-2000 at 1993-94 prices.

Source: *Statistical* data from Economic Reviews 1968, 1982, 1987, 1994, 1997, 2000, State Planning Board, Statistics for planning 1977, Department of Economics, Department of Economics and Statistics, Kerala.

Table 5 gives the annual average growth rates of NSDP and per capita income over the Five Year Plans. This analysis brings forth the fact that in the 1960s and 1970s also the economy was not performing in its full capacity. Except for the period of Annual Plans from 1966-67 to 1968-69 and period of Eighth Plan, NSDP show less than potential growth rate for the economy in 1960s 1970s and 1980s.

The table clearly shows that the rate of growth of state income observed in the 1990s is considerably higher than the rates obtained for the decades of 1950s, 1960s and 1970s. On the whole, the available estimates suggest an upward trend in the long term growth rate of state income during the last 10 years. However, the estimates also indicate clearly that the process of growth did manifest persistent fluctuations on either side of the rising trend, and that there were fairly long sub periods marked by rapid growth, relative stagnation and even slight decline

SECTORAL GROWTH ACCOUNTING–KERALA'S PRE LIBERLISATION PERIOD

The study of the nature and structure of State Domestic Income will not be complete without an analysis of the structural pattern of growth in the Kerala economy. The changes in aggregate values are associated with the shifts in relative importance of different economic units, distinguished by character, organization, ownership and types of income generated. The sectoral transformation, i.e. the share of primary, secondary and tertiary sectors, undertaken during 1980-2000 period reveals the nature of the three economic zones behind the aggregate values.

The role of sectoral performance in economic growth has been a topic of major importance in growth studies from Adam Smith in the 18th century to Angus Madison in the 20th century. Structural change in the process of economic growth involves the transfer of resources from lower to higher productivity sectors and is marked by the decline of agriculture followed in succession by the expansion of industry and services both in terms of employment and output. Structural change is ultimately reflected in the importance of services in a rapidly growing economy and high correlation between services and income.

Over the 20 year period under analysis, as the Kerala economy grew in spurts and scuds, the share of the commodity producing sectors, namely primary and secondary sectors, came down from 39 per cent to 28 per cent in the case of the former and from 24 per cent to 20 per cent in case of the latter. The service sector conforms to the theoretical rule. Its share increased to 50 per cent in 1999-2000 from a mere 36 per cent in 1980-81. Secondary sector shows a stagnant picture. It never had a substantive share of the state economy. The secondary sector never took off and its share averaged around 22 per cent of the state income. But primary sector's share came down and is showing a declining trend. This is revealed by the Table 6 which shows that the sectoral growth in Kerala has taken place in accordance with the theoretical pattern of growth process.

Table 6

Structure of State Domestic Product at Constant Price (%)

Year	*Primary Sector*	*Secondary Sector*	*Tertiary Sector*	*NSDP*
1980-81	39.23	24.37	36.40	100
1981-82	38.19	24.39	37.42	100
1982-83	37.46	24.19	38.35	100
1983-84	35.54	24.60	39.86	100
1984-85	36.54	23.17	40.29	100
1985-86	36.70	23.43	39.87	100
1986-87	35.54	22.21	42.25	100
1987-88	34.76	22.47	42.77	100
1988-89	36.59	22.88	40.53	100
1989-90	33.62	25.62	40.76	100
1990-91	35.99	23.92	40.09	100
1991-92	36.43	23.83	39.74	100
1992-93	34.11	24.59	41.24	100
1993-94	30.14	20.91	48.95	100
1994-95	31.03	21.48	47.49	100
1995-96	29.43	21.64	48.93	100
1996-97	29.09	20.74	50.37	100
1997-98	28.33	20.34	51.33	100
1998-99	27.97	19.98	52.05	100
1999-00	28.72	20.64	50.64	100

Source: 1 for data from 1980-81 to 1992-93. See DES: State Domestic product 1989-90 to Estimates from 1993-94 to 1999-2000 is computed from Economic Review 2000. State Planning Board, Kerala.

Table 7 reveals contribution of three main sectors-Primary, Secondary and Tertiary during the decades of 1980s and 1990s. The years of poor economic activity and negative growth rates of NSDP in the years 1981-82, 1983-84, 1986-87, 1988-89, 1991-92 is accompanied by deceleration of economic activity in the three main sectors.

Table 7
Revised Series of NSDP & Net Domestic Product Originating in Primary, Secondary & Tertiary Sectors 1980-81 to 1999-2000
(% Contribution)

	Average % share for			
Year	*Primary Sector*	*Secondary Sector*	*Tertiary Sector*	*NSDP*
1980-81 to 99-00	34	22	44	100
1980-81 to 89-90	36	22	42	100
1990-91 to 99-00	30	22	48	100

Source: Table 6.

In Kerala, the primary sector accounted for 28 per cent of the SDP and 39 per cent of the workforce in the late 1990s. National Income Accounts include Agriculture, Forestry and Logging, Fishing and Mining and Quarrying as sub-sectors of the primary sector. Agriculture is the main source of income in the primary sector accounting for 87.53 per cent in 1998-99 with the other sectors contributing a meagre 12.47 per cent. (8.4 per cent by Fishing, 4.7 per cent by Forestry and logging and 0.68 per cent by Mining and Quarrying).

Experts trace the reasons for agricultural stagnation as inefficient use of irrigation, insufficiency of inputs, and lack of long-term investment in land improvement, implementation of ill-suited large irrigation schemes, previously unknown summer droughts, neglect of local resource management, absence of regulated markets and failure to promote co-operation among farmers. In the years when agricultural growth had been low or negative, growth of net state domestic product had been low. But as the data on agricultural growth from 1980-81 to 1998-99 shows there has been no stable growth rate. Persistently deteriorating food crops scenario, constraints raised by labour, high wages, defective marketing, poor infrastructure, fluctuating market value of commodities, international competition in the export zone and poor technological up gradation are some of the disheartening features of the primary sector.

There are various views regarding the slow industrial growth of Kerala. Economists have cited the absence of an entrepreneurial class, lack of commitment to development on the part of both labour and management, lack of communication between government, labour and management, attitude of labour towards development, i.e. lack of will to work, and political polarisation as reasons for the tardy growth of secondary sector. Some commentators have considered historical and structural factors as reasons for lopsided industrial development (Pillai and Shanta 1997).

Tertiary sector or service sector forms the foundation of economic growth. It includes transport and communication, trade and hotels, banking and insurance, real estate, public administration and other services.

Other services include educational, scientific and research services, medical and health services, sanitary services, legal, religious and community services in both private and public sector. These services relate to the social and human development of any society. All the other five sectors relate to the basic facilities offered to any society. In other words, the growth of these sectors indicates the general living standards of the society. Thus economic growth requires certain infrastructure of growth, which are termed economic and non-economic factors.. Economic preconditions are adequate basic facilities of transport and communication, power, technical skills, banking and financial organisations and so on. The non-economic factors include literate population, high health status of the population, urbanization, political stability, pure drinking water etc.

The annual compound growth rate of the tertiary sector from 1980-81 to1998-99 has been analysed in Table 6. Except for 1983-84 and 1991-92, the sector has been recording tremendous growth rate. After 1996, more than 50 per cent of the NSDP is originating from tertiary sector as shown in the following table.

Table 8 combines the share of primary and secondary sectors into a single unit and is taken as the commodity or the real sector. Steady level of growth in commodity producing sectors sustains economic growth while growth of service sector tries to meet the accelerated demand for infrastructure.

Table 8 shows that the share of commodity producing sector was 63 per cent in 1980-81 and it was only 49 per cent in 1999-2000. As already noted, the service sector's share had a quantum jump to 50 per cent from 36 per cent in 1980-81.

Table 8
Distribution of Net State Domestic Product by Commodity Producing Sectors and Service Sectors 1980-81 to 1999-2000

Period	*Commodity Producing Sector (%)*	*Service Sector (%)*	*NSDP*
1980-81	63.6	36.4	100
1981-82	62.5	37.5	100
1982-83	61.6	38.4	100
1983-84	60.1	39.9	100
1984-85	59.7	40.3	100
1985-86	60.1	39.9	100
1986-87	57.8	42.2	100
1987-88	57.2	42.8	100
1988-89	59.5	40.5	100
1989-90	59.2	40.8	100
1990-91	59.9	40.1	100
1991-92	60.3	39.7	100
1992-93	58.8	41.2	100
1993-94	51.1	48.9	100
1994-95	52.5	47.5	100
1995-96	51.1	48.9	100
1996-97	49.8	50.2	100
1997-98	48.7	51.3	100
1998-99	47.9	52.1	100
1999-00	49.4	50.6	100

Source: Computed from Table 6.

GROWTH RATE OF SECTORS UNDER FIVE YEAR PLANS

Official support for the development of the three sectors is done through the Five Year Plans. NSDP growth rate under each plan indicates that the growth had been neither stable nor uniform. The following Table 9 shows annual compound growth rates of NSDP, per capita income and the three sectors of Kerala from 1950-51 to 1996-97.

Table 9
Annual Compound Growth Rates of NSDP, PCI and Sectors, Kerala 1950-51 to 1996-97 (%)

1	2	3	4	5	6
Period	*Primary*	*Secondary*	*Tertiary*	*NSDP*	*PCI*
First Plan 1951-56	3.4	2.4	4.1	3.4	1.2
Third Plan 1961-66	0.4	5.8	4.4	2.5	0.2
Annual Plans 1966-69	5.3	4.5	6.6	5.6	3.2
Fourth Plan 1969-74	2.3	5.0	4.5	3.5	3.3
Fifth Plan 1974-78	-0.3	2.7	3.6	1.4	-0.4
Annual Plans 1978-80	0.2	6.7	6.2	3.9	2.3
Sixth Plan 1980-85	0.8	0.8	6.3	2.9	1.2
Seventh Plan 1985-90	2.7	6.5	4.7	4.4	3.0
Annual Plans 1990-92	9.0	1.0	3.4	4.7	3.5
Eighth Plan 1992-97	5.3	6.8	7.9	6.7	5.3

Note: NSDP at constant prices for 1950-51 to 1973-74 at 1960-61 prices, for 1973-74 to 1984-85 at 1970-71 price, for 1984-85 to 1996-97 at 1980-81 prices.

Source: Statistical data from Economic Reviews, 1968,1982,1987,1994, 1997, State Planning Board, Statistics for Planning 1977, Department of Economics and Statistics, Kerala.

During the period of the five year plans NSDP grew from 3.4 per cent in the First Plan to 6.7 per cent in the Eighth Plan. At the same time per capita income increased from a mere 1.2 per cent to 5.3 per cent. A growth rate 3.4 per cent in primary sector, 2.4 per cent in secondary sector and 4.1 per cent in tertiary sector during the first plan changed to 5.3%, 6.8% and 7.9% respectively in the Eighth Plan. Primary and secondary sector's growth had not only been low but was unstable. Only the service sector did relatively well throughout.

Calculating growth rates according to Five Year Plan period also reflects our earlier findings that in the decade of 1980s the NSDP was not able to sustain a growth rate of above 5 per cent. But in the 1990s, the picture is completely different with a 6.7 per cent growth during the period 1992-97.

GROWTH OF THE STATE INCOME IN THE 21ST CENTURY

Economic reforms in Kerala were at a snail's pace till the fiscal crisis of the state in 2001. The state started economic reforms in 2001 as a response to the near default on its payment obligations on account of a bad fiscal position (GOK 2001). Kerala Government announced a number of reform measures for attracting private investment in agriculture, industry, power, infrastructure, tourism, health care and higher education. Improvement of the quality and effectiveness of governance and tiding over the poor fiscal situation of the state was also part of the reforms. During this time the state government took a loan from Asian Development Bank for introducing economic reforms (P.D. Jeromi, 2005). The main objective of the reforms was the faster growth of the state economy. The impressive performance of the state income and the revival of the Kerala economy in the 21st century are unprecedented in the 52 year history of the economy since its formation in 1956. The following table gives the details regarding the turnaround in state income.

Table 10

NSDP at Factor Cost 2000-2007 (Base: 1999-2000 Prices)

Year	*NSDP (Rs. Crores)*	*% change (Rs.)*	*PCI*	*% change*
1999-2000	60643	-	19294	-
2000-2001	62523	3.1	19724	2.2
2001-2002	65594	4.9	20519	4.0
2002-2003	70211	7.0	21699	5.7
2003-2004	74739	6.4	22848	5.2
2004-2005	80091	7.1	24217	5.9
2005-2006	85759	7.0	25657	5.9
2006-2007	92120	7.4	27284	6.3

Source: Handbook of Statistics on Indian Economy 2008, RBI.

It can be seen that the state has been on a stable growth path from 2002 onwards. While Kerala's aggregate growth rate in the pre liberalisation period was considerably below all India level, in the period after 2002, it is on par with all India performance. From 3.1% in 2000 -01 to 7.4% in 2006-07, the economy is showing a turnaround in growth, refuting the stigma of 'high social development and economic backwardness'. In case of per capita income also the change is remarkable, the state has been able to maintain more than 5% growth rate from 2002 onwards. This is also the result of the demographic advantage due to low population growth in the state. Thus it can be stated that Kerala is on a steady growth path. The sectoral growth performance also shows that the tertiary sector is the lead sector contributing 61% to the overall growth of the state. During 2006-07 the contribution from primary, secondary and tertiary sectors constituted 17.8% 21.6% and 60.6% respectively. It can be seen that the primary sector's contribution is declining and service sector's share is increasing. The secondary sector remains almost at the same level of about 22% (*Economic Review, 2007, SPB*).

KERALA ECONOMY *VIS-À-VIS* OTHER STATES

Experts and institutions analysing the economic performance of individual states in the Indian economy during the decades of 1980s and 1990s have noted the dramatic recovery experienced by certain states in the post-liberalization period. Special mention is made in the case of Kerala economy. A brief survey of these estimates is presented in this section.

The publication of the Reserve Bank of India 'Handbook of Statistics on Indian Economy 2000' states that the Net Domestic Product of Kerala registered a growth rate of 59.08 per cent during the period 1989-90 to 1997-98. This is higher than those of Tamil Nadu (58.64%) and Karnataka (51.26%). In fact Kerala ranks fifth among the major states with regard to growth rate of state income during this period. State-wise comparison is given in Table 11.

All the first 6 States mentioned in the table showed increased growth rate in the decade of 1990s. But most notable among them is the recovery of the Kerala economy.

T. R. Satish Chandran makes an in depth analysis of the impact of globalisation on India and the southern states. He analysed the way the four southern states, Andhra Pradesh, Karnataka, Kerala and Tamilnadu, adjusted themselves to the changes brought about by the twin processes of liberalisation and globalisation. He argues that there has been no significant adverse impact on these states. He considers the poverty situation and the human development index and concludes that there is no negative impact of liberalisation on these states.

Table 11
State-wise Growth of Net SDP (At Factor Cost: Constant Prices) (Percentage) (Base 1980-81)

	Growth Rate	
State	*1980-81 to 1989-90*	*1989-90 to 98-99*
Gujarat	63.14	72.58
Maharashtra	71.81	64.80
Andhra Pradesh	57.61	72.82
West Bengal	43.16	65.76
Kerala	27.96	59.08
Madhya Pradesh	38.69	51.65
Tamil Nadu	58.88	58.64
Rajasthan	77.51	52.08
Karnataka	61.91	51.26
Haryana	70.78	45.71
Punjab	65.54	37.71
Orissa	52.02	14.88
Uttar Pradesh	53.45	27.27
Bihar	47.50	13.74

Source: Hand Book of Statistics on Indian Economy 2000-Reserve Bank of India.

His analysis of overall economic performance in terms of per capita NSDP is given below.

Table 12
Per Capita NSDP (at 1980-81 Prices) (Rupees)

State	*1991-92*	*1995-96*
Andhra Pradesh	1,788	1,913
Karnataka	2,262	2,425
Kerala	1,826	2,353
Tamilnadu	2,268	2744

Source: T.R. Satish Chandran (2000).

Montek S. Ahluwalia (2000) makes comparative study of the economic prosperity of 14 states in the post reforms period. He presents the estimated growth rates of SDP in the pre reform period 1980-81 to 1990-91 and in the post reform period 1991-92 to 1997-98. His estimates are given in the following two tables.

Ahluwalia makes a laudable comment on Kerala. "The performance of Kerala deserves special attention. Kerala is justly celebrated for its achievements in human development but it has also been criticised for under performance in economic growth. It is important to note that its performance in the 1990s showed marked improvement compared with the 1980s. From an SDP growth rate much below the 14 states average in the 1980s it accelerated to growth rate only marginally below the average in the 1990s. However, because of the low population growth its performance in per capita SDP growth in the 1990s was actually much better than the average" (*EPW, May 2000, p. 1637).*

Table 13
Annual Rates of Growth of Gross State Domestic Product (SDP)

State	*1980-81 to 1990-91*	*1991-92 to1997-98*
Bihar	4.66	2.69
Rajasthan	6.60	6.54
Uttar Pradesh	4.95	3.58
Orissa	4.29	3.25
Madhya Pradesh	4.56	6.17
Andhra Pradesh	5.65	5.03
Tamil Nadu	5.38	6.22
Kerala	3.57	5.81
Karnataka	5.29	5.29
West Bengal	4.71	6.91
Gujarat	5.08	9.57
Haryana	6.43	5.02
Maharashtra	6.02	8.01
Punjab	5.32	4.71
Combined SDP of 14 States	5.24	5.94
GDP (National Accounts)	5.55	6.89

Source: M. S. Ahluwalia (2000) "Economic Performance of States in Post Reforms period" EPW. May 6, 1637.

Both statistical analyses suggest that Kerala achieved commendable achievement in SDP from 3.57 per cent in pre-reform period to 5.81 per cent growth rate in 1990s. In the case of PCI also Kerala improved her position from 2.19 per cent annual growth rate in 1980s to 4.52 per cent in the 1990s.

Table 14
Annual Rates of Growth of Per Capita Gross State Domestic Product

States	*1980-81 to 1990 91*	*1991-92 to 1997-98*
Bihar	2.45	1.12
Rajasthan	3.96	3.96
Uttar Pradesh	2.60	1.24
Orissa	2.38	1.64
Madhya Pradesh	2.08	3.87
Andhra Pradesh	3.34	3.45
Tamilnadu	3.87	4.95
Kerala	2.19	4.52
Karnataka	3.28	3.45
West Bengal	2.39	5.04
Gujarat	3.08	7.57
Haryana	3.86	2.66
Maharashtra	3.58	6.13
Punjab	3.33	2.80
(Combined SDP 14 states)	3.03	4.02

Source: M. S. Ahluwalia (2000).

Dr. K. K. Subrahamanian & E. Abdul Azeez (2000) also highlight the acceleration in the growth movement in Kerala. Their results are given below.

Table 15
Annual Growth Rates of Net Domestic Product

Period	*Kerala*	*Karnataka*	*Tamilnadu*	*All India*
1971-72 to 1980-81	3.43	-	-	3.44
1981-82 to 1990-91	4.83	5.39	5.35	5.36
1991-92 to1997-98	6.05	5.46	6.26	5.64
1971-72 to 1990-91	2.88	-	-	4.30
1981-82 to 1997-98	4.90	5.41	5.65	5.38

Source: Subrahamanian & Azeez (2000).

Table 16
Annual Growth Rates of Per Capita NDP

Period	*Kerala*	*Karnataka*	*Tamilnadu*	*All India*
1981-82 to 1990-91	3.39	3.51	4.37	3.23
1991-92 to 1996-97	5.10	4.02	4.90	3.80
1981-82 to 1996-97	3.57	3.65	4.58	3.36

Source: Subrahamanian & Azeez (2000).

Keen interest is shown by economists in analysing the dramatic achievements of the state. Some of the recent studies are by K. P. Kannan, Achin Chakraborty and PD Jeromi. All these studies and estimates indicate that the Kerala economy was facing severe constraints in its growth process in the 1970s and 1980s. But in 1990s, the economy was able to overcome some of these constraints but it is still too early to state whether the economy has achieved sustainable growth rate and will able to achieve commendable growth rates in future.

CONCLUSION

Kerala's trajectory of development has been marked by social investment, redistribution reforms by the State, relatively poor growth rates in the commodity producing sectors, and high quality of living standards. Despite the fact that there are growth-enhancing effects of social investment, the stagnation of the Kerala economy in the 1970s and 1980s raised serious questions about the viability and sustainability of its developmental trajectory. But the state began to show recovery in the1990s which culminated in the stable growth rate of 6 to 7%from 2002 onwards. "The record of economic growth and human development over the past 30 years shows that no country can follow a course of lopsided development for such a long time where economic growth is not matched by advances in human development or vice versa."(Human Development Report 1996). Kerala's experience can be analyzed in the light of this theory. But the resurgence in growth rate highlights the positives in the state and at the same time camouflages the negatives lying hidden in its growth process.

The positives are

1. Kerala's unique social development has successfully tackled the first generation problems–illiteracy, high infant mortality rate, high maternal mortality rate, high birth rate and related indicators of under development far ahead of many other Indian States. This has been primarily due to the fact that the state has followed a different development path and rapid

strides have been made in extending the two major public goods namely education and health.

2. The decadal growth rate of Kerala's population was 14.32%from 1981-1991, while it declined to 9.42% in 1991-2001.
3. Estimates of HDI for the Indian states place Kerala at the top- the index is 0.773with the rank one. (*Economic Review 2007)*
4. The state benefits from the remittances from expatriates which were estimated to be Rs. 18364 crores in 2003-04 from all countries.
5. Highly educated labour force with a literacy rate of 94.20%
6. Growth of the service sector which generates 60% of income and two thirds of employment in the state.

The negatives are

1. Declining budgetary support to capital formation in Kerala in all the three sectors..
2. The dismal power situation in the state. Power shortage is likely to result in a slowing down of overall growth in the economy.
3. Another constraint Kerala economy faces is the high increase in the number of job-seekers.
4. Increases in the total debt of the state from Rs. 11420.91crore in 1996-97 to Rs. 57138.71crore in 2007-08(*Economic Review 2007*) which is an area of major concern.
5. The state is witnessing the increase in the number of the aged in the population with the consequent socio–economic problems.
6. Deteriorating public health facilities and environmental problems like waste disposal, high incidence of lifestyle diseases, suicides and consumption of alcohol, frequent hartals etc are black spots in the shining armour of the high growth of the state.

In sum, for accentuating the momentum of growth achieved by the Kerala economy there is a need for a new vision on modernising both agricultural and industrial sectors. A clear and pragmatic approach of the State in its response to reform process and a positive approach in its own policies for encouraging private investment in the regional economy are the need of the hour. Private investment becomes necessary as the state coffers are dwindling, and the state no longer can be expected to herald the growth process in the economy. In this context, an investor friendly climate must be brought in at the initiative of the State Government. This new vision will be able to take full advantage of Kerala's comparative advantage in knowledge generation and human resource development and on that basis promote knowledge based and service industries. All this could change Kerala as a value-added service provider in a globally competitive environment.

REFERENCES

Ahluwalia M. S. (2000), 'Economic Performance of States in Post-Reform Period', *Economic and Political Weekly*, May 6, p. 1637.

Centre for Development Studies (1977), Poverty, Unemployment and Development Policy Bombay Orient Longman.

Chakraborty Achin (2005), 'Kerala's Changing Development Narratives', *Economic and Political Weekly*, Feb. 5.

Chandran, Satish T. R. (2000), 'Globalisation Impact on India and the Southern States', *Journal of Social and Economic Development*, Vol. III, No. 1, January-June.

Choudhary, Umadatta Roy (1993), *'Inter State and Intra State variations in Economic Development and Standard of Living'*, National Institute of Public Finance and Policy, *Monograph Series*, IV.

Dholakia, Bakul H. (1974), *The Sources of Economic Growth in India'*, Good Companions, Baroda.

Economic Review, 1985, 1992, 1994, 1996, 2000, 2001, 2007, State Planning Board, Thiruvananthapuram.

Handbook of Statistics on Indian Economy 2000, 2008, Reserve Bank of India, Bombay.

Jeromi P. D. (2005), 'Economic Reforms in Kerala' *Economic and Political Weekly*, July 23.

Kannan K. P. (2005), 'Kerala's Turnaround in Growth: Role of Social Development, Remittances and Reform', *Economic and Political Weekly*, Feb. 5.

Pillai M. P. and Santha N. (1997), 'Industrialisation in Kerala', Kerala Studies Series, Centre for Development Studies, Trivandrum.

Subrahamanian K. K. and Abdul Azeez (2000), *'Industrial Growth in Kerala: Trends and Explanations"*, Working Paper 310, Centre for Development Studies, November.

World Bank: World Development Report 2001, UNDP.

World Bank: Human Development Report 1996.

2

OCCUPATION STRUCTURE IN KERALA: SOME OBITER DICTA

B. N. Ghosh

INTRODUCTION

In Chaucer's famous *Canterbury Tales*, the clerk always seems to be busy without any productive engagement. In the same way, in a country like India, which is basically a labor-surplus economy, one can always discover occupations where there are more laborers than what is really needed. The overstaffing is accompanied by low productivity, high cost and gross inefficiency. This sums up the situation of the Indian economy even after economic reforms. The economy of Kerala, however, is not an exception in this regard. Backward countries are mainly characterised by many types of rigidities and inelasticities which are too difficult to remove within a short-period of time. Just as in many other areas of economic activities, the occupation pattern in a country, often called the occupational distribution of labour force, reflects formidable structural rigidities. Under such circumstances, what is needed is to remove structural rigidities and initiate development-oriented structural changes. The structural change in the economy in fact is a social and institutional change which is inextricably associated with the process of economic development. This is so because economic development is expressed through institutions as institutions are expressed through economic development.

Occupations are broadly classified under three distinct categories: primary occupations that include mostly jobs in the rural-agricultural sector such as farming, working for livestock, forestry, fishing, mining and similar preoccupations. Secondary occupations relate to industrial-manufacturing sector occupations where jobs are located in different types of organised and unorganised industries, large and small scale industries and household and non-household industries. In a developing country like India, an important constituent sub-sector of the industrial sector is the construction sector which is employing an increasing number of labourers every year n India. The tertiary sector, which is also called the services sector, includes many types of services such as trade and commerce, transport, storage and communication, education and health services, banking services, tourism and similar other services.

Occupation structure is a critical reflection of the degree of economic development that a country has achieved. We can classify a country on the basis of its occupation structure. In a developed country (DC), primary occupation is a negligible proportion of the total employment in all sectors and generally, labour employment in the non-agricultural sectors is the highest. The opposite is the situation in a backward country. Thus, in 1946, Canada had nearly 26 per cent of its labour force in the primary sector and 74 per cent in the non-agricultural sector. In the same year, Britain had only 6 per cent of its labour force in the agricultural sector and 94 per cent in the non-agricultural occupations. In 1940, the United States had nearly 20 per cent of the labour force in the primary sector and 80 per cent in the non-primary occupations (Ghosh, 1998, pp. 80-81). In general, most of the less developed countries (LDCs) have surplus labour force in agriculture in the sense that the marginal productivity of labour there is either zero or negative, and if a portion of that surplus labour is shunted out to the non-agricultural sector, agricultural output will not diminish. In such a case, apparently, all workers are engaged in work but the intensity of work remains very low and there are unnecessary work-stretching and work-making (Ghosh, 1977, ch. 2). However, with economic development, the changing dynamics of occupation structure gradually reduces the percentage of people dependent on the agricultural sector and correspondingly increases the percentage of labour force in the non-agricultural occupations. The necessary changes take place as a result of inter-sectoral changes in productivity and demand for labour. Before analysing the case of Kerala, let us take a look at the theoretical scaffoldings of the problem.

THEORETICAL SCAFFOLDINGS

As economic development progresses, more people are shifted first from agriculture to industry and then from industry to services (Kuznets, 1966). Whereas the percentage of people depending on agriculture is very low in developed countries (10 per cent or less), it is very high in underdeveloped countries (80 per cent or more) (Table 1). The Table reveals the fact that in developed countries including Austria, Sweden, Australia, Japan and France, less than 5 per cent of the labor force depends on the agricultural sector. But this dependency is much higher in Afghanistan, Ethiopia, Cameroon and Nigeria, all of which are developing countries with low per capita income. Economic growth and the dependency load on the agricultural sector are negatively correlated. The rate of economic development may be described by the rate at which the 70: 30 occupation ratio in underdeveloped countries is changed to 20: 80 approximately (Singer, 1952). The transfer of population from the agricultural to the non-agricultural sector must be accompanied by a rise in productivity in the former sector for providing food and raw materials to the latter sector. An upward change in agricultural productivity has to be accomplished with the help of many structural changes in the economy, for instance, in socio-economic institutions, production frontier, market mechanism, incentives, and so on.

A change in the occupational structure is necessary, desirable and practicable in LDCs.

Economic progress is generally associated with certain distinct, necessary and predictable changes in occupational structure. Clark observes that a high average level of real income *per capita* is associated with a high proportion of labor force in the tertiary sector (Clark, 1952, p182). Similarly, low *per capita* real income is associated with high proportion of population in agriculture. High average real income *per capita* compels a large proportion of population to engage in the tertiary sector. Clark contends that the proportion of population engaged in commerce and finance is a precise measurement of the degree of the economic development (Clark, 1952, pp. 395-97).

Clark gives two main explanations for the shift of population from agricultural to non-agricultural sector:

1. With the increasing real *per capita* income in agriculture, less would be spent on consumption (because of low elasticity of demand for primary products). It follows then that the labor force engaged in agriculture must decrease.
2. Output per worker may be increasing more rapidly in some sectors than in others. If average output per head in the primary industry is increasing faster than in other fields, it will accelerate the movement of labor from agriculture to other sectors.

Jean Fourasite (1951, p. 224) explains further the occupational shift of labor force with the help of technical change. He says that for the above two reasons, agricultural population will shift to the industrial sector which will have increased employment due to increased demand for manufactured products. But ultimately, the industrial sector will be saturated and hence, people will be shifted to the tertiary sector, where the goods and services will remain in demand. The shifts of employment from the primary towards secondary and tertiary production revealed by the census are the inescapable reflection of economic progress (Fisher, 1964, pp. 6-7).

The Clark-Fisher thesis leads to a few important generalisations (Dutta, 1952):

1. Real per capita income is very low in those countries where the percentage of population engaged in the primary occupation is very high.
2. Per capita value productivity is higher in secondary and tertiary sectors than in the primary sector.
3. Agricultural productivity is higher in countries with small percentage of agricultural labor force than in countries with high percentage.
4. In the industrial countries, the percentage of secondary employment tends to fall whereas that of tertiary employment tends to rise.

However, it should be noted that there are some differences between the tertiary occupations in developed and those in under-developed countries (Dutta, 1952, p. 129):

First, in developed countries, tertiary occupation emerges out of high level of income in other sectors. But in under-developed countries, this occupation emerges not out of high level of income but out of scarcity of employment in other sectors. Personal services, which are an important part of tertiary occupation, arise out of inequality in income and wealth distribution in backward countries. People enter in this sector because low productivity jobs require very low capital intensity. Petty traders and shoe-shining boys in India (and Kerala) are good examples. Cheap supply of labour and social prestige consideration of the upper strata of population make possible the employment of a large number of domestic servants in underdeveloped countries (Lewis, 1954). But they are disguisedly unemployed and their productivity is near zero; whereas *per capita* productivity in tertiary occupation is the highest in developed countries. Second, in underdeveloped countries, the distributive services in the tertiary occupation are low-income type and poverty-induced; but those in developed countries are high income types and property-induced. Third, tertiary occupations in developed countries are highly capital-intensive whereas those in underdeveloped countries are highly labour-intensive. Thus, in a developed country, tertiary occupation is the citadel for highest income and productivity; but in an underdeveloped country, it is the problematic abode of low income and low productivity from where people are required to be shifted to higher productivity occupations. A large part of the Indian services sector consists of the expanding informal sector which is low-productive and unorganised.

In this context, it is interesting to compare the occupational distribution of labour force in India and China, the two Asian super-powers and fast developing economies, to know partly why China is growing faster than India. In China, the greatest value-added is made by the manufacturing sector, where output has increased three times with the doubling of the labor force. China has become virtually 'the workshop of the world'. In India, it is the services sector which has contributed the most, but it is basically low-income and low-capital induced. The manufacturing sector in India could not make much headway. India is still a capital-deficient country. India's investment is only about 26 per cent of its GDP. A large chunk of India's private saving is dissipated to finance the escalating public sector deficit. With lower capital endowment per worker, the productivity of labour has also remained low in India. The labour productivity in the secondary and tertiary sectors in 2004 was respectively seven and five times that of the agricultural sector in China. For India, this was four and five times respectively. In India, labour productivity in the non-agricultural sector is three times that of the agricultural sector. India's primary sector still contains a huge amount of labour force (60 per cent), a large proportion of which is underemployed, both open and hidden. However, over the years, China has changed the occupational distribution of the population in a remarkably substantial way. The primary sector in China now contains 50 per cent of the total labour force. But China's output per worker in the primary sector was 0.7 compared to 0.5 in India between1993-2000. For the period 1980-2000, the growth rate of GDP per capita in the two countries was basically due to increased sectoral productivity. Increased labor force participation rate and better occupational shift of population from the low-productivity agriculture accounted for higher growth momentum in both these countries (2.6 per cent for China and 0.3 per cent for India). It is instructive to note that economic development can be measured by the extent to which a country is successful in shifting its labor force from agricultural to non-agricultural occupations over time: the higher the proportion of population in the non-agricultural sector, the higher is the rate of economic development. This type of favorable structural change in the realm of occupational distribution of population has been spectacular in China. India's achievement in this regard has been rather marginal. The meat of the matter is that sectoral occupational ratios are changing very slowly India in spite or because of a modicum of economic growth.

As sated earlier, in developed countries, the proportion of total labour force engaged in the agricultural occupation is the lowest and it is the highest in the services sector. The situation is quite different in developing countries including India (vide Table 1). Kerala is not an exception.

Table 1
Occupation Structures in Selected Countries

Country	*Primary Sector (%)*	*Secondary Sector (%)*	*Tertiary Sector (%)*
Afghanistan	80	10	10
Ethiopia	80	8	12
Cameroon	70	13	17
Nigeria	70	10	20
Bangladesh	63	11	26
India	60	12	28
Albania	58	15	27
China	50	22	28
Indonesia	43.3	18	38.7
Romania	41	27	32
Azerbaijan	41	7	52
Turkey	36	22.8	41.2
Egypt	32	17	51
Iran	30	25	45
Brazil	23	24	53

Contd...

Country	*Primary Sector (%)*	*Secondary Sector (%)*	*Tertiary Sector (%)*
Macedonia	21.7	32.6	45.7
Kazakhstan	20	30	50
Poland	16.1	29	54.9
Malaysia	14	36	50
Uruguay	14	16	70
Venezuela	13	23	64
Russia	10.8	29.1	58.2
Portugal	10	30	60
Barbados	10	15	75
North Cyprus	14.5	29	56.5
South Cyprus	7.4	38.2	54.4
Taiwan	5.5	36	58.5
Australia	5	22	73
Japan	4.5	27.8	67.7
Switzerland	4.6	26.3	69.1
France	4.1	24.4	71.5
Czech Republic	4.1	37.6	58.3
Antigua and Barbuda	3.7	22	74.3
Austria	3	27	70
Sweden	2	24	74
Belgium	1.3	24.5	74.2
British Virgin Islands	0.6	40	59.4

Source: CIA World Factbook; *www.cia.gov/cia/publications/factbook*

THE KERALIAN SCENARIO

Structural changes in the realm of occupations are very conspicuous in the case of Kerala as compared to India as a whole. This bespeaks of a more dynamic nature of the economy of Kerala. As development proceeded steadily, occupational shift of labour force followed the suit in the right direction in Kerala although the speed of the shift is not still the optimum or ideal. The trend in the occupation structure in Kerala is shown in Table 2.

A cursory glance at the Table shows that within a period of nearly two decades, Kerala's occupation structure has changed tremendously. The primary sector which used to absorb 53 per cent of the labour force in 1981 had been able to work only with 32per cent in the year 2001. Apparently, in terms of development, it is a commendable achievement. The 32:68 ratio of agricultural *vis-à-vis* non-agricultural occupations

Table 2
Occupation Structure in Kerala (% of Labour Force)

Sector	*1961*	*1981*	*1991*	*2001*
Primary	57.5	53.2	47.24	32.0
	(69.0)	(68.8)	(69.9)	(64.5)
Secondary	20.1	19.4	18.34	28.0
	(13.0)	(13.5)	(12.5)	(14.5)
Tertiary	22.4	27.4	34.	42 40.0
	(18.0)	(17.7)	(20.6)	(21.0)

Source: Compiled from Census Reports (Data for India are shown in the parentheses).

is *per se* a great accomplishment. The rate of progress in this direction is more remarkable than the one achieved by the whole country which is still languishing with 60 per cent of the labour force in the primary sector. Whereas the agricultural sector in Kerala is undergoing the process of structural slimming, the secondary and tertiary sectors have started gaining weight. The industrial sector which accommodated about 20 per cent of the labour force in 1961, was able to absorb 28 per cent of the labour force in 2001. This demonstrates the continuous expansion of the industrial sector albeit at a low rate. This is indeed a salutary sign of industrial development of the state. This observation appears to be pretty convincing because there has been a simultaneous growth of productivity of the labour force employed in industries. The industrial sector is poised for further expansion if the strategy accepted by the state government is fully implemented. The saturation point for labour employment is still far away. It has partly absorbed a proportion of the labour force of the agricultural sector in the process of structural transition.

The story of Kerala's services sector is far more interesting. Its achievement is the highest. It used to absorb 22 per cent of the labour force of the state in the year 1961. However, in the year 2001, its absorptive capacity was almost doubled. The productivity of the services sector is the highest among all sectors in Kerala. Productive absorption of labour is rapidly taking place in the tertiary sector. It has absorbed a sizeable portion of the labour force of the agrarian sector by generating higher income and employment. Although both the industrial and the tertiary sectors are growing in importance, the performance of the latter sector in terms of income generation and employment creation is far more overwhelming. Obviously, therefore, the services sector has become the target destination of many labourers from the agricultural and the industrial sectors. However, if this unplanned trend is not restricted to some extent, it may lead to the hypertrophy of the sector, which will plummet income and productivity.

The occupation structure of Kerala is related to relative sectoral productivity. Out of the three sectors, the productivity per labour in terms of average annual growth rate of NDP is the lowest in the primary sector (0.35), and highest in the tertiary sector (1.88). In terms of per labour productivity, the industrial sector occupies the middle position (1.01). During the period 2000-2005, the average annual growth rate in NDP in Kerala was 1.68 per cent in the primary sector, 4.19 per cent in the secondary sector and 9.21 per cent in the tertiary sector. The tertiary sector consisting of trade, transport and communication, banking services and tourism has been doing exceptionally well. This sector is further poised for higher value-added in the coming years. The industrial sector though is doing well, has still not been able to show the dynamism that it should have in the process of industrialisation of the economy. However, it is accommodating a large percentage of labour force from the agricultural sector. The industrial sector in Kerala does not generate sufficient pull forces to absorb all the surplus from the primary sector with higher productivity. An analysis of employment patterns by sectors and sub-sectors shows that whilst some sectors are gaining importance, others are losing the luster.

As Table 3 reveals, the percentages of cultivators and agricultural labourers have been declining in Kerala. The percentage of labour force engaged in livestock, forestry, fishing and mining has also shown a declining trend over the years. Sizeable proportions of agricultural labour force and cultivators are trying their fortunes in the industrial and services sectors as part-timers and commuters. They are

Table 3
Employment by Sector in Kerala (% of Labour)

Sector	*1961*	*1981*	*1991*	*2001*
Cultivators	20.9	17.80	13.7	12.27
Agricultural Labourers	31.2	30.7	29.5	26.58
Livestock, Forestry, Fishing, Mining, etc.	8.6	7.4	10.0	8.39
Household Industry	8.7	4.2	4.0	3.92
Other than Household Industry	9.4	11.4	12.5	10.52
Construction	1.3	1.7	2.9	3.90
Trade & Commerce	5.7	9.9	10.2	11.47
Transport, Storage and Communications	2.7	3.8	4.9	5.43
Other Services	11.5	13.5	12.3	17.52
Total	100	100	100	100

Sources: Census of India 1961, vol. 7, Kerala Part IIB (1)
Census of India 1981, Series10, Kerala, Part II (1)
BES 1977, Statistics for Planning 1977.

concentrated mainly in the construction sector and other services including auto-drivers, hotel boys, coolies and similar unskilled manual and odd jobs. Lack of proper education and skill prevent them from being employed in the professional works. The importance of the primary sector in terms of job creation and income-generation is perceptibly declining in Kerala.

It sounds as a paradox that Kerala's primary sector which employs only 32 per cent of the total labour force, perhaps the lowest among the Indian states, is having the largest rural unemployment (around 20 per cent) and per labour productivity is the lowest among all the three sectors in the state. However, in spite of low income, there is labour shortage at the going wage rate (Patrick, 2005). What one normally expects is that, given all the paraphernalia of a traditional agriculture, Kerala should have an unlimited supply of labour at the current wage rate *a la* Lewis. However, although there is a conspicuous existence of open and disguised unemployment and underemployment in the agricultural sector of Kerala, at least in some pockets of the agricultural sector, there is often a situation of labour shortage. The seemingly paradoxical situation can be explained by the fact that, the unemployed cultivators, marginal farmers and casual labouerers do not wait all the time in the primary sector but move out to other sectors to earn higher level of income even if there are risks and uncertainties. True, there is also the prevalence of unemployment in the non-agricultural sector but workers, particularly the young workers, from the rural areas are often desperate and do try their luck in the non-agricultural sector. Since the rate of unemployment in the non-agricultural sector is much lower, there is a higher probability of getting some openings. The situation is like the Todaro model of migration where rural-urban migration takes place in spite of the existence of urban unemployment, if the probability value of getting a job is higher, effective wage rate is higher and the age of the migrant is favourable.

The development of the primary sector is constrained by a number of factors like frequent failure of monsoon, and also occasional floods, increasing cost of inputs in the face of falling prices of agricultural commodities, fall in profitability, increase in wages and apparent shortage of labour. Over the years, the terms of trade have moved against the agricultural sector in Kerala, and this has adversely affected the development of the primary sector. The mechanisation of agriculture has been prevented by fragmentation and sub-division of land holdings. The situation of late is alarming. As high as 94 per cent of the total land holdings in Kerala are now classified as marginal holdings that prevent the modernisation of those holdings (Prakash, 2007, p. 25). It is interesting to note that for many of the cultivators and farmers in Kerala, agriculture is no longer a primary occupation, but a subsidiary activity. The proletarianisation of cultivators is a new development in the Keralian agriculture, which is not a salutary sign particularly in the context of recent global food crisis and the extreme lack of food security in Kerala and also of India as a whole. In fact, the contradiction between the market access and lack of food security has produced many types of food policy dilemmas in less developed countries in general and India in particular, which I have discussed elsewhere in detail (see Ghosh, 2009). Suffice it to say here that in Kerala, the recent trend shifting the preference from the cultivation of food crop to the cultivation of cash crop is an uncanny signal. The recent paradigm shift that valorises industries and completely trivialises agriculture is not a suitable strategy for a developing state like Kerala. However, there is nothing wrong in an unbalanced strategy of development in the short-run but in the longer run, such a line of approach for a state which is suffering from the lack of basic food security is likely to prove detrimental. Moreover, a lot of agricultural land in Kerala is being devoted for making industrial hubs and houses. One of the offshoots of industrialisation is that it favours the strategy of commodification of land. There is no doubt that such a policy is consistent with the profit calculus of concerned industrialists but will make the marginal landowners and cultivators a pauper class.

It needs to be borne in mind that the natural migration of people from agriculture to industry and then to the tertiary sector that happened in the case of industrialisation of today's developed countries, was induced by agricultural prosperity and technological development so that the necessary food and fibre could be produced by lesser number of work force. In the absence of such a type of technological development, the whole idea of shifting labour from agriculture to industries by force or by manipulation is indeed preposterous (Ghosh, 1977). The agricultural sector in Kerala has already reached a state where it has the smallest percentage of labour force, and perhaps the lowest figure in the whole of India. What is now necessary, at least in the short-run, is to make the agricultural sector more productive, viable and buoyant so that it can supply the food needs of the country, create a marketable surplus and generate sufficient employment opportunities for the existing labour force. The bottom line is: changes in the occupation structure *have to be* natural, demand-based and prosperity induced.

The development of the industrial sector is limited by many factors and forces. Perhaps the most serious factor is the lack of reforms in the labour market. There are frequent strikes, *bandhs*, lock-out and inter-union conflicts. Inimical activities by trade unions often clamouring for higher wages and many other unreasonable demands have vitiated the climate of industrial development in Kerala. The disquieting feature is that such unreasonable demands by trade unions are often backed up by political parties that often instigate troubles. Private investors both local and international are afraid to invest in Kerala because of labour market instability, labour aristocracy, high nuisance value of labour, high wages and uncertain political climate. The policies are, more often than not, pro-labour and not pro-market. This is borne out by the fact that wages are higher than productivity of labour in Kerala (Table 4).

Table 4
Wage-Productivity Nexus in Kerala's Manufacturing Sector

Year	*% Variation in Employment*	*% Variation in Emolument*	*Emoluments/ Employment*	*Average Productivity of Labour*
1981-82	8.40	15.50	6.90	5.50
1982-83	-11.10	10.41	7.45	5.54
1983-84	-5.95	7.37	8.51	7.86
1984-85-	-1.46	11.66	9.64	8.81
1985-86	-4.70	12.90	11.43	8.49
1986-87	-4.80	4.90	12.61	9.34
1987-88	9.00	17.60	13.60	10.52
1988-89	-4.20	10.40	15.69	11.0
1989-90	9.90	14.70	16.36	13.48
1990-91	6.60	8.00	16.59	9.75
1991-92	2.70	27.40	20.56	12.32
1992-93	16.60	14.90	20.27	9.62
1993-94	6.50	9.00	19.73	9.45
1994-95	6.20	12.00	17.30	8.96
1995-96	4.80	11.50	16.00	25.96
1996-97	5.10	8.00	18.20	12.29
1997-98	4.20	9.80	17.00	11.91
1998-99	4.00	12.00	18.10	18.16

Source: ASI Dataset as given in Patrick (2005), p. 88 (Table 4.16).

In Table 4, column four stands for the average wage of labour (AWL). When it is compared to the data on the average productivity of labour (APL) in Kerala, it becomes clear that in the manufacturing sector, the AWL was higher than the APL in all the years except two years (1995-96 and 1989-99). This stands in the way of maximisation of labour employment in the manufacturing sector as it creates losses to employers.

The demand for higher wages by trade unions regardless of lower productivity of labour has no economic justification. As the Table reveals, the changes in wages were much higher than the changes in productivity in Kerala between 1981-82 and 1998-1999. In this situation, the secondary sector cannot make any sustainable efforts for industrial development and expansion. Because of this unhealthy milieu, some of the industries in the past were converted from factory-type to household type establishments to save themselves from the uncertain onslaught of labour unions and uneconomically high minimum wages. It is then not surprising that many of the local industries are shifted to other states like Tamil Nadu and Karnataka for their development. The outflow of capital and de-capitalisation have been a serious constraint in the industrial development of Kerala. The state is evidently having a pro-labour policy frame which is making the macroeconomic fundamentals weaker and weaker. Moreover, many basic facilities like good infrastructure, transport and communication, electricity supply and technology have not been adequate and satisfactory. The industrial sector in Kerala falls short of many of the basic requirements of growth-promoting capitalist sector to absorb all the unemployed and underemployed labour productively from the primary sector.

If occupation structure is an index of economic progress, then it can be said that in a sense, Kerala is more developed than the Indian union. The pattern of its occupation structure is much better than the national scenario. Kerala's primary sector contains lesser percentage of labour force and the other two sectors absorb more workers compared to the national average. The agricultural sector in Kerala is carrying with nearly one-third of the total labour force. The burden is much lower than that of many of the developing economies, and reasonably, one can expect that all going well, the occupational structure will improve further in the foreseeable future. The pattern of Kerala's occupation structure is perhaps better than that of many of the Asian countries. In countries like Bangladesh and Pakistan, to name only a few, the occupation ratio has remained static at around 65:35 for the agricultural and non-agricultural occupations respectively in spite of economic growth. But the rate of growth of GDP has remained much lower in Kerala than all these countries. However, all these countries including Kerala, are plagued by three fundamental constraints. First, very low average productivity of labour; second, declining per capita productivity in agriculture and finally, slow and sluggish growth of the industrial sector. These constraints are conspicuous by their absence in DCs.

In Kerala, the services sector is poised to be the largest employer in the near future. But the expected hypertrophy of the services sector does not always imply a rapid and sustainable growth of productivity unless it is backed up by modern technology. Large capital intensity and high-tech services sector cannot be expected in Kerala in the foreseeable future. Hence, the extra jobs that will be created in this sector may not be accompanied by a high level of productivity. The services sector contains many different types of services, and persons without much technical skill can easily enter into some of these services which are low-productive and low value-added. Thus, this sector will be a happy hunting ground of both low and high-skilled jobs-seekers juxtaposed side by side, and probably there will be disguised unemployment and underemployment. The services sector in a state like Kerala is partly an informal sector where productivity is palpably low but is infested by redundant labour. All these are less likely in the industrial sector which needs technically competent and experienced people and is managed by heard-headed profit-maximising private entrepreneurs. The plausibility of the existence of surplus labour in the industrial sector is much less. However, the expansion of private industries and privatisation may be potentially limited in a state dominated by the philosophy of communism. Hence, employment growth in industries may not be as high as is often expected in a growing state. At present, the share of employment in the public sector is much higher than that of the private sector. If this trend continues, there will be more surplus labour and loss of sectoral productivity. Government offices and enterprises are the citadel of most of the surplus labour in LDCs. Having said about the downside of the service sector, it needs to be added that in Kerala, the services sector will remain the major employer for quite some time to come because of its increasing expansion of domestic demand-oriented activities, and also because of its highest per capita income and productivity. As a matter of fact, in Kerala in recent years, both industrial and services sectors are gradually undergoing structural transformation towards higher value-added, and the utilisation of technology which, though not the best, is better than the type of technology used in yesteryears.

CONCLUDING OBSERVATIONS

A number of interesting facts emerge from the discussion on Kerala's occupation structure. First, although the primary sector is shedding labour at the highest rate compared to other sectors, the unemployment in the rural sector stands out to be still much higher than that of the urban sector. Second, there exists some scope for the absorption of additional labour in both tertiary and industrial sectors with higher productivity provided these are modernised with better technology, and capital per worker is adequately augmented. The fact that an increase in capital per worker can significantly improve productivity has been recognised by many economists including Robert Solow. The Solow model of growth (1956) clearly states that output (income) per worker is given by the square root of capital per worker. Thus, a large amount of capital is indeed necessary to bring about some perceptible change in labour productivity. Finally, a sustainable increase in labour productivity is not possible unless human capital and skill endowment of the labour force are significantly improved.

The Keralian economy has not yet attained optimum occupational distribution, for a sectoral reallocation of labour force from agriculture to non-agricultural sector will enhance labour productivity. While this is factually true, it seems to be practically problematic to transfer labour from agriculture unless the primary sector is re-organised, modernised and technologically refurbished, and at the same time, the non-agricultural sector generates sufficient pull factors. But to reorganise the agricultural sector in a slowly-developing state like Kerala will indeed be a heroic undertaking.

REFERENCES

Clark, Colin (1952), *The Conditions of Economic Progress*, Macmillan, New York.

Dutta, B. (1952), *Economics of Industrialisation*, World Press, Calcutta.

Fisher, A. G. B. (1964), *Economic Progress and Social Security*, Macmillan, London.

Fourasite, Jean (1951), " Productivity and Economies", *Political Science Quarterly*, June.

Ghosh, B. N. (1977), *Disguised Unemployment in Underdeveloped Countries*, Heritage Publications (published with the support of IDRC, Canada), New Delhi.

Ghosh, B. N. (1998), *Malaysia: The Transformation Within*, Addison–Wesley–Longman, Pvt. Ltd., Kuala Lumpur.

Ghosh, B. N. (2009), "Globalisation and Food Policy Dilemmas in Developing Countries: Contextualising the Indian Scenario", *Journal of Third World Studies.*

Kuznets, Simon (1966), *Modern Economic Growth*, Oxford and IBH, Calcutta.

Patrick, Martin (2005), "Labour Market and Employment", in D. Rajesenan and Gerard de Groot (eds.), *Kerala Economy-Trajectories, Challenges and Implications*, Directorate of Publications and Public Relations, CUSAT, ch. 4.

Lewis, Arthur W. (1954), "Economic Development with Unlimited Supplies of Labour", *Manchester School*, May.

Praksah, B. A. (2007), *Fifty Years of Kerala's Economy* (1956-2006), Department of Economics, University of Kerala, Tiruvananthapuram.

Singer, H. W. (1952), "The Mechanics of Economic Development", *Indian Economic Review*, August.

Solow, Robert (1956), "A Contribution to the Theory of Growth", *Quarterly Journal of Economics*, Vol. 70, February.

3

AN OVERVIEW OF KERALA'S POWER SECTOR

N. Madhava Menon

Infrastructure means both social and economic overhead capital. Economic infrastructure includes services from public utilities, public works and other transport sector. Public utilities in turn include power, telecommunications, water supply, sanitation and sewage, solid waste collection and disposal. Since energy is an essential input of all productive economic activity, it is considered as the most important single factor for economic development.

The present paper focuses on the power scenario of Kerala with a brief review of the power scenario in India. The history and growth of the power sector in Kerala, plan wise achievement of power in Kerala, growth of Kerala's power system in terms of installed capacity, generation per annum, per capita consumption of power, import and export of power, growth of transmission and distribution lines, number of consumers and connected load, number of villages electrified, category wise consumers...etc. also come within the purview of the study.

POWER SCENARIO IN INDIA

There are three broad sources of commercial energy such as coal and lignite, oil and gas and electricity. Electric power is an important pre-requisite for economic development and it is required for commercial and non-commercial uses. Commercial uses of power refer to the use of electric power in industry, agriculture and transport. Non commercial uses include electric power required for domestic lighting, cooking, use of domestic mechanical gadgets like the refrigerators, air conditioners etc. There are three main sources of generation of electric power, viz., hydro electric power, thermal power and nuclear energy.

The per capita energy consumption, a proxy to energy stock reveals that India's per capita consumption is relatively low comparable to other developed and developing world. The per capita consumption of energy in India in 2003 was 520 kg of oil equivalent. The per capita consumption of energy in India was only 13% of that in Japan and only 6.6% of that in USA. In 2008-09 it is estimated to become 612 kg.. But the production of energy has increased steadily after 1950-51. Between 1951and 2005, the electricity (installed capacity) increased by over 68 times (i.e. installed capacity in thousand MW) increased from 2.3 in 1950-51to 143.8 in 2005-06 and generation (in billion Kwh) from 7 to 650. Despite this tremendous growth, India has always faced chronic power shortage since 1950-51.

Table 1
Installed Power Capacity 1950 to 2006

Year	*Total capacity (1000 MW)*
1950-51	2.3
1970-71	16.2
1990-91	74.7
2005-06	143.8

Source: Economic Survey.

The Table 2 shows the targets and achievements of power generation under various Five Year Plans. In the first plan there was 15% short fall in achievement, in the fourth plan 50% and in the tenth plan 40%.

Table 2
Power Generation Targets and Achievements in India under Various Plans Additions to Installed Capacity (MW)

Plan	*Targets*	*Achievements*	*% Shortfall*
First	1300	1100	15
Second	3500	2300	36
Third	7000	4500	36
Fourth	9300	4600	50
Sixth	19670	14230	28
Seventh	22250	21500	4
Eighth	30540	16420	46
Nineth	40250	19015	53
Tenth	41110	23250	40

Source: Various Five Year Plans.

According to Central Electricity Authority, the shortage will aggravate further. The country's overall deficit in terms of net energy will be 8.8% and in terms of demand during peak hours, around 18%. In absolute terms, the figures of deficit are 70, 616 MU and 201,701MW.

Table 3
Projected Power Supply Scenario 2008-09

Region	*Requirement (MU)*	*Availability (MU)*	*Surplus/ Deficit (MU)*	*Demand (MW)*	*Met (MW)*	*Surplus/ Deficit (MW)*
North	2,35,718	2,20,895	-14,823 (-6.3%)	36,180	29,150	-7,030 (-19.4%)
West	2,69,218	2,18,715	-50,503 (-18.8%)	42,036	30,501	-11,536 (27.4%)
South	1,99,707	1,83,298	-16,409 (-8.2%)	30,943	25,124	-5,819 (18.8%)
East	85,173	95,974	10,801 (12.7%)	13,673	13,930	257 (1.9%)
North East	9,762	10,080	318 (3.3%)	1,885	1,600	-285 (15.1%)
All-India	7,99,578	7,28,962	-70,616 (-8.8%)	120,109	98,408	-21,701 (-18.1%)

Source: Central Electricity Authority's Load Generation Balance Report 2008-2009.

POWER DEVELOPMENT SCENARIO IN KERALA

The History and Growth

The history of electrification started with the establishment of first hydro electric power generator of 200 Kw in 1960 by Kannan Devan Hill Produce Co. The First public sector power project, designed on a large scale for commercial uses, in Kerala came in 1940 with the installation of the first unit of 5 MW project at Pallivasal hydro- electric power station. Then the Sabarigiri hydro- electric power station of 300MW installed capacity was commissioned in 1966-67.This was the first major power project in Kerala. Idukki project with 780MW of installed capacity commissioned in 1976(I stage) and in 1985-86 (Stage II) is the largest hydro-electric power station of Kerala. These two stations together constituted about 62% of the total hydro power installed capacity of Kerala. Kerala has at present 26 hydel power plants, 2 state owned Diesel projects of 234.60 MW (Brahmapuram 106.6MW and Kozhikode 128 MW), one thermal plant under private sector (BSES) at Kochi of 160MW and KPCL at Kasargode of 20 MW and Central Public sector NTPC, a naphtha based thermal project plant at Kayamkulam of 350 MW, wind farms at Kanjikode and Ramakkalmedu of 18.53 MW and two private captive power plants at Maniyar and Koothungal of 33 MW. At present 69.54% of our power generation is contributed by hydro power stations.

Table 4

Generation Capacity of Kerala Power System as on December 2008

Various sources of power	*Installed capacity MW*
KSEB Hydro Power	1879.10
Private Hydro Power	33.00
KSEB Thermal	234.60
IPP Thermal	177.44
NTPC	359.58
Wind	18.53
Grand total	2702.25

Source: www.kseboard.com

The Kerala system consists of 13 hydel stations, 11 small hydel stations, 2 captive power plants, 2 thermal stations, 3

IPPs and 2 wind mills. The grid is connected to the Southern Region Transmission system through two 400 KV double circuit line at Madakkathara and Thiruvanathapuram. There are 5 major inter-state transmission lines. The major sub-stations include one 400 KV sub-station, and fourteen 220 KV sub-stations and four 220 KV sub-stations under construction.

The Kerala State Electricity Board (KSEB) was set up on 31-03-1957 as per the Supply act 1948 with the objective of rationalization of power development at the state level, with on inherited installed capacity of 93.5 MW that rose to 2657.24 MW by December 2007. KSEB from its very inception acted as a service organization instead of a business organization. KSEB has the monopoly in generation, transmission and distribution of power in Kerala.

Table 5
KSEB–Statistics of 1958

The Domestic Tariff	1.5 Annas
Installed Capacity	109.5 MW
Transmission Lines	
110 KV Lines	220.176 Ckt miles
66 KV Lines	835.3 Ckt miles
33 KV Lines	26 Ckt miles
22 KV Lines	114.05 Ckt miles
11 KV Lines	2365.31 Ckt miles
Distribution Lines	
3.3 KV Lines	24.6 miles
LT Lines	3826.36 miles

Source: www.kseboard.com.

Plan wise Achievements of Power in Kerala

During the first three plan periods 155 MW were added to the power system where as during the annual plan period (1966-69) 379MW were added. In the 5th and 7th plan period the increase was to the tune of 390 MW and 502.50 MW respectively. During the eighth plan the installed capacity increased only by 20 MW. This was followed by an increase of 1092.68 MW during the 9th plan period. During the 10th plan period an additional installed capacity of only 55.6 MW were added to the power system. The following table shows the plan wise achievement of installed capacity from first to tenth plan periods. The table reveals the fact that there is no planned uniform increase in the installed capacity in Kerala and consequent deficit of power occurs.

Table 6
Plan wise Achievement of Power

Plan Period	*Installed Capacity (MW)*
First three plan	155.00
Annual plan (1966-69)	379.00
Fifth plan	390.00
Sixth plan	-
Seventh plan	502.50
Eighth plan	20.00
Ninth plan	1092.68
Tenth plan	55.6

Source: Economic Review, Various issues.

Growth in Installed Capacity

The total installed capacity increased-from 85.5MW in 1956-61 period to 2657.22MW in 2006-07.This increase in installed capacity is also not at a uniform rate. With the commissioning of Idukki hydro project there is a steep increase in installed capacity during 1976 and 1986. After that no major projects were commissioned and hence a decline in this rate up to 1997-98 period. Later the minor hydro projects, thermal projects and diesel power plants with public and private participation were initiated and consequent rise in the power generation took place.

Growth in the Generation, Consumption, Import, and Deficit in Power System

Electricity generation in Kerala state increased from 591MU in 1960-61 to 7745.78 MU in 2006-07. In December 2008, it became 2702.25 MU. Even though the generation of electricity in our state is increasing, the rate of increase in consumption exceeds the generation of power. This necessitates the import of electricity from other states and Central station. The purchase of electricity from other states and central station increases from a mere 56.80 MU to 8149.84 in 2006-07. This

Table 7
Growth in Installed Capacity

Period	Installed Capacity MW	Cum. Instaled Capacity MW
1951-56	48	85.5
1956-61	47.00	132.50
1961 66	60.00	192.50
1966-69	379.00	571.50
1969-74	50.00	621.50
1974-78	390.00	1011.50
1978-80	-	1011.50
1980-85	-	1011.50
1985-90	465.00	1476.50
1990-94	7.50	1484.00
1994-95	19.50	1503.50
1995-96	2.02	1505.52
1996-97	3.00	1508.80
1997-98	267.28	1775.80
1998-99	270.52	2046.30
1999-2000	304.38	2350.70
2000-01	70.00	2420.70
2001-02	180.50	2601.20
2002-03	-	2601.20
2003-04	13.00	2614.22
2004-05	3.00	2617.22
2005-06	27.00	2644.22
2006 07	13.00	2657.22

Source: KSEB, Power System Statistics, Various Issues.

continuous and fast increase in consumption led to deficit of power in our state. It increased enormously from 1299.10MU in 1991 to 8149.84MU in 2006-07.

This deficit is further caused by the increase in the number of consumers and connected loads as well as the number of villages electrified. The number of consumers increases from 11.72 lakhs in 1978-79 to 87.14 lakhs in 2006-07and in December 2008 this figure comes to 92.35 lakhs. Similarly the connected load in KW (lakhs) also increases from 17.38 in 1978-79 to 114.66 in 2006-07. The table given below highlights these facts.

Table 8
Generation, Import, Consumption and Deficit of Power from 1960 to 2007

Year	*Generation (MU)*	*Import (MU)*	*Consumption (MU)*	*Deficit (MU)*
1960-61	591.00	56.80	636.20	45.20
1970-71	2126.00	21.00	1807.90	-318.10
1980-81	5241.60	43.60	3552.70	-1688.90
1990-91	5075.15	1159.75	6789.85	1299.10
2000-01	6967.00	5543.00	12510.00	5543.00
2001-02	7142.18	5447.51	12577.79	5435.61
2002-03	5475.74	7330.80	12685.34	7209.60
2003-04	4488.06	8015.41	12503.47	8015.41
2004-05	6377.06	6390.79	12719.77	6341.94
2005-06	7600.78	6700.50	14254.86	6654.08
2006-07	7745.78	8149.84	15895.62	8149.84

Source: KSEB, Power System Statistics, Various Issues.

EXPORT OF POWER

There is surplus in the power supply from 1968-69 to 1985-86. The commissioning of the Sabarigiri Project in 1966 - 67 led to power surplus situation in Kerala. This gave rise to export of power from our state to other neighbouring states. With the commissioning of Idukki project (stage I) export increased at a very high rate. In 1969-70 export of power became 306.80 MU. The export continued to increase and in 1978-79 it was 2097 MU. This high export trend continued up to 1981-82. Thereafter export declined steadily due to fast increase in the internal consumption and a continuous deficit in the power scenario in our state was seen. The table given below illustrates the export performance of power from 1960-61 to 200

PER CAPITA ENERGY CONSUMPTION IN KERALA

As mentioned earlier per capita consumption is a proxy to energy stock, it increased from 30Kwh in 1960-61 to 465 in 2006-07.Eventhough there is an increasing trend in the per capita consumption of energy in Kerala, it is very low compared with other states and all India figures.

Table 9
Increase in the Number of Consumers and Connected Load

Year	*No. of Consumers (Lakhs)*	*Connected Load (KW Lakhs)*
1978-79	11.72	17.38
1979-80	13.37	18.87
1980-81	15.72	20.46
1981-82	18.37	23.60
1982-83	19.70	25.89
1983-84	20.56	27.74
1984-85	22.18	28.03
1985-86	23.97	31.45
1986-87	26.07	33.80
1987-88	27.70	35.69
1988-89	29.37	37.58
1989-90	31.93	41.66
1990-91	34.50	46.43
1991-92	36.98	55.26
1992-93	39.31	65.76
1993-94	41.55	49.33
1994-95	44.18	53.98
1995-96	46.86	57.70
1996-97	49.24	60.61
1997-98	52.11	64.61
1998-99	56.40	72.75
1999-00	60.29	81.50
2000-01	64.47	85.51
2001-02	66.62	89.18
2002-03	69.48	93.94
2003-04	73.01	99.10
2004-05	77.99	103.34
2005-06	82.95	109.08
2006-07	87.14	111.66

Source: KSEB, Power System Statistics, Various Issues.

Table 10
Villages Electrified in Kerala from 1978-2007

Year	*Villages Electrified*
1978-79	1248
1980-81	1268
1985-86	1268
1990-91	1384
1995-96	1384
2000-01	1384
2005-06	1384
2006-07	1384

Source: KSEB, Power System Statistics, Various Issues.

Table 11
Export of Power

Year	*Export*	*1983-84*	*90.60*
1960-61	11.60	1984-85	329.00
1961-62	14.60	1985-86	396.00
1962-63	-	1986-87	19.00
1963-64	13.10	1987-88	17.42
1964-65	-	1988-89	10.74
1965-66	-	1989-90	103.59
1966-67	10.90	1990-91	4.73
1967-68	5.10	1991-92	2.18
1968-69	28.20	1992-93	186.77
1969-70	306.80	1993-94	15.95
1970-71	339.10	1994-95	-
1971-72	340.40	1995-96	4.09
1972-73	301.20	1996-97	1.97
1973-74	307.30	1997-98	0.73
1974-75	363.60	1998-99	-
1975-76	302.50	1999-00	-
1976-77	555.30	2000-01	-
1977-78	1605.40	2001-02	11.90
1978-79	2097.20	2002-03	121.20
1979-80	1933.80	2003-04	-
1980-81	1732.50	2004-05	199.44
1981-82	1777.50	2005-06	635.90
1982-83	668.00	2006-07	1046.89

Source: KSEB, Power System Statistics, Various Issues.

Table 12
Per Capita Consumption of Energy

Year	*Per Capita Consumption (Kwh)*
1960-61	30.00
1970-71	72.00
1980-81	109.40
1990-91	185.00
2000-01	311.67
2001-02	395.00
2002-03	392.00
2003-04	386.00
2004-05	400.00
2005-06	427.00
2006-07	465.00

Source: KSEB Power System Statistics Various Issues.

TRANSMISSION AND DISTRIBUTION LINES

The growth of power system is further reflected in the growth of transmission and distribution lines (220,110, 66, 33, 22, and 11KV lines) in our State. The table shows the growth of various lines from 1978-79 to 2006-07.

Table 13
Transmission and Distribution Lines in Circuit KM

Year	*220kv*	*110kv*	*66kv*	*33kv*	*22kv*	*11kv*	*LT (Km)*
1978-79	854.00	1545.00	1879.00	-	160.00	12645.00	42507.00
1980-81	887.00	1545.00	2046.00	-	160.00	14189.00	55963.00
1985-86	887.00	1897.00	2373.00	-	160.00	16917.00	76141.00
1990-91	1064.22	2329.00	2492.00	-	160.00	20221.00	101834.00
1995-96	1175.99	2425.09	2669.46	-	120.52	25807.00	129893.00
2000-01	2577.89	3465.92	2911.37	29.80	99.94	30035.67	187170.00
2001-02	2577.89	3518.55	2924.65	150.10	102.94	30971.19	191930.80
2002-03	2577.89	3554.94	2933.08	252.85	102.94	32054.42	196974.02
2003-04	2582.15	3730.64	2943.33	358.92	156.59	33280.22	201637.62
2004-05	2594.35	3802.50	2948.37	530.69	156.59	34235.70	207711.00
2005-06	2640.85	3873.80	2996.82	623.40	156.59	34596.00	217899.00
2006-07	2640.85	3901.54	3027.09	738.45	156.59	36419.00	226128.00

Source: KSEB Power System Statistics, Various Issues.

Except 22kv lines almost all lines in circuit KM increased in Kerala. There is a three fold increase in the 220 KV lines, two fold increase in 110, 66 KV lines, one and half times in the case of 11KV lines from 1978-79 to 2006 07. In the case of 33 KV lines there is a twenty times increase. Similarly the LT lines increases from 42507 KM in 1978-79 to 226128 KM in 2006-07.

MAXIMUM DEMAND AND TRANSMISSION AND DISTRIBUTION LOSSES

Internal maximum demand has been growing at a faster rate than the installed and generating capacity in the state. This causes power shortage and was met through import of power from other states. The peak demand of the state increased from 116.3MW in 1960-61 to 2880 MW in 2006-07.

In Kerela the T&D loss on an average is 20%. It increased from 18.30% in 1960-61 to 30.76% in 2001-02 and again declined to 23.43% in 2006-07.

Table 14
Maximum Demand and T&D Losses

Year	*Peak Demand (MW)*	*T&D Loss (%)*
1960-61	116.3	18.3
1965-66	173.7	20.20
1970-71	318.2	15.20
1975-76	482.4	18.10
1980-81	735.4	21.10
1985-86	1001.8	26.80
1990-91	1271.6	21.52
1995-96	1651.4	20.4
2000-01	2501.0	17.21
2001-02	2520.0	30.76
2002-03	2409.0	29.08
2003-04	2495.0	27.44
2004-05	2451.0	24.95
2005-06	2624.0	24.59
2006-07	2880.0	23.43

Source: KSEB, Power System Statistics, Various Issues.

CATEGORY WISE CONSUMERS AND PERCENTAGE OF SALES AND REVENUE

The category wise consumers in Kerala show that the industrial and domestic sectors dominate the other sectors. 70% of total consumption of electricity in our state is by these two groups. In December 2008 the number of domestic consumers increased to 70.25 lakhs, commercial consumers 16.46 lakhs, industrial consumers 1.28 lakhs and agriculture consumers are 4.35 lakhs. The sale of electricity is a proxy for consumption. The following table explains all these facts.

Out of the total sale of power in 1970-71, the industrial sector accounted for 65.9%, domestic sector 4.36% and agriculture sector 2.2% .The share of domestic sector has been increasing to 42.12% where as the industrial sector declines to 32.45%. The share of other sectors is constant. Revenue from various sectors shows that domestic sector contributes only 21% of total revenue even though this consumes 42% of the total electricity. The industrial sector's contribution to revenue increased from 11% in 1970-71 to 40% in 2006-07.

The power shortage and power crisis led to load shedding and power cut. At the start of the third five year plan period a

Table 15
Percentage of Sales and Revenue from 1970-71 to 2006-07

Year	*Domestic*		*Commercial*		*Industrial*		*Agriculture*		*Public Lighting*		*Others*		*Total*	
	S%	*R%*	*S%*	*R%*	*S%*	*R%*	*S%*	*R%*	*S%*	*R%*	*S%*	*R%*	*S%*	*R%*
1970-71	4.36	-	3.55	-	65.90	-	2.20	-	1.07	-	22.91	-	100	-
1980-81	9.84	-	4.11	-	42.51	-	1.78	-	0.93	-	40.82	-	100	-
1990-91	30.34	24.90	9.37	13.46	50.58	11.1	3.87	1.33	2.06	2.87	11.10	3.81	100	100
2000-01	45.44	21.78	8.02	20.89	36.67	49.68	3.39	1.35	1.75	1.25	4.73	3.71	100	100
2001-02	42.81	20.80	12.81	23.99	34.38	47.43	2.16	0.87	1.74	1.18	6.10	5.34	100	100
2002-03	43.42	22.41	13.85	20.97	36.24	50.90	2.09	0.68	1.78	1.02	2.62	4.02	100	100
2003-04	49.93	25.53	14.73	20.99	33.47	49.74	2.37	0.71	1.86	1.02	2.62	0.61	100	100
2004-05	44.43	25.76	13.71	21.72	37.78	48.20	2.31	0.63	1.95	1.14	2.71	2.52	100	100
2005-06	42.81	23.68	10.02	21.51	34.45	44.27	1.74	0.56	1.91	1.13	9.07	13.84	100	100
2006-07	42.12	21.68	10.06	2 0.53	32.45	39.95	1.78	0.56	1.85	1.07	11.75	16.21	100	100

Source: KSEB , Power System Statistics, Various Issues.

major power cut was introduced in Kerala. From that time onwards Kerala is facing power cut and load shedding.

POWER SECTOR REFORMS

The power crisis in Kerala necessitates urgent power sector reforms. The E. Balanandan Committee to study the Development of Electricity in Kerala (1997) recommended to set up a Government owned company viz., The Kerala Power Development and Finance Corporation Ltd., to develop, finance and manage generation of electricity, construction and installation of power stations and transmission lines in Kerala. The Task Force on Policy Issues Relating to Power Sector and Power Sector Reforms (1997) and the Expert Committee to Review the Tariff Structure of the KSEB (1998) provided detailed discussion on reform process. The then UDF Government accordingly initiated necessary steps to restructure the functioning of the Board in terms of profit centres at the levels of generation, transmission and distribution, three regional centres with head quarters at Thiruvananthapuram, Ernakulam and Kozhikode were also to be established. These regional centres would have the control over the electricity supply in the state. The profit centres would have wide autonomous powers in decision making in several areas including capital investment, resource generation, appointment of personnel etc.

In August 2001, Government of Kerala signed a MoU with the Union Power Ministry, expressing its willingness to undertake power sector reforms. As per the MoU, the KSEB is now to be run on commercial lines and also to securitise all its due to the Central Public Sector Undertakings. Accordingly, in April 2002, the KSEB was divided in to three independent profit centres with separate administrative set up and account.

The Kerala State Electricity Regulatory Commission was constituted on 14 th November 2002 under the provisions of The Electricity Regulatory Commissions Act 1998. With effect from 10 th June 2003 the Commission has come under the purview of the Electricity Act 2003. The important functions vested in the Commission are:

- Determine the tariff for generation, supply, transmission and wheeling of electricity, wholesale, bulk or retail, as the case may be, within the state.
- Regulate Electricity Purchase and Procurement Process of distribution licensees including the price at which Electricity shall be procured from the generating companies or licensees or from other sources through agreement for purchase of power for distribution and supply within the state.
- Issue licenses to persons seeking to act as transmission licensees, distribution licensees and electricity traders with respect to their operations within the state.
- Promote cogeneration and generation of electricity from renewable sources of energy.
- Levy fee for the purpose of the Electricity Act 2003.
- Promotion of competition, efficiency and economy in activities of the Electricity Industry.

As per the Sub section (2) of the Section 131 of the Electricity Act 2003, KSEB was to be transformed in to a corporate entity. Accordingly as per the G.O dated 25.9.08 , all interests, rights in property and all liabilities of KSEB was vested into the Government of Kerala until a new company as per the provisions of the act is registered.

In addition to these administrative and structural reforms, KSEB is planning many renovation and modernization Programmes for Generation, Distribution and Transmission sectors to meet the ever increasing demand for power in future. 429.55 MW hydel schemes, 100 MW wind farms at Ramakkalmedu are planned to be added in the Eleventh Plan Period for enhancing the generation. The proposed 400 KV power highway, many 220 KV Substations, 33 KV Substations are envisaged to strengthen the transmission grid. In distribution side Voltage Improvement schemes under Accelerated Power Development and Reforms Programmes are planned. All these efforts are expected to reduce the T&D loss and to ensure better service to the customers. Hence these reforms are to be implemented urgently and properly in the Kerala Power System to save our state from darkness.

REFERENCES

Government of Kerala, Economic Review (Different Volumes), State Planning Board, Trivandrum.

Government of Kerala (1997), Report of the Committee to Study the Development of Electricity (Chairman E. Balanandan).

Kerala State Electricity Board, Power System Statistics (Various Issues), Thiruvananthapuram.

Government of India (1996), The India Infrastructure Report, Volume III, Sector Reports, NCAER, New Delhi.

Government of India, Economic Survey (2006-2007), Chapter 9.

Planning Commission, An approach to the Eleventh Five Year Plan, (2007-12).

www.kseboard.com, Official Web site of Kerala.State Electricity Board.

4

DECENTRALIZED PLANNING IN KERALA: PERFORMANCE AND PROBLEMS

G. Gopikuttan

INTRODUCTION

The participatory mode of Democratic Decentralised Planning implemented in Kerala has been appreciated as a 'model' to be emulated in the rest of the country. The way in which the state has devolved functions, functionaries and finances to the lower levels and the process of decentralised development administration, fiscal decentralisation and local governance has been adjudged as the best practice among the Indian states. At present the Local Self Governments (LSGs) have more than a decade of experience in development planning through a democratic and participatory process. Grama Panchayats and urban local bodies are mandated to identify the felt needs of the local people and to prepare projects and implement development plans through a participatory process that ensures direct democracy. LSGs belonging to the higher tiers do not have any hierarchical control over the lower tiers. Grama Panchayats (GPs) are not controlled by Block Panchayats (BP) and the BPs are not under the supervision of District

Panchayats (DPs). District Planning Committee[1] (DPC) ensures the coordination of plans both the rural and urban areas. The LSGs in Kerala were able to evolve a fairly elaborate methodology[2] for participatory plan formulation and implementation. Further, in spite of periodic change in government, the participatory approach to local level planning has been sustained and carried forward into 10th and 11th five-year plan periods. The decentralisation experiment has proved that the scope of public action could be improved through democratisation of planning process (Isaac & Franke 2000; Parameswaran 2005).

There may be many problems related to planning, financial administration and local governance. But the fact is that the LSGs prepare development plans and handle more than one-third of the state's annual plan funds. Most of the human development and social security and welfare functions are now being implemented through the LSGs. In this context, the present paper attempts to evaluate the performance and challenges of the decentralised planning process. It first examines the history of decentralisation, and then analyses the financial administration, and the institutions and processes involved in planning. The paper then evaluates the production sector planning, plans for the disadvantaged categories and also the plans dealing with education and health. Lastly it concludes with an overview of major challenges to be addressed for strengthening the democratic decentralised planning process.

HISTORY OF DECENTRALISATION

Earnest efforts for decentralisation[3] began ever since the first Kerala Ministry assumed in 1957. 'The first ministry appointed an administrative reform committee to suggest measures for the democratisation of the government at various levels. The committee recommended the strengthening of Panchayats in the state as viable and basic units of administration and development. Subsequently, the Kerala Panchayat Bill (1958) and District Council Bill (1959) were placed in the state assembly, but could not be enacted as the ministry was dismissed and the assembly dissolved. The new government passed the Kerala Panchayat Act (1960), which incorporated various recommendations of the Balwantray Mehra Committee (1957). Based on the Act, the first Panchayat election was held in 1963 and a total of 922 village Panchayats came into existence in 1964 (Oommen 2004). But the Panchayats had very little autonomy and freedom. Though there was an elected body in charge of panchayats, the government had tremendous power over them (Ramachandran 2004). In 1964, the Kerala Panchayat Union Councils and Zilla Parishad Bill was formulated, but that was not passed as the ministry fell. Again in 1967 another bill, the Kerala Panchayat Bill (1967) that envisaged a two-tier structure with panchayats as the basic unit and Zilla Parishad at the district levels was introduced in the state legislature. That bill was also lapsed with the fall of the ministry and dissolution of the Assembly. After several setbacks, the government of Kerala in 1986 appointed a committee to study the existing legislations and to make specific recommendations for democratic decentralisation at the local level. Based on the Report on the Measures to be taken for Democratic Decentralisation at the District and Lower Level (1988) elections were held for district councils, which then came into existence in 1991. But the subsequent government reduced the annual plan outlay for district councils, and later dissolved them altogether. Fortunately, it was at this time that the central government proclaimed the historic Constitutional Amendment (Oommen 2004, p. 110).

With the adoption of 73rd and 74th constitutional Amendment Acts and subsequent legislations at the state level, Local Self Governments has become the basic unit of governance. The state of Kerala has transferred most of the functions, responsibilities, authority and resources to the LSGs[4]. The elected representatives got the power, freedom and authority to govern the panchayat. The participatory mode of Democratic Decentralised Planning in Kerala began as a 'big bang' namely 'participatory people's campaign' (PPC) in 1996. High autonomy was given to the local bodies to determine their own priorities and to chalk out plans and programmes. Mass campaigns, public participation in decision making and the opportunity for the poor to articulate their felt needs and the proclaimed transparency in selection of beneficiaries and allocation of funds associated with the decentralization process aroused high expectations among the people. A rich pool of committed and dedicated social workers rendered voluntary service to the development programmes of LSGIs during the early years of PPC. It was expected that the Micro-level institutions (MLIs) such as neighbourhood groups (NHGs), Grama Sabha/Ward Sabha, Task forces, and Expert committees[5] would take a civil society role. DPC was expected to integrate various development plans into a comprehensive district plan. Irrespective of ideological differences local units of all the political parties and political coalitions worked for strengthening the new development consciousness generated in the state through the democratic decentralised planning process.

During the 10th Five Year Plan (FYP) period the PPC was re-christened as 'Kerala Development Plan' with the main thrust of institutionalising and sustaining capacities created in the LSGs; improving the quality of service delivery especially in the field of health and education; and catalysing local economic development through LSGs. With a view to further consolidate the positive impacts of the decentralised planning during the 9th and 10th FYP periods, the government of Kerala has launched the 2nd phase of People's Plan programme during the Eleventh FYP that began in 2007. Following are the core objectives at this phase[6]:

- Sustainable institutionalisation of decentralisation in the state.
- Improve the quality of local level planning with active participation of people
- Revival of agriculture and promoting local economic development with special emphasis on improvement of public service by targeting the weaker sections of the society.
- Increasing the production and productivity of agriculture and other allied sectors by preparing Integrated Watershed Management Plans.

- Generating additional income and job opportunities by promoting primary sectors supplemented by strengthening of micro-enterprises, small and medium enterprises and traditional industry.

FINANCIAL ADMINISTRATION

The Panchayats are expected to have acquired the capacity to handle its finances by now. Prior to the launching of the decentralised planning programme, 'the village Panchayats in Kerala had a fairly good revenue base. Their receipts consisted of own tax revenue from taxes assigned by state government but collected and appropriated by Panchayats; taxes assigned to Panchayats but collected by the state government and passed to them; shared taxes; non-tax revenue; grants in aid from the state government; loans from the state government or financial institutions; and funds received for Centrally Sponsored Schemes' (Oommen 2004). With the introduction of decentralised planning, the finances of the LSGs increased several folds. Among the various sources, grant-in-aid is the dominant one. Source-wise expenditure of the LSGs shows that own fund accounted for only a little more that 10 per cent of the total expenditure, and the share of grant-in-aid was 57.3 per cent during the 9th plan period. The share of grant-in-aid in total expenditure has further increased to 73.6 per cent during the 10th plan period (Table 1).

Table 1
Source-wise Expenditure of LSGs during 9th and 10th Five-Year Plan Period (Per cent)

Source of fund	*9th Plan*	*10th Plan*	*Total*
Grant-in-aid	57.3	73.6	66.0
Own fund	10.1	7.4	8.7
State Sponsored	7.6	2.3	4.8
Centrally Sponsored	10.6	7.6	9.0
Loan from Co-operative	1.9	0.2	1.0
Externally aided	0.0	0.3	0.1
Institutional Finance	3.3	1.5	2.4
Voluntary Contribution	1.3	0.2	0.7
Beneficiary Contribution	5.6	4.2	4.9
Others	2.2	2.7	2.4
Total	100	100	100

Source: Estimated from GOK (2008), *Economic Review*, 2007, p. 571.

Despite the buoyancy in economic activities and prosperity of the state during the past one-decade, the share of own source revenue (OSR), declined substantially during the 10th plan period. That may be partially due to the laxity in the collection of OSR.

Plan funds to LSGs are allocated in two different streams: (i) for centrally sponsored and state sponsored schemes; and (ii) for local development. All schemes included in the first stream have been transferred to the LSGs for implementation.[7] For the second stream, funds are allocated on the basis of a well-defined criterion[8] and the LSGs have full freedom in deciding their priorities, formulating and implementing schemes subject to an overall framework designed at the state level. The plan fund is in the form of untied grant (grant-in-aid). Absolute amount devolved to the three tires of LSGs, which was Rupees 4614 crores during the 9th FYP, increased to Rupees 6784 crores during the 10th FYP. However, grant-in-aid as a percentage of state plan outlay declined from 29.29 per cent in 9th FYP to 26.81 per cent in the 10th FYP period. It is observed that the LSGs were not spending the full assistance allotted for developmental purposes. Total expenditure as a percentage of grant-in aid has been stagnating at about 74 per cent during the two plan periods (Table 2).

Table 2

Grant-in-aid Outlay and Expenditure of LSGs during 9th and 10th Plan Periods (Rs. Crore)

Year/Plan	*Grant-in-aid Outlay*	*Expenditure*	*% of Expenditure*
1997-98	949.0	702.31	93.77
1998-99	950.0	589.15	62.02
1999-2000	1020.0	941.06	92.26
2000-01	1045.0	732.28	70.07
2001-02	850.0	486.97	57.29
9th Plan Total	4614.0	3451.77	74.81
2002-03	1342.0	602.26	44.87
2003-04	1317.0	1350.34	102.53
2004-05	1350.0	923.09	68.37
2005-06	1375.0	986.21	71.72
2006-07	1400.0	1209.83	74.76
10th Plan Total	6784.0	5071.73	74.76

Source: GOK (2008), Economic Review, 2007, p. 568.

Among the three tiers of LSGs the GPs showed an impressive performance in spending grant-in-aid. Their expenditure as a percentage of grant-in-aid allotted to them increased from about 73.0 per cent during the 9th Plan to more than 77.0 per cent during the 10th Plan period. Corporations, on the other hand, exhibited a poor performance. The tier-wise grant-in-aid and expenditure of the LSGs during the 9th and 10th Plan periods is given in Table 3.

Table 3

Tier-wise Grant-in-aid and Expenditure during 9th and 10th Plan Periods

(Rs. Crore)

	9th Plan			*10th Plan*		
Tier of LSG	*Outlay*	*Expenditure*	*%*	*Outlay*	*Expenditure*	*%*
GP	2567.68	1938.75	72.95	3826.65	2952.96	77.17
BP	652.24	496.55	76.13	936.66	714.52	76.28
DP	683.39	505.52	73.97	960.78	661.84	68.89
Municipality	396.29	302.78	76.40	589.51	438.17	74.33
Corporation	224.40	208.17	92.77	470.40	304.24	64.68
Total	4614.00	3451.77	74.81	6784.00	5071.73	74.76

Source: GOK (2008), *Economic Review*, 2007, p. 569.

Under-utilization of plan funds allotted for local development may be due to the lack of vision and commitment of the decision makers at the local level. Projects taken without considering economic feasibility and social acceptance might have abandoned half-the way. Before taking up the issues of projects and plans let us have an overview of the major institutions created for ensuring democratic and participatory decision-making.

Institutions for Ensuring Democratic Participation

Participatory planning is expected to operate mainly through the Grams Sabhas, Development Seminar, Working Groups/ Technical Advisory Committees, Committee systems at the LSG level and District Planning Committees.

Grama Sabha

People's participation in decentralization was ensured mainly through meetings of the GP ward level Grama Sabha, chaired by the ward member. Ten per cent of the voters of the ward constitute the quorum. Implementing officials are required to attend the GS meetings. It is envisaged that the needs articulated at the Grama Sabhas be recorded, processed, prioritized, projectised and harmonized into an integrated plan for the village.

Development Seminar

Based on GS recommendations, a one day Development Seminar (DS) would be held every year at the LSG level to which experts, elected members, representatives nominated by the GSs are expected to discuss the draft annual plan document of the LSG, suggest the broad priorities of development projects and select members of Task Forces (Working Groups/Technical Advisory Groups) to provide technical support to projects and programmes as and when needed.

Technical Support Group (Working Groups/Technical Advisory Groups)

Working Groups (at GP, BP and DP levels) were to translate the demands and recommendations of Grama Sabhas and Development Seminars into technically feasible, economically viable and socially beneficial projects. WG members are supposed to be trained and experienced persons capable of providing technical support to projects and programmes. They are also expected to have skills to recognise, acknowledge and address the reality of diverse social relations. For each local body, there were about 8-12 Task Forces/working groups dealing with different sectors. Each WG is headed by an elected Member and convened by specified government official. Working Groups/Technical Advisory Groups (TAG) (evolved from earlier expert committees) at block and district levels consists of experts from and outside the Government. They are expected to provide technical advice to LSGs, technical vetting projects of LSGs and giving technical sanction for works, wherever required.

Present Plight of the Structures and Institutions

The structures and institutions created for ensuring face-to-face democracy and participatory planning were vibrant during the initial years of PPC. Gradually, Grama Sabha, which was conceived as a forum for direct democracy, lost its vibrancy. Since beneficiary selection is its preferred and significant role, social and economic groups who have no expectation of individual benefit abstain from GS meetings. Therefore, participation in GS dwindled. Majority of those who participate expect individual benefit. In the absence of realistic information (scientific and accurate data) objective selection of households for individual benefit and plan formulation for lasting solutions to the development problems becomes difficult. Similarly in several places TAGs lost its significance. For, nominated members who have no expertise or interest in factual data based planning dominate TAGs. Development seminars have become a mockery. Consequently, major proportion of the projects prepared by the LSGs is destined to fail, since they are not factual data based.

Project and Comprehensive Plans

Projects are supposed to be the documentation of technically feasible, economically viable and socially beneficial action programmes aimed at solving specific problems that people face. They form the applied or practical part of planning for economic development and social equity based on a comprehensive strategy. Long and short-term strategies based on issues, possible solutions suggested at the forums such as GS are clearly spelt in the Panchayat Development Reports (PDR). To convert these needs into projects and plans factual data on issues to be tackled, physical targets and financial planning are required. Unless it is meticulously planned based on factual data, it would be difficult to yield the desired results. Though there were attempts to use scientific planning methods in the initial phase of participatory planning, that has not been sustained.

In the absence of data based comprehensive planning and GP level prioritisation of programmes, governing body members of the LSGs representing political parties fought for not less than equal share plan funds to their constituencies. That often resulted in the division of plan funds equitably among the wards, which is detrimental to the spirit of comprehensive planning. Shortage of funds to any ward is counted as an indication of inefficiency of the member representing that ward. Since nobody wants to risk their political support and vote banks, every member fights for more projects and funds to their constituency. Also, spatial balancing in infrastructure sector planning has not been practiced. With the result the correlation between backwardness of GP wards and allocation of expenditure under infrastructure appears to be weak. Productive sector planning failed to generate any impact.

Productive Sector Planning

Decentralised planning was perceived as a means to challenge the problem of poor performance of productive sectors, especially agriculture. But micro level studies (Gopikuttan and Joseph 2007) and state level data indicate that a sense of ad-hocism must have guided most of the productive sector projects and plans. It is also noted that the major proportion of productive sector projects designed were meant for individual benefit. Physical targets were seldom planned. Even in financial terms there exists wide disparity between estimated and actual expenditure incurred for the projects each year. This fact is well documented by the State Planning Board[9]. Therefore, there is no reason to believe that productive sector projects have developed into a comprehensive plan that is capable of addressing the issue of poor performance.

Moreover, prioritisation of plans require scientific information that in turn would require constant vertical communication of planning processes (through officials, academia and other willing collaborators) from GP to district level. That system of vertical communication and integration based on the principle of subsidiarity[10] was lacking throughout. LSGs did not seem to have used the freedom they have to set priorities according to the local specificities. The principle of subsidiarity was often violated due to overlapping activities of government departments and the three tiers of LSGs. Involvement of local people in implementation and monitoring and social audit remain only on paper. People with professional skills and experiences are not involved in the local planning process. Many programmes, therefore, remain expenditure oriented and not outcome oriented.

PLANS FOR DISADVANTAGED CATEGORIES

National and sub national governments implement several programmes targeted to the uplift of the disadvantaged sections. Even though the responsibility to identify deserving households for public support is entrusted with the Grama Panchayats and Municipalities, conditionality attached to implementation and the volume of support vary widely among the department and agencies implementing the programme. With the result the true deserving households fails to get the benefit of several schemes. LSGIs also failed to chalk out appropriate strategies to improve the livelihood conditions of the disadvantaged sections. Though the participatory planning visualises the involvement of local people at every stage–from identification of beneficiaries, designing appropriate programmes to implementation and social audit–that was not effective.

Alleviation of poverty calls for proper identification of the rural and urban poor. Programmes for poverty alleviation and social welfare should be targeted to the most deserving. Lack of correct factual information about the most deserving, multiplicity agencies and duplication of schemes with differential rates of subsidies created several problems. Even though there are only few takers for certain schemes, LSGs are forced to set financial targets to comply with government orders. Central government, through line departments, also implement programme for the same target group. Therefore there is utter confusion among the beneficiaries. Primarily due to the lack of co-ordination and integration of GP schemes/ projects, line department programmes and central government schemes, delivery of services with at least minimum standards, the livelihood conditions of the hard-core poor still remain unchanged.

Most of the projects consisting of individual benefit schemes are implemented and monitored by VEO/LVEOs. Functional control of these officers' rests with the GPs and administrative control remain with the Block Development Officers. They are overburdened with duties[11] in the Block and GPs. Their duties ranging from enquiring the eligibility of identified households to receive a benefit to monitoring and final financial settlement have to be done single-handedly without proper office space, infrastructure and assistance. It is humanly impossible to undertake the diverse types of activities envisaged with ease and equal efficiency. The overburdened work of the VEOs would certainly affect the quality and standard of services that are being provided to the marginalised sections.

Plans dealing with Education and Health

Education and health are critical components of human development. The deterioration of public education would affect the poor people limiting their chances for upward mobility. Similarly, deterioration in quality of public healthcare system and the resultant high cost of healthcare would make the poor more vulnerable. LSGs gave priority to infrastructure development and basic infrastructure of all schools. With the result Kerala stands top in terms of school infrastructure facilities (Mehta 2007). In the health sector also, physical infrastructure of hospitals and heath centres has improved significantly. Panchayats and Municipalities implemented several programmes for sanitation and preventive health care during periods of contingencies. But they never form part of a comprehensive health plan. A health plan consists of preventive, curative and promotive health care, health education, nutrition and drinking water programmes, sanitation and environmental cleanliness, waste managements, waste and rainwater management and so on. Health department, line departments and LSGIs have implemented several programmes of their own. But there is no coordination among the agencies and departments; hence, comprehensive planning is absent.

Overall Performance

Kerala's democratic decentralisation attracted international attention primarily because of its pro-poor development.

Compared to the rest of India, there has been substantial improvement in the livelihood conditions of the disadvantaged sections. Social infrastructure such as roads improved considerably. About 8 lakh new houses, more than 10 lakh sanitary latrines, about 2 lakh new drinking water wells and several other physical assets were provided to the deprived sections during the 9th and 10th FYP periods. However, in this age of global neo-liberalism and market penetration, the decentralisation is facing several challenges.

Major Challenges

Majority of programmes and projects planned under the participatory planning programme were oriented towards the weaker sections of the society, which forms only a minority in the local context. The dominant middle class does not see any significant stakes in such activities. This reduced the interest and hence a threat to the lofty ideal of participation expected in plan preparation and implementation. Hence, democratic and participatory discussions and transparent decision-makings became relatively absent in *grama sabha* meetings and Panchayat Development Seminars. These meeting and seminars are held occasionally by the Panchayat Board to satisfy constitutional obligations. Since the message of an integrated development agenda has not been percolated down to the grass roots, each ward member began to fight for more schemes and benefits to the ward they represents. Hence, it became difficult to achieve an integrated and balanced development of all regions in the Panchayat.

Kerala being a highly politicised State, civil society organizations failed to garner the expected space for democratic dialogues and discussions. They also thought not to invite the ire of the dominant parties. Moreover, voluntarism for regular work such as periodic assessment of the objective realities of the locality, preparation of plans and projects and monitoring of the local development activities would not sustain for long. Cultural attitudes of nucleation with the new media culture of television keeps people, especially the young away form the public space. Young social workers/volunteers keep high aspirations and expectations about personal gains in terms of positions in institutions or democratically elected bodies. When they find that chances for such gains are bleak in PPC, they started withdrawing from the scene. Like in other parts of the globe, the middle class in Kerala that forms the majority pursue neo-liberal attitude and market approach of development, while the marginalized sections, which forms only a minority, look forward to local governments for support to satisfy their basic needs.

A reasonably knowledge oriented participatory methodology of planning from the grass root level has not been developed so far (GOK 2007 p. 578). That was mainly due to the lack of scientific information and professional skills. There is need for a large number of full-time professionals to plan and execute activities with speed and quality. Unfortunately most of the technically qualified persons–the bureaucrats, private doctors, retired engineers and other educated and technically qualified persons- opted to remain outside the institutional structures created for facilitating comprehensive planning.

The bureaucracy and governing body members are overburdened with a host of activities and responsibilities. They can hardly muster their imagination and energy required for data based comprehensive planning for local development and equity. The state government failed to recognise the volume of professional inputs required for local planning. Right-sizing the personnel in commensurate with the functions and responsibilities of LSGIs is an urgent necessity.

There is no integration of programmes initiated and implemented by the three tiers of LSGs, line departments and centrally sponsored schemes (CSS). Lack of integration resulted in unnecessary overlapping and duplication. The centrality of agriculture is not yet recognised. The ecological and environmental aspects are also often neglected. Despite these challenges, we hope that with correct and factual database, professional support, clarity of functions and responsibilities and encouraging political and social environment the democratic decentralisation can definitely be rejuvenated.

NOTES

1. District Planning Committees were set up in each district with the aim of helping the district prepare plans encompassing both the rural and urban areas. In order to ensure co-ordination among the different LSGs in a district Kerala Acts of 1994 (as amended in 1999) provide for a DPC. DPC is empowered to make district perspective plans besides co-coordinating plans prepared by rural as well as urban LSGs (Kerala Development Report 2008, pp. 443-452).

2. Major steps adopted in the methodology of participatory planning are: (i) identification of felt needs of the people in the locality by knowledgeable persons through a participatory and democratic process; (ii) situation analysis; (iii) strategy setting; (iv) project preparation; (v) preparation of comprehensive plans; (vi) plan vetting; (vii) plan approval; (viii) implementation; and (ix) monitoring.

3. "Decentralization brings government closer to the people. It is expected that ordinary citizen to participate and exert influence. When power is brought closer to the citizens, the political process becomes more tangible and transparent and more people can become involved. Decentralization may also create a more open political system in that it implies a division of powers in society; many channels of representation and power sharing become available. This counteracts the monopolization of power by certain elite groups, often the onsequence of centralized political and administrative structures" (Hadenius 2003, p. 1)

4. (i) In the *Health* sector: all institutions other than medical colleges and big regional speciality hospitals have been placed under the control of the local governments.

   (ii) The entire *Public Sanitation* and almost the whole *Rural Water Supply* scheme are now under the local government responsibility.

   (iii) In the *Education* sector: high schools in rural areas have been transferred to the District *Panchayats* and lower primary and upper primary schools to Village *Panchayats;* and in urban areas, all schools have been transferred to the urban local bodies.

   (iv) In the *Agriculture* and allied sectors: the following are now in the domain of the local government functions

   - (a) Agricultural extension including farmer oriented support for increasing production and productivity; (b) Watershed management and minor irrigation; (c) Dairy development; (d) Animal Husbandry including veterinary care; and (e) Inland fisheries.

(v) All the *Poverty Alleviation* schemes, including the centrally sponsored anti-poverty programmes, are now planned and implemented through the local bodies.

(vi) In the field of *Social Welfare*: barring statutory functions relating to juvenile justice, all the functions are now carried out by local governments. The Integrated Child Development Scheme (ICDS) is fully implemented by Village *Panchayats* and Urban Local Bodies. Similarly, care of the disabled has become a local government responsibility to a substantial degree.

(vii) All the *Welfare Pensions* are now administered by the local governments.

(viii) *Connectivity* (roads), except highways and major district roads, has now become a local government responsibility. (Human Development Report 2005, Kerala p. 146).

5. NHG is a territorial association of 25-40 households living in close proximity. At the time of launching PPC, NHGs were conceived as basic or grass-root level socio-political as well as developmental units of society that facilitates participatory and face-to-face democracy. The Technical Support Group was conceived as the Panchayat Planning Board consisting of experts (traditionally trained and academically trained) available within the Panchayats.
6. Government of Kerala, Economic Review 2007, State Planning Board, Thiruvananthapuram 2008, p. 573.
7. The scheme guidelines under this scheme are formulated by the central/state government and the role of LSGs is to act as an intermediary agency for executing the scheme after deciding the location or beneficiary of the scheme.
8. Allocation of funds is based on a composite index of entitlement. Indicators and weights assigned to each indicator for allocation of funds to the three tiers of LSGs are given below:

Indicators	*Weightage (Percentage)*			
	GP	*BP*	*DP*	*Municipality/ Corporatin*
Population (excluding SC/ST)	60	60	50	70
Tribal population	5	5	5	5

Contd...

Indicators	*Weightage (Percentage)* GP	BP	DP	Municipality/ Corporatin
Geographical area excluding area under forests	5	10	15	5
Area under paddy	5	-	-	-
Own income of GP	10			
Composite index of agricultural labourers, persons engaged in livestock, fisheris etc. and marginal workers	15	25	20	-
Composite index of backwardness: houses without latrine, houses without electricity etc.	-	-	10	20
Total	100	100	100	100

Source: GOK (2008), Economic Review 2007 p. 564.

9.Tier-wise estimated and actual expenditure incurred for productive sector projects using grant-in-aid during the 10th Plan period is given below.

(Rupees in Crore)

		Productive sector projects	
Tier	*Allocation*	*Actual expenditure*	*Per cent*
GP	969.99	609.96	62.88
BP	197.57	113.94	57.63
DP	208.97	116.34	55.67
Municipality	65.29	40.53	62.08
Corporation	44.13	18.8	42.60
Total	1485.95	899.57	60.53

Source: GOK (2008), Economic Review 2007, p. 569.

10. Isaac, one of the progenitors of People's campaign for participatory planning, says that 'the basic principle governing the devolution of functions and resources should be that of subsidiarity: what can be done at best at a particular level should be done at that level and not at higher levels. All that can be optimally done at the lowest level should be reserved to that level. Only the residual should be passed to the higher levels' (Isaac 2001, pp. 8-47).

11. Block Panchayat duties: (1) IAY–new houses and renovation (2) IAY credit cum subsidy scheme, (3) SGSY–formation of self-help groups, assistance for self-employment, monitoring (4) Preparation of beneficiary list and muster roll with respect to SGRY, MPLAD, SDF (MLA), NCFRW, NCDRW and (5) other duties including plan and project preparation of BP.

Grama Panchayat Duties: (1) convener of working groups, (2) Coordinator grama sabha (3) Implementing officer of several GP projects, (4) Member secretary, Kudumbasree, etc.

REFERENCES

Gopikuttan G. and Joseph. M. J. (2007), 'Democratic Decentralized Planning in Kerala and Hard-core Poor: Lessons Drawn from Pandalam Grama Panchayat', paper presented at the International Conference on Kerala People's Plan Revisited, on 14-15 December 2007, held at Thiruvananthapram.

Government of India, Planning Commission (2008), *Kerala Development Report*, Academic Foundation and Planning Commission, New Delhi.

Government of Kerala (2006), *Human Development Report 2005: Kerala*, prepared by Centre for Development Studies, State Planning Board, Thiruvananthapuram.

Government of Kerala (2008), *Economic Review 2007*, State Planning Board, Thiruvananthapuram.

Hadenius, Axel (2003), *Decentralisation and Democratic Governance: Experiences from India, Bolivia and South Africa,* Elanders Gotab, Stockholm.

Isaac, Thomas. T M (2001) 'Campaign for Democratic Decentralization in Kerala', *Social Scientist,* Vol. 29, No. 9/10 (Sept–Oct. 2001).

Isaac, T. M. Thomas and Richard Franke (2000), *Local Democracy and Development: Campaign for Decentralized Governance in Kerala,* Left World, New Delhi.

Mehta, Arun C. (2007), Elementary Education in India: Where do we Stand, Vol. 1, National University of Planning and Administration, New Delhi.

Oommen M. A. (2004), 'Fiscal Decentralization in Kerala' in The World Bank (Geeta Sethi (ed), *Fiscal Decentralization to Rural Governments in India,* Oxford University Press, New Delhi).

Parameswaran, M. P. (2005), *Empowering People: Insights from a Local Experiment in Participatory Planning,* Studies in Local-Level Development-2, Centre for Development Studies, Daanish Books, Delhi.

PART–TWO

Transforming Traditional Agriculture

5

KERALA AGRICULTURE IN THE PRE- AND POST-LIBERALIZATION PERIODS

M. Lathika

Agriculture occupies a predominant position in the economy of Kerala and it continues to be the same, even with the remarkable and commendable strides in the non-agricultural sectors of the state. Though the contribution of agriculture towards the state income is coming down substantially from 39.23 per cent of the SDP in 1980-81 to 15.7 per cent in 2006, (GoK, 2006), a considerable proportion of Keralites is reported to be relying still on agriculture for one means of livelihood or other. However, the cultivators and labourers constitute only 23.27 per cent in Kerala as per 2001 census, as against 37.79 per cent in 1991census. Kerala is endowed with a rich resource of land, rainfall, irrigation sources, more educated labour and a wide network of public-funded research and extension facilities–all of which provide a strong production base for agriculture. Twelve agro-climatic zones have been identified in Kerala, which vary widely in their crop suitability and productivity potential, and the state has a total of nearly 22 lakh hectares of net sown area (2004-05) with a cropping intensity of 1.35. (GoK, 2006). Per-cultivator availability of gross cropped area is the highest in Kerala (4.23 hectare) against 1.47

in India (Census, 2001; GoK, 2005). The total surface and replenishable ground water in Kerala is estimated to be 70.165 BCM. But only about 60 per cent of it could be put to beneficial use. The per-capita utilizable ground water availability from both surface flow and replenishable ground flow comes to 1340 M^3 (GoK, 1998). Kerala farmers are having high educational status than those in any other states in India (Kumar and Lathika, 2007).

India chose to adopt import substitution as a development strategy, right from 1950s (Veeramani, 2008), suiting its socialist mode of governance–a development mandate it made itself committed to through a constitutional amendment. Accordingly, its trade environment was relatively closed till 1990s and was subsequently made open following the formation of WTO, free trade agreements (FTA) and removal of quantitative restrictions (QRs). This paradigm policy-shift made the domestic price of the crops getting more integrated with the international prices (Joseph, 2004; Chand), as the domestic markets became more sensitive to the market signals from abroad. A crash in the price of many horticultural crops in the domestic market followed immediately. This dealt a heavy blow on the agricultural economy of many Indian states which had high dominance of commercial crops in their cropping pattern and which had hitherto enjoyed favourable terms of trade (Jeromi, 2007; Joseph and Joseph, 2005; Mohandas, 2005). The capability of a nation to insulate itself from international price volatility depends to a great extent on its comparative advantage. However, comparative advantage is no more considered as having been built solely on the production factors like land, labour and capital. In an open economy environment, apart from these factors, inter-country variations in the level of technology, taxes, subsidies, price of input and output etc., also influence the costs and returns of crop cultivation (Rao, 2005). Productivity and ability of a crop to move up the value chain, possibly through employment of capital and technology, also enhance the comparative advantage of the crop in the nation.

This paper seeks primarily to examine the growth performance of agriculture in Kerala over the two distinct phases of the Indian economy, namely, pre- and post-liberalisation periods, and makes an enquiry into the factors that contributed to the current state of affairs in agriculture in the state. In the process, it also highlights the issues/threats the state is currently encountered with.

DISTRIBUTION OF AGRICULTURAL INCOME

A preliminary analysis of the performance of primary sector of the state, over the years, presents a rather disappointing picture (Table 1).

Table 1
Sectoral Contribution to NSDP (1993-94 base Year)

Sector	*1980-1981*	*1999-2000*	*2000-2001*	*2001-2002*	*2002-2003*	*2003-2004*	*2004-2005*
Primary	39.2	25.38	20.4	19.8	18.8	17.1	16.6
Agriculture[a]	31.58	21.5	16.2	15.4	14.5	13	12.7
Secondary	24.4	20.65	20.9	19.8	19.5	19.3	18.69
Tertiary	36.4	54.0	58.7	60.4	61.8	63.6	64.71

[a]: Share of agriculture in primary sector.

Source: GoK. *Statistics for Planning* (various issues)

Over the years, the primary sector tended to contribute lesser and lesser to the NSDP. While it claimed about 40 per cent stake in 1980-81, it reduced to 16.6 per cent by 2004-05. Agriculture had been a source of great contribution towards the foundation sector. In 1980-81 it had about 32 per cent share on the primary sector. But, over the decades, its tally declined sharply. Thus, along with the weakening of the primary sector, the percentage contribution of agriculture in the primary sector is also on the decline. On the other end of the pyramid, the tertiary sector flourished. It posted a consistent improvement all over the years and this sector continues to lead the growth of the economy.

The annual compound growth rate of different sectors of Kerala also shows the weakening of the foundation sectors. A wider time span is considered here. Table 2 displays the salient results.

Table 2
ACGR of Sectors in the in the Pre- and Post-Liberalization Periods

Sector	*1961-74*	*1974-85*	*1985-92*	*1993-02*	*2002-03*
Primary	2.23	0.7	4.77	-3.92	2.5
Secondary	4.71	2.15	5.36	2.83	1.3
Tertiary	4.24	5.32	5.41	8.03	13.8
Total NSDP	3.21	1.76	5.17	3.42	9.2

Source: GoK, Statistics for planning.

Primary sector grew at a remarkable rate of 4.77 per cent in 1985-92 at the dawn of liberalization. Tertiary sector maintained a high growth rate in both the phases and in the year 2004-05 when the state economy grew at the rate of 9.2 per cent backed by a growth of 13.8 per cent in the service sector, the other two sectors remained more or less indifferent with a growth rate of 2.5 and 1.3 per cent respectively. The decade from 1993-02 shows the fate of primary sector immediately after liberalizing the national economy. Primary sector began to grow at a negative rate of -3.92 per cent from 1993 onwards, where as a quantum jump is experienced in the growth performance of the tertiary sector. Thus, a preliminary analysis of the performance and role of primary sector in the state economy in terms of its contribution towards the growth of state income is quite disappointing.

A review of the area under cultivation and production of different agricultural crops in Kerala during the pre- and post-liberalization eras brings to light certain interesting features. Before setting out to analyze the area under crops, let us at first see the pattern of land utilization in Kerala.

LAND USE PATTERN

The table given above reveals certain interesting facts regarding how the land which is the prime resource of an economy is utilized by Keralites over the years. It is quite clear from the table that land put to non-agricultural use changed its usual trend and began to increase at an increasing rate during the post-liberalisation period (1990-91 to 2001-02). While the increase in the 1980-90 decade was 10.10 per cent from that of its previous decade, the next decade saw a sharp rise by 90.91

Table 3
Land Use Pattern in Kerala (Area in '000 Hectare)

Classification of land	*1960-61*	*1970-71*	*1980-81*	*1990-91*	*2001-02*	*2004-05*
Total geographical area	3858	3885	3885	3885	3885	3885
	(100)	(100)	(100)	(100)	(100)	(100)
Forests	1056	1055	1082	1082	1082	1081
	(27.54)	(27.42)	(27.85)	(27.85)	(27.85)	(27.82)
Land put to non-agricultural use	205	275	270	297	392	409
	(5.3)	(7.15)	(6.90)	(7.65)	(10.10)	(10.53)
Barren & uncultivated land	151	72	86	58	30	29
	(3.9)	(1.87)	(2.21)	(1.49)	(0.77)	(0.75)
Permanent pastures	45	28	5	2	0.2	0.3
	(1.2)	(0.72)	(0.13)	(0.05)	(0.01)	(0.00)
Land under miscellaneous crops	204	132	64	54	14	11
	(5.3)	(3.43)	(1.65)	(0.89)	(0.35)	(0.28)
Cultivable ted waste	144	80	129	95	64	64
	(3.7)	(2.08)	(3.32)	(2.43)	(1.64)	(1.65)
Fallow other than current fallow	62	23	27	25	34	36
	(1.6)	(0.60)	(0.69)	(0.68)	(0.88)	(0.93)

Contd...

Classification of land	*1960-61*	*1970-71*	*1980-81*	*1990-91*	*2001-02*	*2004-05*
Current fallow	67	24	44	44	79	82
	(1.7)	(0.62)	(1.13)	(1.14)	(2.04)	(2.11)
Net Area Sown	1924	2169	2180	2247	2191	2173
	(49.9)	(56.10)	(56.11)	(57.83)	(56.38)	(55.93)
Area sown more than once	425	761	705	796	802	770
	(11.0)	(19.78)	(18.15)	(19.90)	(20.63)	(19.82)
Total cropped area	2349	2933	2885	3043	2992	2942
	(60.90)	(76.26)	(24.26)	(77.72)	(77.01)	(75.73)
Intensity of cropping	1.221	1.352	1.323	1.350	1.370	1.350

Source: GOK. Statistics for Planning (various issues)
Note: Figures in parenthesis are percentage to total geographical area.

per cent. While the proportion of barren and uncultivable land declined steadily from 3.9 per cent to 0.75 per cent during the four and a half decades from 1960-61, the percentage of area under cultivable waste also declined from 3.7 per cent to 1.65 per cent. Quite surprisingly the per cent share of forests is remaining stagnant all over these years. Though the contribution of agriculture towards the primary sector and hence to the GSDP of the nation has plunged alarmingly over the years, the net area under cultivation remained more or less the same over all these periods. The decade till 1970-71 witnessed a commendable increase in the NSA, total cropped area and area sown more than once. The area expansion phase of agriculture in Kerala is found to be over by 1970-71 and all these three parameters remained more or less the same over a long period of 35 years since then. This is quite natural since land, having an inelastic supply, usually responds to demand signals of the market at the risk of either steep price movements, or, shift of crops in favour of more remunerative ones and this leaves the farmers to take to a vertical expansion of the available land to increase the crop acreage. But the intensity of cropping remained almost stagnant around 1.3 from 1970-71 onwards. Thus, the new agricultural scenario in Kerala brought about a situation–so precarious as it is-that not only no land is newly brought under cultivation but the existing available land is also not utilized intensively. However, the cropping intensity showed marginal increase during the post liberalization period, but by 2004-05 it also began to decline.

CROPPING PATTERN

The agricultural sector of Kerala has undergone tremendous changes in terms of cropping pattern, ownership of land, etc. during the pre- and post-liberalisation periods. Traditionally crop choice of farmers was ruled by comparative advantage considerations, which are chiefly governed by productivity of the crop and domestic price of inputs and output. But, as pointed out earlier, the liberalization process made the competitive advantage dictated by, apart from the above said factors, inter-country variations in the level of technology, taxes, subsidies, international price of input and output etc. Thus, a host of factors on which the farmer has virtually no control, also began to influence the costs and returns of crop cultivation. As a result, an altogether different cropping pattern has emerged in Kerala, which had possibly got through the tests of the market. Table 4 shows the crop distribution in Kerala over the years.

The two energy rich food crops prevalent in Kerala, namely, rice and its cheaper substitute (tapioca) registered an alarmingly declining trend in Kerala, over the decades. The area under rice declined from 7.78 lakh hectare in 1960-61 to 2.9 lakh hectares in 2004-05. The per cent share of rice in the total net sown area of the state, declined tremendously from 33 per cent to 9 per cent in 2004-05 constituting nearly one-fourth of the area which Kerala had in 1970s. Rice production in the state also followed the same pattern all these decades, and during 2004-05, Kerala produced only half of what she had produced during 1970s.

A similar pattern is observed in the case of tapioca also. The area and production declined from 1970 onwards. The steep decline in area under tapioca could be explained due to the falling dependence of Keralites on tapioca as a substitute for rice over the years. This is because of the availability of rice at a relatively cheaper price especially after lifting the ban on interstate movement of rice by the Government of India. Moreover, food preferences of Keralites whose per capita income is maintaining an upward trend, has also changed thus reflecting the operation of Giffen Paradox in the case of tapioca. However, the heavy shrinkage in acreage under paddy and tapioca casts shadow on the food security status of Kerala. Many a time the shift from paddy was accompanied by the conversion of paddy land into other forms land, after which it could no longer be recovered and brought under crops like paddy. Conversion of wet lands not only challenges our food security system but also undermines our ecological balance. It has, thus, disastrous consequences harming the interests of the state economy very much.

Table 4
Area and Production of Food Crops from 1960-61 to 2003-04 in Kerala
(Area in Lakhs and Production in Lakh Tones)

Food grains	*Parameter*	*1960-61*	*1970-71*	*1980-81*	*1990-91*	*2001-02*	*2004-05*
Rice	Area	7.78	8.75	8.02	5.59	3.22	2.9
		(33.16)	(20.34)	(27.79)	(18.38)	(10.77)	(9.86)
	Production	10.68	12.98	12.72	10.86	7.04	6.67
Tapioca	Area	2.42	2.94	2.45	1.46	1.1	1.04
		(10.31)	(10.02)	(8.49)	(4.81)	(3.72)	(3.56)
	Production	16.83	46.17	40.61	28.03	24.55	24.36
Banana & plantain	Area	44.42	48.76	49.26	65.64	106.05	110.7
		(1.89)	(1.66)	(1.71)	(2.16)	(3.54)	(3.77)
	Production	321.85	368.98	317.41	491.94	769.09	839.96

Source: Economic Review (various issues), GoK, 2000. Statistics for planning (various issues)
Note: Figures in parenthesis are per centage to Gross Cropped area.

Banana and plantain are the two food crops in Kerala whose area and production are acquiring a comparatively comfortable position over the decades. This is mainly because of the fact that most of the converted paddy lands are used for the cultivation of banana, once they are converted. Although coconut and coconut oil could be categorized under food items it cannot be exclusively classified as a food crop since a considerable proportion of coconut oil is used for industrial purpose. The performance of cash crops during the same years presents an entirely different picture.

The most striking feature of Kerala's agricultural development is that rubber and coconut emerged as the two most prominent crops, gaining area tremendously during the period since 1960s. Currently (2004-05), rubber occupied 16.33 per cent of NSA of the state, and coconut claimed 30.51 per cent. Proportion of area under rubber made a three-fold increase from 5.23% in 1960-61 to 16.33% in 2004-05. Next to rubber comes coconut whose proportion of area increased from 21.32% in 1960-61 to 30.51% in 2004-05. While the area under tea and cardamom remained almost stagnant over the decades, area under coffee increased from 0.72 per cent to 2.9 per cent in 2004-05. Cashew area increased up to 1980-81 and it began to decline thereafter. From the above two tables one could observe that area under food crops declined dramatically from 45.36% in1960-61 to 17.2% in 2004-05 and during the same period area under cash crops increased from 36.7% to 62.4% . It might be accidental that the area gain of cash crops and its increasing trend was triggered immediately after the liberalization policies of the government. Area under cash crops was only 41.3% in the liberalization eve. Thus a quantum jump in the area under commercial crops from 41.3% in 1990-91 to 62.4% in 2004-05 (21.11%) is obtained within a short period of nearly 15 years , where as it took more than three decades to acquire an area increase from 36.7% to 41.3% (4.6%) during the pre liberalization period.

Production is a function of area and yield of crops. Performance of crops with respect to the yield over a long period of time from 1956-2005 is analysed and the kinked

Table 5
Area and Production of Selected Cash Crops in Kerala from 1960-60 to 2004-05
(Area in '000 ha. and Production in '000 Tones)

Crop	*Parameter*	*1960-61*	*1970-71*	*1980-81*	*1990-91*	*2001-02*	*2004-05*
Pepper	Area	56.97	99.70	108.07	168.51	203.96	208.94
		(4.25)	(4.01)	(3.75)	(5.54)	(6.82)	(7.10)
	Production	27.03	25.03	28.52	46.80	58.24	68.36
Rubber	Area	122.87	179.26	237.77	411.62		480.54
		(5.23)	(6.11)				(16.33)
	Production	23.04	78.73	140.33	307.52	580.35	690.71
Coconut	Area	500.76	719.14	651.37	870.02	905.72	897.76
		(21.32)	(24.52)		(28.59)	(30.27)	(30.51)
	Production (Mn. nuts)	3220	3981	3008	4232	5479	5727
Tea	Area	37.63	37.59	36.16	34.71	36.90	36.94
		(1.6)	(1.28)	(1.25)	(1.14)	(1.23)	(1.25)
	Production	40.37	41.45	50.72	60.64	66.09	57.55
Coffee	Area	16.8	31.56	57.56	75.06		84.64
		(0.72)	(1.08)				(2.9)
	Production	7.41	12.57		35.70		57.55
Cashew	Area	54.32	102.71	141.28	115.62	89.72	86.10
		(2.31)	(3.5)	(4.90)	(3.80)	(3.00)	(2.93)
	Production	84.63	115.24	81.90	102.77	65.87	63.29
	Production	1.28	1.25	3.23	3.45	8.38	8.93

Source: Same as in Table 4.
Note: Values in parenthesis are percentage share of the crop to NSA.

exponential model with 1990 as the break year, yields the results that are presented in Table 6.

Table 6
Yield Performance of Crops during the Post Liberalization Period

Crop	*Yield in 2005-06 (in kg.)*	*Growth rate 1990-2005$*
Food crops		
Rice	2285	1.37
Tapioca	27217	1.23
Banana	7734	0.25
Cash crops		
Pepper	315	2.03
Rubber	1495	4.0
Coconut (in nuts)	6682	3.02
Tea	1609	-0.06
Coffee	711	5.35
Cashew	714	1.29
Cardamom	240	12.39

Note $: Based on estimates of kinked exponential model with 1990-91 as the break-yar, for the second period (1990-05). Only the second period estimates are given here.

Source: Computed from Various issues of Statistics for planning, Economic Review, Data book on Agriculture.

All the crops showed a positive growth rate during the post-liberalization period. Growth in yield of rubber, coffee and cardamom was quite impressive during the phase. But yield growth of our staple foods like rice and tapioca was not satisfactory, taking into account the impressive strides elsewhere in India and the massive machinery of research, extension and other support system including the building of infrastructure these crops supposedly enjoyed in Kerala during all the early FYPs. The burgeoning supply deficits and the fairly good public distribution system ensured a stable market for these food crops.

Traditionally, Kerala had been exporting pepper, cardamom, ginger, cashew, tea, coffee etc. Since Kerala economy was relatively closed during the pre liberalization period, cultivation of these crops was profitable, because of the protected internal market. But with the liberalization policies of the government, resulting in the removal of

Quantitative Restrictions (QRs) on imports and lowering of tariff levels, our farmers had to face stiff competition for exports in the international market, particularly since 80 per cent of the agricultural commodities produced in the state are dependent on domestic and/or international market situation (GoK, 2003). Moreover, recently cheaper imports like pepper, tea etc. from other nations negatively affected the domestic prices of these crops. Many of the commodities which are produced and was being exported from Kerala have become cheaper with the Free Trade Agreement (FTA), particularly with countries like Sri Lanka, deprived the farmers of the profit they enjoyed till now. Thus, the integration of international market with the domestic market reduced the prices of the domestic farm produces, as a result of the integration of prices and this made the native farmers to live with the distress induced by the international price volatility.

Table 7
Parity between Prices Received and Paid by Farmers in Kerala–Parity Indices

Year	*Prices received*	*Domestic expenditure*	*Farm cultivation cost*	*Prices paid*	*Parity index*
1980	481	441	607	578	93
1985	783	688	1167	896	87
1990	1072	945	1728	1277	84
1991	1326	1078	1910	1435	92
1992	1486	1201	2255	1646	90
1993	1496	1301	2579	1834	82
1994	1582	1464	2891	2057	77
1995	1802	1641	3312	2331	77
1996	2079	1810	3928	2666	78
1997	2486	1979	4571	3007	83
1998	2447	2107	4895	3212	76
1999	2907	2246	5556	3532	82
2000	2492	2327	5920	3711	66
2001	1927	2489	6584	4048	48
2002	1999	2542	6684	4122	49
2003	2454	2615	7056	4925	57
2004	2651	2705	7360	4459	59
2005	2440	2795	7703	4640	53

Source: Economic Review. Various issues.

Parity Index shows how the consumer price situation of the state affected the farming community. It is the ratio of prices received and prices paid by farmers. The table reveals that farm cultivation cost and domestic expenditure, the twin cost components on the part of farmers, surpassed the receipts they earned. Parity indices were below 100 since 1980 and it remained more or less stagnant around 77 from 1994-98 after which it dipped to less than 50 particularly from 2001 onwards. Thus from the dawn of this century the farmers were not in a position to recoup even half of what they had spent towards cultivation. It is quite natural that they leave agriculture which turned out to be an unprofitable avocation in the neo liberal era. If this tendency of migration of farmers to non-farming activity continues, the peril it may afflict the food security system of the state would be still disastrous.

THREAT TO STATE FOOD SECURITY

As per FAO (1996) food security exists when all people at all times have physical and economic access to sufficient, safe and nutritive food to meet dietary needs and food preferences for active and healthy life. Food security of a state is determined by the domestic production of food grains, net availability through buffer stocks and availability through PDS. The Table 8 provides Kerala's status with regard to the major food security parameters.

Domestic production of food grains is falling continuously and has come down to 15.34 per cent of the total requirement in 2001. But from mid-90s, with the reduction in the supply of food grains through PDS, the supply gap began to widen and by the year 2001 it took a whopping tally of 3,612,000 tonnes.

CURRENT CONCERNS IN THE AGRICULTURAL SECTOR IN KERALA

Large Scale Conversion of Agricultural Land

In the neo-liberal era, with the increasing demand for land for construction activities and for urbanization, paddy land became the first target of demand for non-agricultural uses on account of its relative cheapness. The increasing wage rate and

Table 8
Supply Gap in Cereal in Kerala (000 tones)

Parameter	*1971*	*1975*	*1981*	*1985*	*1991*	*1995*	*2000*	*2001*
Net requirement[a]	3074.0	3310.4	3665.2	3875.2	4170.1	4420.7	4579.2	4584.9
Net internal availability[b]	1216.5	1228.5	1206	1055.7	954.3	828.5	657	703.5
Supply through PDS	892	1007	1623	1494	2084	1830	676	539
Total availability	2108.5	2235.5	2829.0	2549.7	3028.3	2658.5	1333	1242
Estimated supply gap	965.5	1074.9	836.2	1325.5	1131.8	1762.2	3246.2	3612.4

Note: [a] Per capita requirement is estimated to be 12kg. per month.
Requirement estimates made according to ICMR recommendation of balanced Diet. (ICMR 1982).
[b] Production minus 10% for feed, seed, waste etc.

Source: Mohandas (2005).

fertilizer cost and the declining returns from agriculture prompted the relatively resourceful rice cultivators to convert their paddy land for some other profitable activity. Similarly, with the price crash of cash crops, the cultivators of cash crops also diverted their land for non-agricultural activities. This is quite evident from the fact that the land put to non-agricultural use which almost doubled from 2,05,500 hectares in 1960-61 to 4,09,000 hectares in 2004-05. The overall increase in the land put to non-agricultural use from 1960 to 2005 was 99.5 per cent.

Increase in Land Prices and Commoditization of Land

The neo–liberal era is characterized as a period of high growth in non-primary sectors, and is witnessing, among others, unprecedented rise in land prices on account of increasing urbanization and the rising demand for land for construction activities. Land prices have become totally unrelated to the rate of returns that the land could fetch from the cultivation of crops. Land is considered as a commodity-rather than a factor of production-with only exchange value, in total disregard of its capability in agricultural productivity. With increasing inflow of capital, augmented by the liberalized economic policies, the commoditization of land would attract investors who seek quick-profits and who have no inclination to farming. The massive entry of intermediaries in land transactions and large scale speculative deals will soon rule the market. These will shoot up the land prices, corrupt the land market operations and will eventually alienate the practicing cultivators and labourers from the agricultural land that was at their disposal till then. Thus, agriculture will get starved of the basic factor of production, namely, the land. Though reliable data on land transactions are not available, neither are they available on land prices, there is a growing recognition, among the stakeholders including the government, of the fact that these mischievous forces have already set in motion in Kerala land market, especially in urban and peri-urban areas. The Kerala Sashthra Sahitya Parishad (KSSP) in their recent study (KSSP, 2007), concluded that the only top economic-stratum (constituting 8 per cent of the populace) were the net-gainers of the recent spurt in land transfers in Kerala, and all the strata beneath them turned out to be net-loosers.The government has already initiated some steps to contain the evil. The newly introduced system of proving the identity of both the parties, pasting photographs of them etc. was put in place with the intention of restricting land deal to genuine buyers and sellers. The new guideline by the Revenue department to register the 'advance agreement' document for its validity was also a right step towards this. Publishing the minimum prices fixed for land is another measure in this direction. This will increase the state revenue on account of stamp duty on land value during land deals.

Farmer Indebtedness

Declining profitability of farmers in the state resulted in an increase in their debt burden. As per the survey among farmer households (NSSO, 2005) the incidence of indebtedness in Kerala was put at 64.4 per cent and was higher (4th highest incidence among the states), as against the national average of 48.6 per cent (NSSO, 2005). An important and immediate manifestation of the increasing indebtedness of farmers is the distress sale of land for the settlement of debts leading the asset loss. In a primary survey conducted at Wayanad (Mohanakumar and Sharma, 2006), it was found that 24 per cent of the farmers sold their land, which constituted 8.4 per cent of their total land.

However, indebtedness among farming community is not a new phenomenon, but the suicides are. (Rao and Suri, 2006). The kind of wicked operations in the land market that have come fully functional in Kerala, as was averred in the previous section, had thrown the livelihood interests of the practicing farmer-landholders more at bay. The indebted farmers, who were driven to the wall as being unable to repay the debt, sold their land to mitigate the distress they were then put to, by yielding to these mischievous market forces. But note that farmer's distress was the fallout of a crash in the commodity prices, and hence, is crop-dependent. Certain crops emerged stronger after an initial shock. The case of rubber is in point.

Moreover, a major share of the farm loan in Kerala was reported to have been utilized for purposes other than farming. Therefore, the governmental interventions to salvage the farmers of their debt-distress, should stem from a clear appraisal of the economic status of the candidate-farmers as to whether s/he utilized the loan exclusively for farming and whether they incurred heavy losses due to farming during the period. A blanket process of rehabilitation will not only divert the scarce governmental fund allocation to the undeserved but also make the quantum of assistance too insufficient for the really distressed farmers. The recently implemented loan waiver scheme of the centre does not appear to have acted on such prudence and wisdom.

Farmer Suicides

The economic distress of the farmers occurred as a result of the price-crash led losses and a consequent debt trap, is bound to have its psychological impact on the farmer. Maslow's need hierarchy theory of motivation (1943) propounded that human being is motivated by five needs which are sought to be satisfied in a hierarchical order (that is, one after the other), with the physiological and safety needs taking utmost priority. As the farmer finds that even the most primary needs are not satisfied, the farmer sets to undergo severe psychological stress. Many of the farmers are household heads as well. This aggravates the stress level of the farmers, as the whole family is seen suddenly driven to suffer the casualties. Unfortunately, there was no planned or ad-hoc public effort, including that from the governmental agencies, to enable the farmer to stave off his/her personal trauma; although, these farmers had been the nodal person to maintain the food security system of the region, had been the employer of a good number of laboures around, and his/her current distress had caused chiefly due to the imprudent and indiscriminate perpetration of the liberalization policies of the government. And when even the livelihood security of the whole family is perceived to be under threat, the farmer is made to attempt his 'last escape-route'. As per government's estimates (as on November 22, 2006) a total of 804 farmers committed suicide from 2004 to July 2006 alone and another 101 farmers committed suicide thereafter, till February 2007. (Reply in the State Legislative Assembly on March 25, 2007).

Table 9
Age-adjusted SMR[$] for Male Population and for Male Farmers

	Kerala		*India*	
Year	*All*	*Farmers*	*All*	*Farmers*
1995	42.0	127.6	12.5	9.7
1996	40.2	109.4	11.9	12.3
1997	45.7	138.9	12.9	12.7
1998	47.4	172.9	13.8	14.8
1999	49.6	182.5	14.4	15.3
2000	47.4	184.7	14.2	15.7
2001	48.3	161.8	14.0	16.2
2002	50.5	258.3	14.3	18.1
2003	48.5	297.6	14.2	17.5
2004	45.8	183.0	14.4	19.2

Note $: Age-adjusted SMR is suicides per one lakh population of 5 years and above as suicide is medically not defined for the 0-4 population

Source: NCRB–various years, as in Mishra, 2006.

Table 9 shows the age-adjusted Suicide Mortality Rate (SMR) for all male population for male farmers in India and Kerala. The table shows that in India as a whole, farmers as an occupational group, tended to have higher SMR than the general population, except for two years in the period considered. But the suicide rate of farmers in Kerala was awfully higher than the general population since mid-90s. While the number of suicides among the general population in 2004 was 46, it is almost four times among farmers in Kerala. This is really shocking and intriguing as well. Was it just because that farming let them down once and for all? About two-thirds of the farmer-households in Kerala are indebted (in contrast, in India, it is about the half). But about four-fifths of them had utilized their loan for purposes other than farming. In India, only two-fifths of the indebted have utilized the loan for other purposes (NSSO, 2003; report No. 498). The number of farmers who depended solely on farming for a livelihood and who were affected by the severe price instabilities is not known. The area under those cash crops in Kerala for which price crash occurred during late 1990s and early this decade is also not known. But it might not be greater than 20 per cent of the GCA, if coconut is excluded. Rubber is a crop which keeps fetching them riches, as the terms of trade is currently more favourable to them than it had been ever. Very few coconut farmers could be considered as full-time farmers. Paddy farmers comprised a majority of the practicing farmers in Kerala. It is reported that these farmers have been enjoying a meagre benefit-cost ratio for many years now, though they continue to provide employment to a maximum number of agricultural labourers per hectare and play a key role in maintaining food security. Yet, as a farmer-group, they hardly go in for credits and hence do not take to suicide. Therefore, it is the crop that really counts when one speaks of farmer-distress. Not all farmers are distressed. Nor, all of them need an economic rehabilitation. The benefit of the blanket waiving of farm loan by the centre may reach a large number of undeserved also. It becomes amply clear that the number of suicides among farmers may not be a true reflection of the intensity of distress in agriculture sector in Kerala.

CONCLUSION

Kerala maintains a distinct identity in the agricultural map of India, due not only to its highly productive agro-climatic resource-base but also to its peculiar farming behaviour in terms of its diverse crop pattern with heavy dominance of cash crops, and the higher dependence on international demands. However, the evolution of its economy to its current form, in which agriculture takes a consistently declining role in the economy and the food crops getting increasingly replaced by cash crops, is bound to have disastrous consequences on its food and livelihood security. The process of liberalization made the economy open and the resultant integration of domestic market with the global economy witnessed a host of problems emerging in the agricultural scene of Kerala-the main one being the price crash of cash crops. Though some crops grew strongly competitive thereafter, others failed to cope with the shocks. These developments have their social sway as well. The new trend of hectic land transfers shot up land prices. The commoditization of land alienated the peasantry from the land they tilled hitherto. Many of the farmers who ventured new cropping pattern, braving the challenges put up by the newly clamped liberalization regime, suffered great losses. Some of them finally succumbed to the psychological stress they had undergone, leaving the planners and development experts to find urgent ways to salvage the agriculture sector, especially the food grain agriculture, from the maladies it is currently experiencing.

REFERENCES

Registrar General of Census Operations. Census of India (2001), New Delhi.

Chand, Ramesh (undated): Impact of Trade Liberalisation and Related Reforms on India's Agricultural Sector, Rural Food Security, Income and Poverty. Available (as on July 2008) at *www.gdnet.org*.

FAO (1996), World Food Summit: Action Plan. Rome, 13 November.

GoK. (Government of Kerala, 1998), Ninth Five Year Plan 1997-2002. *Report of the Steering Committee on Water Resources*. State Planning Board.

GoK (2001), Data Book on Agriculture 2000. State Planning Board. Thiruvananthapuram.

GoK (2003), 'Building a Sustainable Agricultural Trade Security System for Kerala'. Report of the Commission on WTO Concerns in Agriculture.

Government of Kerala (2005), *Statistics for Planning*, Department of Economics and Statistics, Thiruvananthapuram.

Government of Kerala (2006), *Economic Review*, State Planning Board, Thiruvananthapuram.

ICMR (1982), Recommended Dietary Intake for Indians. New Delhi.

Jeromi P. D. (2007), Farmer's Indebtedness and Suicides: Impact of Agricultural Trade Liberalisation in Kerala. *Economic and Political Weekly*, August 4.

Joseph, Brigit (2004), Trade liberalisation and primary commodity prices. Empirical evidence from select tropical crops in Kerala,

India. (draft version available at: *http://www.gtap.agecon.purdue.edu/resources/download/1799.pdf.).*

Joseph, Brigit and K.J. Joseph (2005), Commercial Agriculture in Kerala After WTO. *South Asian Economic Journal,* June 6:1.

(KSSP) Kerala Sasthra Sahitya Parishad (2006), Kerala Padanam. Thiruvananthapuram.

Kumar, Ajith C. E. and Lathika M. (2007), "Re-visiting Kerala's Performance on the Education Front", *Review of Development and Change.* 12(2). July-December.

Maslow, Abraham H. (1943), A Theory of Human Motivation. Psychological Review.

Mishra, Srijit (2006), Suicide Mortality Rates Across States of India 1975-2001: A Statistical Note. *Economic and Political Weekly,* 22 April. XII(16).

Mohanakumar, S. and R. K. Sharma (2006). Analysis of Farmer Suicides in Kerala. *Economic and Political Weekly,* 22 April. Vol XLI, No. 16.

Mohandas, M. (2005), 'Agricultural Development in Kerala' in D. Rajasenan and Gerard De Grot. *Kerala Economy: Trajectories, Challenges and Implications.* Cochin University of Science and Technology. Cochin.

NCRB (National Crime Records Bureau), Various Years. Accidental Deaths and Suicides in India. Ministry of Home Affairs. Government of India. New Delhi.

Rao, C. H. H. (2005), *Agriculture, Food Security, Poverty and Economy,* Oxford, New Delhi, p. 41.

Rao, Narasimha, P. and Suri K. C. (2006), Dimensions of Agrarian Distress in Andhra Pradesh. *Economic and Political Weekly,* 22 April.

Veeramani, C. (2008), 'India and China: Changing Patterns of Comparative Advantage?' in R. Radhakrishna (Ed.). *India Development Report 2008.* Oxford University Press, New Delhi. (pp. 145-156).

6

LAND USE AND CROPPING PATTERN IN KERALA

P. Rajendran Nair

Land use implies the utilization of the total available land for agricultural and non-agricultural purposes. Out of the total geographical area of 38,86,287 hectares in Kerala, 55% area is used as cultivable land, 28% area is forest and 12% of area is put under other non-agricultural use.[1] Thus the area used for agricultural purpose is only a little more than half of the total area. In Kerala there is diversity of crops and crop regions. The physical features of Kerala reflect it. On the basis of physical features, Kerala can be divided into six major zones. Low land and coastal plains, Malabar midlands, Palaghat region, Southern midlands, Foot hills, and Eastern high lands.[2] In the high land area the major crops cultivated are Rubber, cashew, pepper, tea, ginger, cardamom and coffee. In mid land the major crops are paddy, coconut, tapioca, banana and areca nut. In the low land area paddy, coconut and banana are the most important crops. Lowland and mid land are suitable for vegetables. In the case of fallow land, Palakkad occupies first rank in position with 9565 hectares, followed by Eranakulam and Thrissur.

Out of the total 3886287 hectares the total cropped area is 29,85,727 hectares. The total forest area is 1081509 hectares. Land put to non-agricultural use is 438839 hectares. Area of barren and uncultivable land is 26125 hectares. Area of cultivable waste is 90288 hectares. Water logged area is 5950 hectares.[3] Among the districts Palakkad occupies 4,47,584 hectares, Idukki ranks second with 4,36,328 hectares and lowest is Alappuzha with 1,41,011 hectares. Table I shows the land use pattern in Kerala in 2006-07 and the percentage changes. It is clear from the table that land put to non-agricultural uses increased by 18.5% in between 2005-06 and 2006-07. In the same period cultivable waste land increased by 36.52%, permanent pastures and grazing land increased by 9.85% and fallow other than current fallow increased by 4.37% while total cropped area decreased by 2.28%. There is no change in the forest area during the period.

CROPPING PATTERN IN KERALA

By cropping pattern is meant the proportion of area under different crops at a point of time. A change in cropping pattern implies a change in the proportion of area under different crops.[4] Cropping pattern depends on physical characteristics such as soil, climate, weather, rainfall etc. It also depends on nature and availability of irrigation facilities. If water is available we can follow double or triple cropping system. For example, in a dry area where rainfall is scanty and where there is high uncertainty of monsoons, there will be a greater dependence on jowar and bajra, as these crops can be managed with small quantity of rainfall. Water logging in parts of Ludhiana and Sangur district in Punjab has lead to an increase in area under rice. In Kerala, Kuttanad area is suitable for rice cultivation. In the newly reclaimed lands of Madhya pradesh, millets are grown for a few years after which rice is cultivated.[5]

Economic factors also influence the cropping pattern. The major economic elements are (a) *price and income*: A study of intercrop price parities by Ministry of Food And Agriculture shows that "prices influence the acreage under the crops in two ways. One is that the variations in the intercrop price

Table 1
Land Use Pattern in Kerala

Classification of Land	2005-06	2006-07	Per cent of Geographical Area	Change in Area between 2005-06 and 2006-07	
				Actual	Percentage
Total Geographical Area	3886287	3886287		-	-
Forest	1081509	1081509	27.83	-	-
Land put to non agricultural uses	370322	428839	11.29	68517	18.5
Barren and uncultivated land	26457	26125	0.67	-332	-1.25
Permanent Pastures and Grazing land	274	301	0.01	27	9.85
Land under miscellaneous tree crops	9526	8959	0.23	-567	-5.95
Cultivable waste	66133	90288	2.32	24155	36.52
Fallow other than current fallow	45171	47144	1.21	1973	4.37
Current Fallow	70166	81651	2.10	11485	16.37
Net area sown	2132483	2111471	54.33	-21012	-0.99
Area shown more than once	853244	806034	20.74	-47210	-5.53
Total Cropped area	2985727	2917505	75.07	-68222	-2.28
Cropping intensity	140	138			

Source: Directorate of Economics and Statistics.

parities. Another is that the maintenance of stable level of prices for a crop.......... Provides a better incentive to the producer to increase the output"[6] (b) *farm size*: Farm size also influence the cropping pattern. Small farmers prefer to produce food grains for their requirements. (c) *Government actions*: Government can influence crop pattern through legislative and administrative measures. If government is providing subsidies and farm inputs such as seeds, fertilizers, manures and irrigation facilities and crop insurance for specific crops farmers may show a preference to cultivate those crops. In earlier periods, a choice of cropping pattern was guided by agronomic considerations and consumptions needs of farmers, but now it seems that mainly market forces determine the emerging trend.[7]

TREND IN AREA, PRODUCTION AND PRODUCTIVITY OF CROPS:

Data regarding the area, production and productivity of important crops grown in Kerala are shown in table II.[8] Out of cropped area of 29.18 lakh hectares in 2006-07 food crops comprising rice, pulses, minor mullets and Tapioca occupy only 12.25%. Kerala state, which had a low base in food production, is facing serious challenges in retaining even this meagre area. Kerala agricultural economy is undergoing structural transformation from the mid seventies by switching over large proportions of its traditional crop area, which was devoted to subsistence crops like rice and tapioca to more remunerative crops like coconut and rubber. According to K N Raj "the process of raising land values was further helped by the growth of population and infrastructure investments in irrigation, communication and transport, particularly in regions with rising values of land and expanding opportunity for trade in agricultural products came also the inflow of finance from outside the agrarian society through urban traders and money lenders."[9] Massive land reclamation and conversion of paddy field for commercial construction purposes by land mafias reduces the area of cultivable land. M A Oommen opined that following the gulf booms, land prices have skyrocketed in Kerala. From being a means of production, land has become a prominent commodity in exchange. The conferring of ownership right to tenants of all categories including many for whom farming is not a business occupation but a secure asset or a source of reliable secondary income, paved the way for a shift into perennial crops rather than seasonal crops.[10]

The decline in the profitability of cultivation arising out of the steep increase in cultivation costs is sited as the major factor that led to the decline of paddy cultivation. The steep increase in the wages of agricultural workers and other categorized workers also discouraged the hiring of labours for agricultural and other activities.[11]

RICE

Rice is the staple food in Kerala. During 1961-62 nearly 7.53 lakh hectares were under paddy cultivation and during 2006-07 it was only 2.64 lakh hectares. Thus with in 44 years state witnessed a spectacular fall of 63% paddy area. During the same period production also decreased from 988150 tones to 642000 tones. The fall in production is 36%. The area under paddy cultivation in 2006-07 was 21% of the total food crop area. The paddy fields have been converted for various other crops and for non-agricultural uses. The low profitability in paddy cultivation appears to have contributed to the shifting of paddy land to other crops. Now a major threat to paddy cultivation is the acute shortage of farm workers.

It is clear from the Table 3 that there is a sharp fall in the area of paddy cultivation during the last six years. During 2000-01 area under paddy cultivation was 3,47,455 hectares. But it decreased to 264000 hectares in 2006-07. During the same period production decreased from 751328 tones to 642000 tones.

Coconut: In 1961-62, the area under coconut crop was 5.05 lakh hectares in Kerala. The area under coconut crop has increased to 8.98 lakh in 2005-06. There is an increase of 78% under the area of coconut cultivation over a period 44 years. In the same period production of nuts increased from 3247 million nuts to 7046 million nuts, 96% increment is recorded.

Table 2
Area, Production and Productivity of Principal Crops

	Area (Ha)			Production (MT)			Productivity (Kg/ha)		
Crops	*2004-2005*	*2005-2006*	*2006-2007#*	*2004-2005*	*2005-2006*	*2006-2007#*	*2004-2005*	*2005-2006*	*2006-2007#*
Rice	289974	275742	263529	667105	629987	641577	2301	2285	2435
Jowar	2566	2450	1827	1309	1248	930	510	509	509
Ragi	1383	414	516	1119	335	417	809	809	808
Other Cereals	955	11	625	746	21	489	781	1909	782
Pulses	8428	10562	6870	8390	7940	5211	995	752	759
Sugarcane	1921	1222	1161	15430	9165	6582	8032	7500	5669
Pepper	237669	237998	226094	74980	87605	64264	315	368	284
Chilies	823	1231	1415	775	1192	1363	942	968	963
Ginger	9991	12226	11082	45305	56288	42497	4535	4604	3835
Turmeric	2881	3384	3917	6244	8237	9978	2167	2434	2547
Cardamom	41378	41367	41362	8616	9765	8545	208	236	207
Arecanut	107572	108590	102078	110340	119309	109968	1026	1099	1077
Banana Other	58866	61400	59143	475371	491823	463766	8075	8010	7841
Plantains	54612	55222	53060	416115	445333	435635	7619	8064	8210
Cashew nut	81547	78285	70461	60584	68262	61680	743	872	875
Tapioca	88486	90539	87128	2400043	2568284	2518999	27123	283670	28911
Sweet Potato	836	711	505	10013	9013	6405	11977	12677	12683

Contd...

Crops	Area (Ha)			Production (MT)			Productivity (Kg/ha)		
	2004-2005	2005-2006	2006-2007#	2004-2005	2005-2006	2006-2007#	2004-2005	2005-2006	2006-2007#
Groundnut	1346	3299	2813	996	2441	2081	740	740	740
Sesamum	883	600	732	260	210	294	294	350	402
Coconut*	899267	897823	870939	6001	6326	6054	6673	7046	6951
Cotton**	1472	2665	1300	2370	3452	1690	1610	1300	1300
Tobacco	40	43	31	223	69	50	5575	1605	1613
Coffee	84644	84644	84571	54300	60175	59475	642	711	703
Tea	35040	35043	35364	49508	56384	53659	1413	1609	1517
Rubber	480661	494400	502240	590778	739225	780405	1437	1495	1554

Area Production and productivity for 2006-07 are provisional except Paddy, Cardamom, Coffee, Tea and Rubber

* Production of Coconut in million nuts and productivity in nuts/ha

** Production of Cotton in No. of bales of 170 kg

Source: Directorate of Economics & Statistics.

Table 3
Rate of Change in the Area of Cultivation and Production of Paddy during 2000-01–2006-07

Year	*Total area in hectares*	*Production in tones*
2000-01	347455	751328
2001-02	322368	703500
2002-03	310521	688859
2003-04	287340	570045
2004-05	28930	66750
2005-06	275742	629987
2006-07	264000	642000

Source: Agricultural statistics, Dept of Economics & Statistics.

Table 4
District wise Classification of Area of Paddy Cultivation during 2001 to 2005-06 in Hectares

	Years					
Districts	*2001-2002*	*2002-2003*	*2003-2004*	*2004-2005*	*2005-2006*	*2006-2007*
Thiruvananthapuram	6995	6810	5371	5125	4705	3849
Kollam	14939	11459	10187	9812	7218	5497
Pathanamthitta	6279	5218	5262	4563	3291	2616
Alappuzha	37740	33111	32083	3123	28768	31060
Kottayam	16677	15250	11502	12753	12557	13814
Idukki	3473	4388	3228	3125	2932	2878
Eranakulam	37433	32905	29495	27351	24934	21895
Thrissur	39384	37012	34158	32355	31074	27311
Palakkad	118701	115904	115131	11415	113919	109208
Malappuram	23148	22654	17671	16952	14825	15109
Kozhikode	6737	6402	5185	5085	4703	4295
Wayanad	15000	12855	12343	12252	4503	11833
Kannur	11791	10987	9461	9161	9223	8842
Kassargodu	9158	7413	6263	6115	6030	5323

Source: Agricultural statistics, Dept. of Economics & Statistics. Different years.

Table 4 shows that in all districts of Kerala there is a fall in the area of paddy cultivation.

In the case of coconut cultivation area Kozhikode district occupies the first position i.e. 14.5% of total coconut area of the state. Malappuram district is in second place with 12.6% area and Wayanad occupies the lowest position with 1.3%.

Table 5
District wise and Season wise Area Production and Productivity of Rice for 2006-07

	Autumn			*Winter*			*Summer*			*Total*		
Name of District	*Area (Ha)*	*Production (MT)*	*Productivity (kg/ha)*	*Area (Ha)*	*Production (MT)*	*Productivity (kg/ha)*	*Area (Ha)*	*Production (MT)*	*Productivity (kg/ha)*	*Area (Ha)*	*Production (MT)*	*Productivity (kg/ha)*
(1)	(2)	(3)	(4)	(5)	(6)	(7)	(8)	(9)	(10)	(11)	(12)	(13)
Thiruvananthapuram	1403	3602	2567	2373	6288	2650	72.6	187	2576	3848.6	10077	2618
Kollam	1615	3904	2417	3879	8672	2236	2.6	4	1538	5496.6	12580	2289
Pathanamthitta	230	550	2391	1434	3423	2387	952.3	3128	3285	2616.3	7110	2714
Alappuzha	7594	22287	2935	13696	40111	2929	9770	27763	2842	31060	90161	2903
Kottayam	4149	10767	2595	4192	9896	2361	5473	14877	2720	13814	35550	2574
Idukki	851	2345	2756	1810	4593	2538	216.6	570	2632	2877.6	7508	2609
Eranakulam	5740	11034	1922	13700	28541	2083	2455	4432	1805	21895	44007	2010
Thrissur	5389	9847	1827	16028	34788	2170	5894	20401	3461	27311	65036	2381
Palakkad	44443	100669	2265	58675	151829	2588	6090	17605	2891	109208	270103	2473
Malappuram	4782	10514	2199	8732	17094	1958	1595	5515	3457	15109	33123	2192
Kozhikode	295	397	1346	3429	4745	1384	571.4	950	1663	4295.4	6092	1418
Wayanad	0	0	0	9265	23115	2495	2568	7607	2963	11833	30722	2596
Kannur	4602	8733	1898	4142	8522	2057	98.4	120	1220	8842.4	17375	1965
Kassargodu	2766	6592	2383	2369	5146	2172	188.3	404	2146	5323.3	12142	2281
State	83859	191241	2281	143724	346763	2413	35947	103573	2881	263529	641577	2435

Source: DES.

Table 6
Rate of Change in the Area of Coconut Cultivation during 2000-01 to 2006-07 with Productivity

Year	*Total area in hectares*	*Production in million nuts*
2000-01	925783	5536
2001-02	905718	5479
2002-03	899198	5709
2003-04	898498	5876
2004-05	898133	6233
2005-06	897833	7046
2006-07	871000	6951

Source: Agricultural Statistics, Dept of Economics & Statistics.

It is clear from the table that there is slight fall in the area of coconut cultivation in between 2000-01 and 2006-07. District wise classification of area of cultivation is given in the Table 7, which is given below.

Table 7
District wise Production of Coconut (Area in hectares)

	Years					
Districts	*2001-2002*	*2002-2003*	*2003-2004*	*2004-2005*	*2005-2006*	*2006-2007*
Thiruvananthapuram	88663	88604	87118	85506	85325	84078
Kollam	79709	74956	71310	67531	66815	66134
Pathanamthitta	22794	22696	21764	21660	21580	21375
Alappuzha	59775	57047	55407	55982	55995	56154
Kottayam	41604	39429	41424	39286	39655	39943
Idukki	23811	25603	25810	24383	24360	24343
Eranakulam	67402	62684	61034	57964	58120	58533
Thrissur	89472	85480	86068	87397	86325	85366
Palakkad	46393	50568	53207	55655	55601	55437
Malappuram	40378	104171	107254	109582	109731	113411
Kozhikode	128739	130100	127402	129365	128521	129501
Wayanad	10995	11383	10947	11098	11325	11517
Kannur	96975	95712	94217	95278	94115	93934
Kassargodu	59073	57285	56236	57811	57712	58088

Source: Agricultural Statistics, Dept of Economics & Statistics.

Table 7 shows that in the case of coconut cultivation area, Kozhikode district occupies the first position with 14.5% of the total coconut area of the state.

Arecanut: In 1961-62 the area under arecanut was 56764 hectares. It increased to 108590 hectares in 2005-06. There is an increase of 91% under the area of cultivation over a period of 44 years. During the same period production also recorded a 203% increment. That is production increased from 8091 million nuts in 1961-62 to 24478 million nuts in 2005-06. Malappuram district occupies first rank in the case of arecanut cultivation area. Kasargod and Kannur districts occupy the second and third respectively.

Table 8
Area of Arecanut Cultivation with Productivity during 2000-01 to 2006-07

Year	*Total area in hectares*	*Production of betel nuts (tones)*
2000-01	87360	87947
2001-02	93193	84681
2002-03	97485	107279
2003-04	102504	105490
2004-05	105580	106870
2005-06	108590	109980
2006-07	102078	109968

Source: Agricultural Statistics, Dept of Economics & Statistics.

It is clear from the table that area of cultivation of arecanut increased from 87360 hectares in 2000-01 to 102078 in 2006-07. In the same period production also increased from 87947 hectares to 109968 hectares. District wise cultivation of arecanut is given in table 9 which is given below.

It is clear from the table that in comparison to the area of cultivation in 2000-01 all districts recorded an increase in the area of cultivation in 2005-06.

Other Oil Seeds: Other oil seeds are groundnut and sesamum. There is a decrease in the area under groundnut. In 1961-62, the area under groundnut was 15993 hectares. It decreased to 2813 hectares in 2006-07. The decrease is estimated as 79%. During the same period production also decreased from 13533 tonnes to 2081 tonnes in 2006-07. The fall in production is estimated as 82%. Seasamum also recorded a fall both in area of cultivation and production. During the same period the area of sesamum cultivation decreased from 11953

Table 9
District wise Cultivation of Arecanut (Area in hectares)

	Years					
Districts	*2000-2001*	*2001-2002*	*2002-2003*	*2003-2004*	*2004-2005*	*2005-2006*
Thiruvananthapuram	1104	1106	1216	1220	1230	1249
Kollam	2442	2382	2502	2322	2360	2485
Pathanamthitta	1269	1345	1343	1488	1450	1462
Alappuzha	2205	2389	2441	2416	2403	2353
Kottayam	1443	1587	1767	1952	2020	2081
Idukki	3682	3942	4096	3831	3935	4009
Eranakulam	4238	4662	4886	5275	5412	5644
Thrissur	7099	7179	7526	8052	8110	8116
Palakkad	4241	4026	4936	5963	6100	6466
Malappuram	16123	17735	19622	20476	20353	20022
Kozhikode	10692	11189	10584	11499	12200	12478
Wayanad	6033	6636	7201	8689	9650	10499
Kannur	13274	14436	14182	13489	13680	14104
Kassargodu	13515	14579	15183	15832	16500	17622

Source: Agricultural Statistics, Department of Economics & Statistics.

hectares to 600 hectares. The fall is 95% production also decreased from 2539 tonnes to 210 tonnes. The fall is 92%. If this trend will continues the cultivation of sesamum may not be seen in the state with in a few years. The Table 10 given below shows the area and production of oilseeds except coconut during 2000-01 to 2006-07 in the state.

Table 10
Area and Production of Oilseeds Area in Hectares Production in Tonnes

Year	*Ground nut*	*Sesamum*	*Ground nut*	*Sesamum*
2000-01	3677	2002	1800	398
2001-02	2437	878	1812	284
2002-03	2422	811	1801	260
2003-04	2687	1204	1980	285
2004-05	2933	935	2200	210
2005-06	3299	600	2441	210
2006-07	2813	732	2081	294

Source: Agriculture Statistics, Department of Economics & Statistics.

It is clear from the table that in the state both area and production of oil seeds, ground nut and sesamum, fall tremendously but there is some improvement in the production of groundnut.

Spices and Condiments: The important spices and condiments cultivated in the state are black pepper, ginger, turmeric and cardamom. In 1961–62 the area under ginger crop was 12050 hectares. After 44 years, it stands almost the same. But during the same period, i.e. from 1961-62 to 2005-06, production increased from 11185 tonnes to 56288 tonnes. The increment is estimated as 403%. In the case of pepper the area of cultivation increased by 138% i.e. from 99887 hectares in 1961-62 to 237998 hectares in 2005-06. In the same period production too recorded 230% increment. Production increased from 26550 tonnes to 87605 tonnes. In the case of Turmeric area of cultivation decreased by 30% i.e. from 4847 hectares in 1961-62 to 4267 hectares in 2005-06. But production increased at a ratio of 93% in the same period i.e. from 4267 tonnes to 8237 tonnes. In the case of cardamom the area of cultivation increased from 38330 hectares to 41367 hectares in the same period.

Table 11 shows that in the case of pepper, ginger and cardamom, there is an increase in the area of cultivation but in the case of turmeric area of cultivation falls. During the same period production of pepper, ginger and cardamom recorded an increment but in the case of Turmeric there is a fall in the volume of production. In 2006-07 areas of production and quantity of production of pepper, ginger, cardamom decreased in comparison to 2005-06. But in the case of Turmeric both area and output increased in the same period.

PLANTATION CROPS

Important plantation crops cultivated in Kerala are Tea, Coffee, Rubber and Cocoa. Among the plantation crops the most important one is Rubber. It is extensively cultivated in all districts of Kerala. Kottayam district occupies first position in the case of Rubber cultivation. In between 1961-62 and 2005-06 the area of cultivation increased from 133133 hectares to

Table 11
Shows the Area and Production of Major Spices in Kerala during 2000-01 to 2006-07

	Area in hectares				*Production in tonnes*			
Years	*Pepper*	*Ginger*	*Turmeric*	*Cardamom*	*Pepper*	*Ginger Cured*	*Turmeric Cured*	*Cardamom Processed*
2000-01	202133	11612	4127	41288	60929	42699	9037	7580
2001-02	20395	10706	3558	4133	58240	40181	7895	7850
2002-03	208607	8998	3140	41412	67358	32412	6938	8680
2003-04	216440	8516	2774	41332	69015	32972	5652	8740
2004-05	225530	10350	3954	4132	75073	45380	7630	9300
2005-06	237998	12226	3384	41367	87605	56288	8237	9765
2006-07	226094	11082	3917	41362	64264	42497	9978	8545

Source: Agricultural Statistics, Dept of Economics & Statistics.

494400 hectares i.e. an increment of 271%. In the same period production also increased from 24589 tonnes to 739225 tonnes i.e. a record increase of 2906 %. In the case of Tea area of cultivation decreased from 37426 hectares in 1961- 62 to 35043 hectares in 2005-06. Decrease is estimated as 6%. But production increased from 37428 tonnes to 56384 tonnes during the period. Increment is 51%. In the case of coffee the area of cultivation increased from 18807 hectares in 1961 – 62 to 84644 hectares in 2005-06. Increment is 350%. During the period production also increased from 8145 tonnes to 60175 tonnes. Increment is 639%.

Table 12 given below shows the area and production of major plantation crops in Kerala during 2000-01 to 2006-07.

Table 12

	Area in hectares				*Production in tonnes*			
Years	*Tea*	*Coffee*	*Rubber*	*Cocoa*	*Tea*	*Coffee*	*Rubber*	*Cocoa*
2000-01	36847	84735	474364	8501	69132	70550	579866	3845
2001-02	36899	84795	475039	8676	66090	66690	580350	4096
2002-03	37068	83113	476047	9295	55348	63322	594917	5709
2003-04	38327	84684	478402	9433	57553	63850	655134	4877
2004-05	36230	84530	48690	9520	56408	62230	68980	5125
2005-06	35043	84644	494400	9570	56384	60175	739225	5362
2006-07	35364	84511	502240	-	53659	59175	780405	-

Source: Agricultural Statistics, Dept of Economics & Statistics.

It is clear from the table that in the case of Rubber and Cocoa area of cultivation increased from 474364 hectares to 502240 and 8501 to 9570 respectively during 2000-01 to 2006-07. But in the case of Tea and Coffee area of cultivation decreased from 36847 to 35364 hectares and 84735 to 84571 hectares respectively during 2000-01 to 2006-07. In the case of production also Rubber and Cocoa achieved good progress. Rubber production increased from 579866 tonnes to 780405 tonnes during the period. Cocoa production increased from 3845 tonnes to 5362 tonnes. While in the case of Tea and Coffee there is a fall in the volume of production. Tea production decreased from 69132 tonnes to 53659 tonnes and coffee production also witnessed a fall.

Table 13
District wise Cultivation of Plantation Crops during 2000-01 to 2005-06, (Tea Area hectares)

	Years					
Districts	*2000-2001*	*2001-2002*	*2002-2003*	*2003-2004*	*2004-2005*	*2005-2006*
Thiruvananthapuram	965	965	966	9685	965	965
Kollam	1258	1258	1258	1349	1910	1258
Pathanamthitta	91	91	91	91	91	91
Alappuzha	-	-	-	-	-	-
Kottayam	2168	2168	2176	2196	2035	1963
Idukki	24754	24792	24953	25748	24200	23702
Eranakulam	2	2	2	3	3	2
Thrissur	530	530	530	530	530	530
Palakkad	852	852	852	852	852	852
Malappuram	192	192	192	192	174	174
Kozhikode	-	-	-	-	-	-
Wayanad	6035	6049	6049	6492	5850	5506
Kannur	-	-	-	-	-	-
Kassargodu	-	-	-	-	-	-

Source: Agricultural Statistics, Dept of Economics & Statistics.
Table shows that in the cultivation of Tea Idukki district ranks first and Wayanad bagged 2nd position.

Table 14
District wise Cultivation of Plantation Crops during 2000-01 to 2005-06, (Coffee Area in hectares)

	Years					
Districts	*2000-2001*	*2001-2002*	*2002-2003*	*2003-2004*	*2004-2005*	*2005-2006*
Thiruvananthapuram	-	-	-	-	-	-
Kollam	-	-	-	-	-	-
Pathanamthitta	-	-	-	-	-	-
Alappuzha	-	-	-	-	-	-
Kottayam	1800	-	-	-	-	1735
Idukki	10725	12635	11490	12605	12605	10870
Eranakulam	-	-	-	-	-	-
Thrissur	-	-	-	-	-	-
Palakkad	4650	4650	4650	4650	4650	4650
Malappuram	-	-	-	-	-	-
Kozhikode	-	-	-	-	-	-
Wayanad	67560	67560	66973	67429	67398	67389
Kannur	-	-	-	-	-	-
Kassargodu	-	-	-	-	-	-

Source: Agricultural Statistics, Dept of Economics & Statistics.
It is clear from the table that in the Coffee cultivation Wayanad ranks first next is Idukki.

Table 15
District wise Cultivation of Plantation Crops during 2000-01 to 2005-06, (Rubber Area in hectors)

Districts	*Years*					
	2000-01	*2001-02*	*2002-03*	*2003-04*	*2004-05*	*2005-06*
Thiruvananthapuram	28196	28296	28415	28432	28630	28920
Kollam	36771	36863	36797	36741	36820	36860
Pathanamthitta	47869	47862	47905	47820	47890	47969
Alappuzha	3801	3849	3825	3844	3895	3934
Kottayam	111196	111301	111776	111775	111750	112235
Idukki	38076	38123	38250	38376	38515	38844
Eranakulam	56644	56710	56737	56892	56950	57288
Thrissur	13373	13402	13396	13448	13550	14057
Palakkad	28933	28985	29064	29612	29980	31951
Malappuram	29209	29263	29335	29831	30565	32588
Kozhikode	17690	17575	17591	17642	17645	18237
Wayanad	6430	6450	6451	6636	6938	7777
Kannur	33944	34012	34085	34581	37210	38366
Kassargodu	22232	22348	22420	22772	23415	25374

Source: Agricultural Statistics, Dept of Economics & Statistics.

Rubber is extensively cultivated in all districts of Kerala. In all districts the area of cultivation increased during the last six years. In its cultivation Kottayam district ranks first. 2nd is Eranakulam District.

Table 16
District wise Cultivation of Plantation Crops (Cocoa Area in hectares)

Districts	*Years*					
	2000-01	*2001-02*	*2002-03*	*2003-04*	*2004-05*	*2005-06*
Thiruvananthapuram	126	134	132	120	112	108
Kollam	35	26	28	13	11	9
Pathanamthitta	671	778	810	845	818	729
Alappuzha	178	182	181	166	167	169
Kottayam	2129	1720	1744	1642	1450	1327
Idukki	3058	3363	3831	4250	4625	4908
Eranakulam	1214	1335	1428	1158	1195	1225
Thrissur	156	139	132	94	89	81
Palakkad	28	33	44	72	68	66
Malappuram	46	52	63	154	132	124
Kozhikode	399	458	494	549	535	500
Wayanad	124	141	134	104	99	91
Kannur	217	206	177	184	178	166
Kassargodu	120	109	97	82	78	67

Source: Agricultural Statistics, Dept of Economics & Statistics.

Cocoa is also cultivated in all districts of Kerala. In the area of cultivation Idukki ranks first. 2nd is Kottayam.

TAPIOCA

Tapioca is a major food crop in Kerala. It is termed as the food of the poor. But its nutritional value is very high. A good portion of the land under tapioca was transformed into Rubber Estate. In between 1961-62 and 2005-06 the area of cultivation decreased by 62% i.e. from 236776 hectare to 90539 hectares. But the volume of production increased by 59%. The production increased from 1618713 tonnes in 1961-62 to 2518999 tonnes in 2006-07.

Table 17
Given below Shows the Area of Production and Production (in tones) of Tapioca during 2000-01 to 2006-07

Year	*Total area Fresh fruits*	*Production in tonnes*
2000-01	114609	2586908
2001-02	111189	2455880
2002-03	104179	2316422
2003-04	94297	2540790
2004-05	92312	2540790
2005-06	90539	2568284
2006-07	87128	2518999

Source: Agricultural Statistics, Dept of Economics & Statistics.

FRESH FRUITS CULTIVATION

In the case of fruit production there is an increment in the area of cultivation (except mango) and in the volume of production during 2000-01 to 2006-07. This is shown in the above two tables. In the case of fruits and vegetables Kerala's production is insufficient. In comparison to market demand, Kerala depends on Tamil Nadu and Karnataka for meeting their excess requirement.

Area in Hectares

Year	*Jack*	*Mango*	*Banana*	*Plantain*	*Pineapple*	*Papaya*	*Other Fresh fruits*
2000-01	93698	90571	45059	54353	10692	14066	12571
2001-02	93472	86308	50871	55183	11159	16016	12629
2002-03	92651	86344	55668	54811	10943	17385	12329
2003-04	92861	85428	55906	53496	11484	17699	10856
2004-05	93350	86623	57812	54755	11862	17925	10698
2005-06	94902	87965	61400	55222	12775	18895	10556
2006-07	-	-	59143	53060	-	-	-

Source: Agricultural Statistics, Dept of Economics & Statistics.

Production in Tonnes

Year	*Jack*	*Mango*	*Banana*	*Plantain*	*Pineapple*	*Papaya*
2000-01	313	259635	327955	403695	84599	63008
2001-02	308	305545	375903	393182	83873	72009
2002-03	320	347154	421809	409282	94842	77788
2003-04	341	384190	442220	399717	95001	80755
2004-05	345	438160	445215	408816	96831	83865
2005-06	350	511131	491823	445333	109325	85481
2006-07	-	-	463766	435635	-	-

Source: Agricultural Statistics, Dept of Economics & Statistics.

Table 18
District wise Cultivation of Fresh Fruits during 2005-06

Area in hectares

Year	*Jack*	*Mango*	*Banana*	*Plantain*	*Pine-apple*	*Papaya*	*Other Fresh fruits*
Thiruvananthapuram	6448	4723	2575	5506	300	1178	515
Kollam	6204	5065	1772	4213	531	1218	449
Pathanamthitta	3134	1727	2583	2203	301	730	712
Alappuzha	2941	5346	578	2897	89	1215	716
Kottayam	4202	3144	3342	3884	934	1226	882
Idukki	7403	3203	1828	3311	1626	830	115
Eranakulam	4502	4406	6308	4641	7603	1491	889
Thrissur	5446	8286	2919	6771	202	1752	1258
Palakkad	5871	9991	11248	7092	185	1349	1083
Malappuram	10593	11477	9897	3780	313	2638	911
Kozhikode	11502	10656	2185	3230	525	2287	697
Wayanad	10284	4734	12842	1732	56	439	456
Kannur	13500	11824	2554	3446	255	1827	769
Kassargodu	2782	3383	789	2516	128	715	534
Total	94902	87965	61400	55222	12775	18895	10586

Source: Agricultural Statistics, Dept of Economics & Statistics.

During 2005-06, 94902 hectares of land were used for the cultivation of Jack, 87965 hectares were used for mango, 61400 hectares were used for Banana, 55222 hectares were used for plantain, 12775 hectares were used for Pineapple, 18895 hectares were used for Papaya and 10586 hectares were used for the cultivation of other fresh fruits.

Table 19
District wise Production of Fruits in Tonnes 2005-06.

Districts	*Jack*	*Mango*	*Banana*	*Plantain*	*Pineapple*	*Papaya*
Thiruvananthapuram	36	30652	17794	46499	1634	7763
Kollam	30	31910	12846	38018	4114	1133
Pathanamthitta	15	13557	23302	29980	1753	4030
Alappuzha	6	26035	3927	18042	397	6038
Kottayam	23	17606	28817	33886	6072	8827
Idukki	18	21524	13883	30531	13318	2067
Eranakulam	22	21281	47906	37399	73855	7217
Thrissur	20	41596	25285	41874	1793	7657
Palakkad	19	95114	82643	63159	954	8944
Malappuram	39	55893	69993	32956	1402	11393
Kozhikode	27	31861	15605	21195	1610	3293
Wayanad	27	15528	115160	15766	228	2928
Kannur	56	87261	27532	18707	1391	9793
Kassargodu	12	21313	7130	17321	804	4398
Total	350	511131	491823	445333	109325	85481

Source: Agricultural Statistics, Dept of Economics & Statistics.

During 2005-06, 350 million Jack nut, 511131 tonnes of Mango, 491823 tonnes of Banana, 445333 tonnes of Plantain, 109325 tonnes of Pineapple and 85481 tonnes of Papaya were produced in Kerala.

Table 20
Area under Crops 2005-06 (Area in hectares)

Districts	*Tapioca*	*Tubers*	*Sweet Potato*
Thiruvananthapuram	19619	1483	45
Kollam	23814	4833	19
Pathanamthitta	7868	3952	7
Alappuzha	2668	840	2
Kottayam	5727	1678	3
Idukki	6608	1568	10
Eranakulam	5636	972	0
Thrissur	1417	667	4
Palakkad	3994	2003	129
Malappuram	5346	2124	229
Kozhikode	2476	1170	111
Wayanad	2348	4111	11
Kannur	2442	575	38
Kassargodu	576	212	173
Total	905390	26188	711

Source: Agricultural Statistics, Dept of Economics & Statistics.

Table 20a
Production in Tonnes 2005-06

Districts	*Tapioca*	*Tubers*	*Sweet Potato*
Thiruvananthapuram	463702	-	510
Kollam	694984	-	209
Pathanamthitta	255006	-	77
Alappuzha	62286	-	24
Kottayam	182262	-	24
Idukki	205293	-	115
Eranakulam	182605	-	0
Thrissur	28254	-	44
Palakkad	105321	-	1190
Malappuram	164029	-	2634
Kozhikode	61311	-	469
Wayanad	85599	-	129
Kannur	63880	-	432
Kassargodu	13752	-	3156
Total	2568284	-	9013

Source: Agricultural Statistics, Dept of Economics & Statistics.

Table 20 shows that during 2005-06, 90539 hectares of land were used for the cultivation of Tapioca, 26188 hectares were used for Tubers and 711 hectares were used for sweet potato.

Table 20 A shows that during 2005-06 the volume of tapioca produced was 2568284 tonnes and the quantity of sweet potato amounted to 9013 tonnes.

VEGETABLES

The major vegetables cultivated in Kerala are Drumstick, Bitter gourd, Snake gourd, Ladies finger, Brinjal, Green Chilies, Elephant yam, peas etc. In between 2001-2006 there is an increment in the area of cultivation. In the case of drumstick the area of cultivation increased from 19632 hectares to 21138. In bitter gourd area increased from 1817 hectares to 2129, in snake gourd area increased from 871 hectares to 1153 hectares, in ladies finger 933 hectares to 1134, In brinjal 735 hectares to 965 hectares, in green chilies 226 hectares to 1231 hectares and in the case of other vegetables area increased from 19415 hectares to 19506 hectares in the same period. This is shown in the table given below.

Table 21

Area of Vegetables Cultivation: Area in hectares 2000-01 to 2005-06

Year	Drum Stick	Bitter Gourd	Snake gourd	Ladies Finger	Brinjal	Green Chilies	Other Vegetables
2000-01	19632	1817	871	933	735	226	19415
2001-02	21283	2489	833	1116	669	692	21390
2002-03	21252	2339	912	871	574	783	20529
2003-04	21293	2162	828	930	762	682	23876
2004-05	21200	2152	935	980	763	780	21393
2005-06	21138	2129	1153	1134	965	1231	19506

Source: Agricultural Statistics, Dept of Economics & Statistics.

VEGETABLE AND FRUIT PROMOTION COUNCILS PROGRAMME

Vegetable and Fruit production council, Kerala was involved in the implementation of vegetables and fruit promotion programme. The programme covers production, formation of SHGs, credit management and marketing. During the year 2006-07 13965 farmers were inducted and 720 SHGs were formed and 27 farmer markets were established. 25215 farmers were covered under the Karsha Rakshaka Medical Insurance scheme. During the year Rs. 113.16 lakh was disbursed as crop loan, 39 MT of vegetables and fruits were exported during 2006-07 and 40022 hectares of area was covered under vegetable cultivation.

Table 22

District wise Cultivation of Vegetables–2005-06

Districts	Drum Stick	Bitter Gourd	Snake Gourd	Ladies Finger	Brinjal Green	Chilies	Other Vegetables
TVM	2174	47	142	37	80	77	458
Kollam	1815	109	31	36	56	156	671
Pathanamthitta	604	136	102	47	96	19	1061
Alappuzha	790	109	77	22	53	54	673
Kottayam	800	258	283	24	65	11	1169
Idukki	583	275	5	2	7	21	2296
Eranakulam	807	194	161	55	48	72	1480
Thrissur	1641	192	39	62	116	256	999
Palakkad	2171	318	151	617	338	412	5719
Malappuram	3198	158	131	111	54	83	1441
Kozhikode	3049	69	11	30	5	2	727
Wayanad	880	136	6	15	17	0	759
Kannur	1978	88	7	32	21	1	1103
Kassargodu	708	40	7	44	19	67	950
Total	21138	2129	1153	1134	965	1231	19506

Source: Agricultural Statistics, Dept of Economic & Statistics.

Table 23
District wise Cultivation of Cereals/millets and Pulses Including Tur during 2005-06

Districts	*Cereals/ Millets*	*Pulses including Tur*	*Total Food Grain*
TVM	4705	517	5222
Kollam	7218	550	7768
Pathanamthitta	3291	20	3311
Alappuzha	28768	112	28880
Kottayam	12557	102	12659
Idukki	2943	229	3172
Eranakulam	24934	787	25721
Thrissur	31074	653	31727
Palakkad	116779	4761	121540
Malappuram	14885	906	15791
Kozhikode	4703	176	4879
Wayanad	11504	484	11988
Kannur	9224	726	9950
Kassargodu	6032	539	6571
Total	278617	10562	289179

Source: Agricultural Statistics, Dept of Economics & Statistics.

In Kerala 278617 hectares of land was used for the cultivation of cereals/millets during 2005-06. The area for pulses including Tur is around 10562 hectares and the area for total food grains is around 289179 hectares in 2005-06.

In the case of the non-food crops the total area under cultivation was around 1667083 hectors in 2005-06. In fodder grass cultivation Idukki district ranked first. Fodder grass is cultivated in 3811 hectares of land. As for manure crops the total area of cultivation is 19756 hectares. Medicinal plants are cultivated in 239 hectares.

AGRICULTURAL INCOME

The trends in agricultural income in Kerala during the last seven years are shown in the table. The estimate for 2005-06 indicated an increase of 6.72%. The estimate for 2006-07 showed an increase of 6.17 % over the previous year. While the share of agriculture in state's income decreased from 16.38% in 2002-03 to 14.55% in 2006-07.

Table 24
Area under Cultivation Non Food Crops 2005-06, (Area in hectares)

Districts	*Fodder Grass*	*Manure Crops*	*Other Crops*	*Medicinal Plants*	*Total Food Crops*
TVM	125	325	3106	40	117327
Kollam	243	1049	2788	13	108552
Pathanamthitta	237	1422	4086	5	76056
Alappuzha	194	349	3740	6	64808
Kottayam	148	652	5767	20	163909
Idukki	1324	667	33170	2	138385
Eranakulam	172	625	4340	41	122404
Thrissur	100	1485	3954	36	106118
Palakkad	808	2420	18005	50	121639
Malappuram	19	6300	8721	13	162198
Kozhikode	51	1831	3545	3	153717
Wayanad	188	457	3601	7	96620
Kannur	148	886	10359	1	144049
Kassargodu	54	1288	5939	2	90901
Total	3811	19756	111121	239	1667083

Source: Agricultural Statistics, Dept of Economics & Statistics.

Table 25
Agricultural Incomes in Kerala during 2002-03 to 2006-07

Year	*Agricultural income Rs. in crores*	*Rate of Change over Previous years*	*% Contribution to state income*
2002-03	13132	1.37	16.36
2003-04	12819	2.38	15.04
2004-05	13762	7.35	14.95
2005-06	14673	6.72	14.85
2006-07	15539	6.17	14.55

Source: Economic review 2007, State Planning Board Trivandrum.

It is clear from the table that in Kerala agricultural income increased from Rs. 13132 crores in 2002-03 to Rs. 15539 in 2006-07. While the percentage contribution of agriculture to state income has decreased.

CONCLUSION

Agriculture in Kerala is passing through a crisis, which the state has never experienced since the formation of the state in 1956. Progressive land reform policies of erstwhile communist government of 1957 provided Kerala a unique model for social transformation and agricultural development. But none of these steps enabled to uplift Kerala agriculture from the deplorable stage. Massive transformation of agricultural land for non agricultural purposes, conversion of paddy fields for economic crops, reclamation of paddy lands for commercial purposes, massive growth of real estate business and it's profitability, growth of land mafias with political patronage and growing demand for house plots reduces the acreage of net cultivable land. Change in the lifestyle accompanied by attitudinal changes towards agriculture further bleakened the glory of agriculture. Non-profitability of agriculture with soaring costs pulled the farmers to bankruptcy. Massive suicide of farmers marked a symbol of present agriculture crisis in Kerala. In order to surpass the crisis, Government of Kerala is now introducing a number of steps to promote agriculture through people's participation programmes. Financial support is given to NeighbourHood Groups (NHGs) of both men and women to initiate agricultural activities. Kudumbasree has introduced Haritha Sree programme to cultivate fruits, vegetables and paddy through Lease Land Farming. Last year Lease Land Farming was done in 57436.28 acres. A total of 3,54,513 families hailing from 35130 Neighbour Hood groups were engaged in agricultural activities.[17] Moreover National Rural Employment Guarantee Programme is being implemented in Kerala through which good support can be given to agricultural promotion.

NOTES

1. Agricultural Statistics (2006), Government of Kerala, Department of Economics and Statistics, Trivandrum.
2. George S and Chadopadhyaya (2001), "Population and Land use in Kerala, in Growing, Population Changing Land Scapes-From Studies from India", Chinaand, the United States, National Academy Press, Washington D C.
3. Economic Review (2007), Government of Kerala, State Planning Board Trivandrum, p. 56.
4. Ruddar Datt, K. P. M. Sundaram (2007), Indian Economy, 57th edition, S. Chand and Company Limited, New Delhi, p. 494

5. Ruddar Datt, K. P. M. Sundaram, *Op.cit*, p. 495.

6. *Indian Journal of Agricultural Economics,* Volume XVIII, No. 1 Conference "Agricultural Price Policy in India", Directorate of Economics and Statistics, Ministry of Food and Agriculture, Government of India.

7. Jose V. T. (2007), "Changes in Land use pattern in Kerala- recent trends and future prospective" Kerala's Development Issues in the New Millennium edited by Prakash B.A and Prabhakaran V.R, Serial Publications New Delhi, p. 125

8. Economic Review (2007), Government of Kerala, State Planning Board Trivandrum, and Appendix: 4.5.

9. Raj K. N. (1985), "An Introductory Overview of Commercialization of Indian Agriculture", Working Paper No. 208 CDS Trivandrum.

10. Oommen M. A. (1994), "Land Reforms and Economic Change: Experience and Lessons from Kerala, Kerala's Economic Performance, Problems and Prospects" edited by Prakash B.A Sage Publications New Delhi, P: 132

11. Prakash B.A. (1994), "Kerala's Economy-An Overview" Performance Problems and Prospects, p. 32.

12. Agricultural Statistics (2001), Government of Kerala, Department of Economics and Statistics, Trivandrum.

13. Agricultural Statistics (2002), Government of Kerala, Department of Economics and Statistics, Trivandrum.

14. Agricultural Statistics (2003), Government of Kerala, Department of Economics and Statistics, Trivandrum.

15. Agricultural Statistics (2004), Government of Kerala, Department of Economics and Statistics, Trivandrum.

16. Agricultural Statistics (2005), Government of Kerala, Department of Economics and Statistics, Trivandrum.

17. Kudumbasree Mission (2007), Government of Kerala.

PART–THREE

Dimensions of Human Development

7

RURAL AND URBAN UNEMPLOYMENT IN KERALA–STRUCTURE AND TRENDS

P. Kumari Latha Devi

INTRODUCTION

India is emerging as a major power with the growing economy registering a high growth rate. Our cities and metropolitan urban centres began to display the marks of development and affluence. But due to lack of uniform economic and social development, the rural hinterland has not been able to march in tandem with urban India. Large scale unemployment has become the prime social, economic and political issue in the developing economy of India. Unemployment is the negative aspect of the economic process and it is a condition of being without gainful work. At the macro level unemployment is seen as there is a disparity between the total labour force in the working age group seeking work and the total demand for labour by the employers. Demographic pressure on the economy, especially, on rural sector over the time has reduced the size of farms leading to increased marginalization of the self employed cultivators. At the same time there has been a considerable decline in the proportion of agricultural workers and an increase in the proportion of non-agricultural workers.

This is partly due to the inability of the agricultural sector to generate adequate employment opportunities, and partly due to increased industrialization and expansion of construction activities in the urban areas. Hence there has been an increase in the volume of unemployment from one plan period to another. The latest NSSO survey reports of 2004-05 (61st and 62nd Round) reveals that the overall unemployment rates are not high at national level. It has been estimated that the urban unemployment rates are higher than the rural unemployment rates. The unemployment rates for women are higher than those for men and it is highest among urban women. As on December 2004, the number of employment seekers in the live register of employment exchanges in India was 405 lakhs. This number decreased to 394 lakhs in December 2005 and increased to 407 lakhs in June 2006. Of the total of 407 lakhs job seekers, 294 lakhs are men and 113 lakhs are women.

CONCEPTS OF UNEMPLOYMENT

The number of persons unemployed per thousand persons in the labour force (employed and unemployed together), is defined by the NSSO as unemployment rate. For convenience, we may express the unemployment rate as percentage of labour force unemployed. Keeping in view the recommendations of the Committee of Experts on Unemployment, the NSSO has developed the standardized concepts and definitions of labour force, employment and unemployment suitable to Indian conditions. The three concepts of unemployment developed by the NSSO are;

1. Usual Status Unemployment,
2. Current Weekly Status Unemployment, and
3. Current Daily Status Unemployment.

The Usual Status Unemployment rate is a person rate, and indicates chronic unemployment, because all those who are found 'usually' unemployed in the reference year, are counted as unemployed. A person is considered as unemployed if the person was not working but was either seeking or was available for work for a relatively longer time during the past year.

On the basis of Current Weekly Status, a person who had not worked for even one hour or any one day of the reference week, but had been seeking or was available for work at any time, treated as unemployed.

Current Daily Status is based on the reported time-disposition of the person on each day of the reference week. A person, who works for a period of one to four hours, is considered having worked for half-day and if he works for four hours or more during a day, he is considered as employed for the whole day. A person who has not worked for even an hour in a day of the reference week is classified as unemployed.

It has been widely observed that the estimates based on daily status is the most inclusive rate of 'unemployment' giving the average level of unemployment on a day during the survey year. It captures the unemployed days of the chronically and intermittently unemployed during the reference week.

Estimates on employment and unemployment on CDS basis indicate that employment growth during 1999-2000 to 2004-05 has accelerated significantly as compared to the growth witnessed during 1993-94 to 1999-2000. Employment growth accelerated from 1.25 per cent per annum to 2.62 per cent per annum. However since the labour force grew at a faster rate of 2.84 per cent than the work force, unemployment on CDS basis increased from 7.31 per cent in 1999-2000 to 8.28 per cent in 2004-05. The following table illustrates the growth of population, labour force, work force, number of unemployed and rate of unemployment in India from 1983-84 to 2004-05 based on the NSSO reports. (See Table 1).

Table 1
Unemployment in India during 1983-84 to 2004-05 on CDS basis (in million)

Year	*1983-84*	*1993-94*	*1999-2000*	*2004-05*
Population	718.10	893.68	1005.05	1092.83
Labour force	263.82	334.20	364.88	419.65
Work force	239.49	313.93	338.19	384.91
Unemployed	24.34	20.67	26.68	34.78
Unemployment rate (%)	9.22	6.06	7.31	8.28

Source: Various NSSO Survey Reports.

NSSO data shows that the rate of unemployment among rural males increased from 5.6 per cent in 1993-94 to 9 per cent in 2004-05 and for rural females from 5.6 per cent to 9.3 per cent. Urban unemployment rates have also risen for both males and females during 1999-2000 to 2004-05. Thus at national level, unemployment rates on CDS basis have risen for all labour force categories–rural/urban and male/female between 1999-2000 and 2004-05.

RURAL AND URBAN UNEMPLOYMENT IN KERALA

The unemployment of a large section of the labour force has been the most serious socio-economic puzzle of Kerala during the last fifty years. In spite of the economic development during the last half a century, Kerala was not able to solve the basic problem of massive unemployment. The structure of the labour market was largely characterized by casual employment with small share of regular employment. Unemployment exists in the State due to the prevalence of labour supply which exceeds the demand. It has been noticed that the growth of supply of labour is determined by the growth of population, and the participation of population on the total work force. In Kerala, from the decade of 1970's onwards, there has been a rapid rise in the labour supply because of an increase in the number of women seeking wage employment. Thus though the supply of workers increased, the demand for them did not increase. As a consequence there has been an alarming increase in the unemployment rate in Kerala. It has been noticed that the basic deficiency of the development process is its failure to generate adequate regular and remunerative jobs in organized sector to meet the rapid growth of educated unemployment.

The NSSO surveys conducted throughout the country during 1993-94, 1999-00 and 2004-05 revealed the fact that Kerala has the highest rate of unemployment compared to other Indian States. The analysis of inter-state unemployment rate shows greater regional disparities in 2004-05 compared to 1999-00. It has been noticed that the unemployment rate was invariably high in Kerala during 1993-94 to 2004-05. (See Table 2).

Table 2
Inter-State Unemployment Rate (on CDS basis)

States	*1993-94*	*1999-2000*	*2004-05*
Kerala	15.51	20.97	25.6
West Bengal	10.06	14.99	11.2
Tamil Nadu	11.41	11.78	15.1
Assam	8.03	8.03	9.0
Andhra Pradesh	6.69	8.03	10.9
Orissa	7.30	7.34	10.2
Bihar	6.34	7.32	6.8
Maharashtra	5.09	7.16	9.3
Haryana	6.51	4.77	6.2
Gujarat	5.70	4.55	4.1
Karnataka	4.94	4.57	6.7
Madhya Pradesh	8.56	4.45	5.6
Uttar Pradesh	3.45	4.08	3.7
Punjab	3.10	4.03	9.7
Rajastan	1.31	3.13	4.4
Himachal Pradesh	1.80	2.96	5.7
All India	5.99	7.32	8.2

Source: NSSO Survey Reports.

Thus it is evident that the unemployment rate in Kerala is abnormally high and this may be demarcated as the single largest problem of Kerala economy. The worsening unemployment problem is obviously related to the inability of the State economy to generate any fresh employment especially during the last decade. Though this phenomenon of 'Jobless Growth' is observable in all the States in the country, the situation in Kerala appears to be particularly distressing, because, most of the labour intensive traditional industries are facing severe crisis in the present era.

According to the live register of employment exchanges, the total number of work seekers in Kerala was 36.7 lakh in 2005. This number increased to 38.6 lakh in 2006, registering an increase of 5.2 per cent. The total number in September 2007 was 40.5 lakh, of which 38.9 lakh were general work seekers and 1.6 lakh were professional/technical work seekers. The total number of work force in different sectors of the economy as on March 2007 amounts to 1110980. Out of this, 603893 (54.36%) were in public and the remaining 507087 (45.64%) were in private sector.

WORK PARTICIPATION RATE

Work participation rate denoting the percentage of workers to the total population provides the idea about the participation of the population in economic activity. Kerala, which ranks first among the Indian States in terms of Human Development Index (HDI) and Gender Development Index (GDI), presents however a poor picture in terms of male and female work participation. According to the 2001 census, the male work participation rate has increased to 50.2 per cent from 47.6 per cent in1991, while the female work participation has declined slightly to 15.4 per cent from 15.8 per cent in 1991. It is well known that Census underestimates work participation rate, in particular of women, while the methodology and concepts used by the NSSO ensures a better enumeration of the work force. The latest NSSO round data for the year 2004-05 reveals much higher work participation rate for men and women compared to the Census reports. The male and female work participation rate in Kerala and India is given in the table below.

Table 3
Work Participation Rates in Kerala and All-India by Usual Principal Status (in %)

	Kerala			*India*		
Year	*1993-94*	*1999-00*	*2004-05*	*1993-94*	*1999-00*	*2004-05*
Rural						
Male	53.7	55.3	55.9	55.3	53.1	54.6
Female	23.8	23.8	25.6	32.8	29.9	32.7
Urban						
Male	55.9	55.8	54.7	52.1	51.8	54.9
Female	20.3	20.3	20.0	15.5	13.9	16.6

Source: Various rounds of NSSO Reports.

It has been noticed that there was not much change in rural-urban and male female work participation rate. The rural female work participation rate in Kerala was much lower compared to other states and the all-India average. The urban work participation rate for both males and females was higher in Kerala compared to the all-India average. The female work participation rate for rural and urban areas was much lower than their male counterparts. Economic, social and demographic factors influenced the participation of the population in economic activities [B.A. Prakash, 2004]. The recession experienced in the State during the second half of the 1990's was a major factor contributing to the decline in the work participation rate. Factors such as the decline in agricultural activities due to low productivity and profitability, small and marginal agricultural land holdings, changes in cropping pattern, decline in traditional cottage and rural industries, changes in the occupational preference of educated young rural labour force, occupational and geographical shifting of the rural labour force through migration, etc have contributed to the lower work participation rate in the rural areas of Kerala.

MALE-FEMALE UNEMPLOYMENT

A peculiar feature of Kerala's unemployment situation is that women outnumber their male counterparts seeking employment. If we consider the last three quinquennial rounds of NSSO, viz. 50th, 55th, and 61st round for the years 1993-94, 1999-2000 and 2004-05 respectively to see the trend in unemployment in Kerala, we can notice that both rural and urban female unemployment rate increased dramatically during 1999-00 to 2004-05. Incidence of urban male unemployment came down slightly during the same period. Apart from that, all other unemployment rates viz. unemployment rates among rural male, rural female, urban female, went up. This position is reflected in all the 14 districts of Kerala. Out of the total number of 38.99 lakh job seekers in March 2007, women constituted 22.59 lakh (58%). The district-wise analysis showed that Thiruvananthapuram district ranks first in the number of work seekers in both general and professional categories. It has been estimated that the total number of work seekers in Thiruvananthapuram district is 5.53 lakh, of which 3.38 lakh are women and 2.15 lakh are men, as on 31st March 2007. The second largest number of work seekers is from Kollam district and the lowest number of work seekers is in Wayanad followed by Kasaragod district.

In 2003, the total number of unemployed men was estimated at 979,000 against the total number of unemployed women at 1,292,000. The unemployment rate was found to be very high among females compared to their male counterparts. When compared to all-India level, female unemployment is higher than that of men. Male and female unemployment rate for the period from 1977-78 to 2003-04 in Kerala is shown in the table below. (See Table 4).

Table 4
Unemployment Rate by Sex in Kerala (in percentage)

Year	*Male*	*Female*	*Person*
1977-78	14.0	30.6	19.8
1983-84	10.8	18.4	13.1
1987-88	12.8	26.3	17.1
1993-94	7.3	18.2	10.1
1999-00	7.4	21.5	11.4
2004-05	11.23	41.21	19.15

Source: Various NSSO surveys. [On the basis of Usual Principal and Subsidiary Status].

It has been evident that female unemployment is more acute than the male unemployment in the state. There is a vibrant increase in the female unemployment rate during the period 1999-00 to 2004-05. The crucial difference observed in the women unemployment should be considered seriously in the state of Kerala where the sex-ratio is the highest (1058/1000 in 2001). The main reason for this upward trend in female unemployment is the lowest female work participation rate. On the basis of 2001 census report, it may be noticed that although both male and female work participation rate was lower in Kerala compared to national level, the disparity looks sharper for women when female work participation in rural India was 31 per cent as against Kerala's 15.09 per cent. In the case of male workers, the total work participation rate has increased between 1991 and 2001 in rural areas and in the case of female workers, a reverse trend has been observed in rural areas. It has been also noticed inter-district variations in the male-female work participation rate. District-wise male and female work participation rate (in %) is given in the Table 5.

From the data it is clear that both male and female work participation rate is the highest in Iddukki district whereas it is the lowest in Malappuram district. District-wise analysis reveals that economic, social and demographic factors influenced the participation of the population in economic activities.

Table 5
District-wise Male and Female Work Participation Rate

District	*Male*	*Female*
Kasaragod	49.3	20.8
Kannur	50.0	15.2
Wayanad	55.7	22.8
Kozhikode	48.8	8.1
Malappuram	42.8	6.6
Palakkad	52.2	21.1
Thrissur	50.8	15.1
Ernakulam	55.4	17.1
Iddukki	58.4	28.1
Kottayam	52.4	13.9
Alapuzha	49.7	20.2
Pathanamthitta	47.6	13.2
Kollam	48.5	16.7
Thiruvananthapuram	51.5	14.4
Kerala	50.4	15.3

Source: Census of India-2001.

DISTRIBUTION OF POPULATION AS WORKERS AND NON-WORKERS

The structure of the work force is a reflection of the macro processes at work in the economy. Economic development is associated with shifts in the sectoral allocation of the work force which in turn is related to shifts in the production structure. In Kerala, according to 2001 Census, there are 10.3 million workers which constitute 32.3% of total population. Main workers constitute 8.2 million and out of them 6 million (73%) are in rural areas and 2.2 million (27%) are in urban areas. Similarly there are 2.05 million marginal workers. Non workers constitute 21.6 million (67.7%) in the state. Total population has been classified as workers and non workers and the total workers can be divided into the main workers and the marginal workers. Main workers are those who work for the major part of the year (183 days or above) preceding the date of enumeration. Marginal workers are those who work at any time but not worked for the major part of the year (183 days). Non workers are the persons who have not worked any time at all in the year preceding the date of enumeration. Male and female distribution of the workers in rural and urban areas is given below. (See Table 6).

Table 6
Distribution of Population as Workers and Non workers in 2001.
(in Million)

	Category of workers	*Total population*	*Total workers*	*Main workers*	*Marginal workers*	*Non workers*
Total	Person	31.8	10.3	8.2	2.1	21.5
	Male	15.4	7.8	6.5	1.3	7.6
	Female	16.4	2.5	1.8	0.7	13.9
Rural	Person	23.6	7.7	6.0	1.7	15.8
	Male	11.5	5.8	4.7	1.1	5.7
	Female	12.1	1.9	1.3	0.6	10.1
Urban	Person	8.2	2.6	2.2	0.4	5.7
	Male	4.0	2.0	1.7	0.3	2.0
	Female	4.2	0.6	0.5	0.1	3.7

Source: Census of India, 2001.

From the table it can be seen that the number of non-workers are higher in all categories of workers. The number of female workers is very low both in rural and urban areas. It is also noticed that there is significant fall in the percentage of both male and female main workers.

RURAL UNEMPLOYMENT

The NSSO survey results show that there has been an increase in the rates of rural unemployment during the second half of the 1990's. According to Dr. B.A.Prakash, the principal reason for the increase in rural unemployment has been the continuous fall in the price of agricultural commodities during the second half of the 1990's resulting in serious crisis in the agricultural sector. Due to the factors such as very small size of agricultural land holdings, the increase in the cost of production, fall in the productivity and profitability of cultivation, changes in the crop pattern, a large section of cultivators and self employed farmers have shifted from agriculture to non-agricultural operations in the urban areas. The decline of traditional labour intensive industries such as handloom, coir, handicrafts, coir, cashew, beedi, etc has also contributed to the decline in rural employment.

On the basis of the estimate of the NSSO survey of 2004-05, Kerala is identified as the State with the highest rate of rural unemployment. It has been estimated that 26 per cent of the rural labour force are unemployed in Kerala. The structure of rural employment in Kerala has been undergoing several changes during the last three decades. The rural work force engaged in agricultural activities has declined considerably and in non-agricultural activities has increased to a greater extent. This shift towards the non-farm sector has influenced not only casual wage employment but also self-employment opportunities of the rural labour force. The most distinguishing feature of the magnitude of rural unemployment is that it has been increasing for a pretty long period. The shift from more labour intensive food crops to less labour intensive cash crops also increased rural unemployment. The new jobs created within agriculture and outside agriculture have failed to absorb the new entrants into the labour force in Kerala. Thus the backlog of rural unemployment in Kerala is mounting day by day due to the rise in rural labour force on one side and diminishing productivity in agriculture is on the other. The following data illustrates the extent of rural unemployment in Kerala and in India based on NSSO reports. (See Table 7).

Table 7
Rural Unemployment Rate in Kerala from 1972-73 to 2004-05 on CDS basis (in Percentage)

Year	*1972-73*	*1977-78*	*1983-84*	*1987-88*	*1993-94*	*1999-00*	*2004-05*
Person	23.5	25.8	26.2	20.0	14.7	21.7	25.6
Male	22.5	25.0	24.3	16.7	13.1	20.0	21.1
Female	25.4	27.4	31.0	27.4	19.0	26.1	34.6

Source: NSSO Survey Reports.

It has been noticed that 26 per cent of rural labour force is unemployed in Kerala based on the NSSO current daily status definition of unemployment in 2005-05. The NSSO surveys also found that Kerala has the highest unemployment rate in rural areas. A sex-wise distribution shows that the rural unemployment rate for males is 21 per cent and for females it has gone up to 35 per cent in 2004-05.

URBAN UNEMPLOYMENT

According to the NSSO surveys, the urban employment rate based on current daily status has increased from 17.7 per cent in 1993-94 to 25.2 per cent in 2004-05. A distinct feature of urban employment is the high incidence of unemployment among women compared to their male counterparts. Another notable feature is the rate of unemployment in Kerala is the highest compared to other States of India. According to Dr B.A. Prakash, the high rate of urban unemployment was attributed to factors such as low growth of employment opportunities, structure of labour market characterized by informal and casual employment, casualisation of labour, low work participation rate, low participation of women in economic activities, preference of regular and white collar jobs by the educated youths and the recession in Kerala since the second half of the 1990's. The high incidence of educated unemployment in urban areas is attributed to factors such as excess supply of labour due to ever increasing supply of educated youth labour force, high literacy rate, preference of the educated for regular and white collar jobs, decline of self employment and more engagement in casual activities. The extent of unemployment in urban areas can be better under stood from the NSSO data given below.

Table 8

Urban Unemployment Rate in Kerala from 1972-73 to 2004-05 on CDS Basis (in %)

Year	*1972-73*	*1977-78*	*1983-84*	*1987-88*	*1993-94*	*1999-00*	*2004-05*
Person	22.9	25.1	24.3	27.1	17.7	19.1	25.2
Male	22.7	25.0	22.7	22.4	14.1	15.5	17.4
Female	23.4	25.5	29.01	40.2	27.8	28.2	42.3

Source: NSSO Survey Reports.

It has been noticed that unemployment in urban areas increased over time. The data also reveals that there was a decline in the male unemployment rate while the female unemployment rate in the urban areas increased very rapidly. The increase during the period from 1999 to 2004 was steeper than the previous increase. Thus female unemployment problem in the urban areas now a days, is an unsolved puzzle in Kerala.

EDUCATED UNEMPLOYMENT

A characteristic feature of unemployment in developing countries is the high incidence of unemployment among young people. The educated are those persons who have attained an educational level of secondary and above including those completed diploma/certificate courses. Normally, one can attain this educational level at the age of 15 years or above. Thus the study among the educated is restricted to persons of age 15 years and above. The 61st and 62nd NSSO rounds survey in 2004-05 revealed that in both rural and urban areas, among the educated, the unemployment rate was much higher for women than for men in India. This disparity was even more prominent among those whose educational level was higher secondary or graduate and above. It was estimated that compared to 1993-94, these rates for 1999-00 among the educated had declined. The decline was more for women than for men. On the other hand, between 1999-00 and 2004-05, the corresponding rates have increased for women, while they declined for rural men and remained stable for urban men.

Education is an important factor in determining the level of unemployment in Kerala, as most of the unemployed are educated. In the state, educated unemployment has assumed alarming proportions in recent times. The rate of educated unemployment in the state rose from 29.3 to 35.0 per cent between 1983 and 1987-88 in sharp contrast with experience at the national level. The NSSO survey reports showed that one-fourth of the educated labour force in rural areas and more than one-fifth of the educated labour force in urban areas is unemployed. In 2003, the highest unemployment rate was among secondary level educated persons, almost 40 per cent. The rate among the degree holders was not much lower, 36 per cent.

The number of work seekers below SSLC increased from 6.29 lakh in 2005 to 6.40 lakh in 2006 and again to 6.45 lakh in September 2007. The total number of work seekers who possess SSLC and above increased from 30.41 lakh in 2005 to32.19 lakh in 2006 and to 34.10 lakh till September 2007. The percentage of work seekers below SSLC to the total work seekers is decreasing since 1999 and the percentage of work seekers who possess SSLC and above is increasing rapidly. The number of work seekers with PDC or HSC increased from 5.75 lakh in 2005 to 6.17 lakh in 2006 and again to 6.57 lakh in September 2007. The number of graduates registered in employment exchanges stood at 2.30 lakh in 2005. It increased to 2.33 lakh in 2006 and again to 2.38 lakh in September 2007. The number of job seekers with Post graduate degree decreased from 0.55 lakh in 2005 to 0.54 lakh in 2006 and further decreased to 0.53 lakh in September 2007. The share of job seekers according to different level of education from 1996 to 2006 is given in the table below. (See Table 9).

Table 9
Percentage Share of Employment Seekers According to Level of Education in Kerala

Level of education	*1996*	*2001*	*2006*
Below SSLC	25.0	21.8	16.5
SSLC	60.4	58.1	60.1
PDC or HSC	8.7	12.3	16.0
Degree	4.9	6.3	6.0
Post Graduate	1.0	1.5	1.4
Total Work Seekers	100	100	100

Source: Directorate of Employment.

It has been estimated that, of the total employment seekers in 2006, 16.5 per cent are below SSLC, 60.1 per cent SSLC, 16 per cent PDC or equivalent, 6 per cent are degree holders and only1.4 per cent Post graduate. It is also noted that the number of professional and technical work seekers in 2005 was 1.77 lakh and this number decreased to 1.64 lakh in 2006 and again to 1.57 lakh in September 2007. The share of employment seekers with various professional and technical qualifications is given below. (Table 10).

Table 10
Percentage Share of Professional and Technical Work Seekers in Kerala

Educational level	*1996*	*2001*	*2006*
Medical Graduates	1.53	1.52	1.78
Engineering Graduates	5.64	5.85	5.16
Diploma in Engineering	22.15	26.19	25.40
ITI Certificate holders	69.67	65.38	66.88
Agricultural Graduates	0.98	0.85	0.46
Veterinary Graduates	0.03	0.21	0.32
Total	100	100	100

Source: Directorate of Employment.

It has been noticed that the job seekers with engineering degree increased from 6389 in 2005 to 8466 in 2006 and decreased to 7431 in September 2007. The number of medical graduates who had registered their name in the employment exchanges decreased from 3428 in 2005 to 2925 in 2006 and again to 2418 in September 2007.

UNEMPLOYMENT AMONG YOUTH

A characteristic feature of unemployment in Kerala is the high incidence of unemployment among young people. The NSSO survey results suggested that the rate of unemployment is very high among young people belonging to the age group of 15-29 years. It has been estimated that 32.3 per cent of young men and 45.8 per cent of young women are unemployed in Kerala. Nearly 32 per cent of rural young men and 68.5 per cent of urban young women are unemployed in Kerala during 2004-05. (Table 11).

It has been noticed that unemployment rate varies considerably by age. The recent estimates shows that the unemployment rate is very high (above 50 per cent) among women at ages below 30 years. At higher ages the unemployment rates are in general lower among both men and women. Sex differentials are maintained at all ages with women showing the higher rates.

Table 11
Unemployment Rates among Youth in Kerala during 1999-00 and 2004-05

Year	*1999-00*				*2004-05*			
Age groups	*15-19*	*20-24*	*25-29*	*15-19*	*15-19*	*20-24*	*25-29*	*15-29*
Rural								
Male	43.7	32.6	26.4	32.3	49.0	32.4	24.5	31.9
Female	50.6	53.8	33.8	45.8	59.1	65.2	56.1	60.6
Person	45.9	38.9	28.5	36.3	52.1	44.5	36.0	42.1
Urban								
Male	44.7	30.3	15.7	26.6	46.0	28.5	21.0	28.3
Female	48.4	61.9	38.8	50.4	83.4	60.0	72.2	68.5
Person	45.7	41.8	22.7	34.3	56.1	39.8	38.6	41.8

Source: NSSO Survey Reports. (On CDS basis).

DISTRICT-WISE UNEMPLOYMENT RATE

An important noteworthy feature of the unemployment situation in Kerala is that the rate differed widely across the different parts of the State. In 2003, the rate varied from 34.3 per cent in Thiruvananthapuram district to 9.6 per cent in Iddukki district. It has been noticed that Thiruvananthapuram, Kasaragod, Kannur, Ernakulam and Pathanamthitta are the major districts with relatively high rates of unemployment. Iddukki, Thrissur, Palakkad, Malappuram and Kozhikode are the districts with relatively low rates of unemployment. It has been also noticed that the districts which experienced large increases in the unemployment rate are Thiruvananthapuram, Kasaragod, Pattanamthitta, Kottayam, Ernakulam and Kannur. (See Table 12).

Table 12
District-wise Unemployment Rate in Kerala

Districts	*1998*	*2003*	*Increase*
Thiruvananthapuram	8.8	34.3	25.5
Kollam	7.0	15.0	8.0
Pathanamthitta	12.9	22.9	10.0
Alapuzha	14.5	21.7	7.2
Kottayam	6.8	16.5	9.7
Idukki	12.1	9.6	-2.5
Ernakulam	14.8	24.5	9.7
Thrissur	10.8	10.4	-0.4
Palakkad	14.1	11.2	-2.9
Malappuram	10.1	12.3	2.2
Kozhikode	13.1	13.1	0.0
Wayanad	12.0	13.2	1.2
Kannur	16.1	25.5	9.4
Kasaragod	5.8	27.7	21.9
Kerala	11.2	19.2	8.0

Source: Directorate of Employment.

CONCLUSIONS

Unemployment rate in Kerala, both rural and urban has been increasing and has already reached an alarming level in the beginning of this millennium. On the basis of NSSO survey reports, it was estimated that the rates of both urban and rural unemployment is the highest among the Indian States. It has been noticed that the rise in both rural and urban unemployment rates after 1999-2000 till 2004-05 was much larger than the rise during the period between 1993-94 and 1999-2000. The high incidence of rural unemployment in Kerala may be attributed to factors such as the existence of small and marginal farmers, uneconomic land holdings, low productivity of major crops, changes in the crop pattern from more labour intensive crop like paddy to less labour intensive commercial crops, decline of traditional labour intensive rural cottage and small-scale industries, occupational shifting of workers from agricultural to non-agricultural activities, rural-urban migration, fall in the prices of agricultural commodities, agricultural price instability, distress sales, lack of agricultural research and other institutional factors like poor implementation of land reform measures, agricultural marketing problems, non-availability of cheap credit facilities to the farmers,etc. The incidence of high urban unemployment in Kerala is mainly due to the fact of growing unemployment among the educated and youth. It is also due to the structure of urban labour market which is highly characterized by casual employment. It has been noticed that female unemployment is comparatively higher in Kerala especially in urban areas and it is in the nature of educated unemployment. Female work participation rate is low compared to national level. It has been already estimated that nearly 50 per cent of the rural female educated labour force and 42 per cent of the female urban labour force are unemployed. The incidence of unemployment among females in the state is higher than among males by two times in the rural areas and by three times in the urban areas. Thus it can be concluded that the problem of unemployment in Kerala is not just one of unemployment among the urban educated youth alone, but unemployment and under-employment among rural workers in primary sectors like agriculture and household industries and women unemployment are really the major concerns.

REFERENCES

Government of India (2007-08), *Economic Survey*, Ministry of Finance, New Delhi.

Kumari Latha Devi P. (2006), "Employment Profile of Women In Kerala- Recent Trends," *Quarterly Journal of the Institute for the Study of Developing Areas*, No. 4, Vol. 16, October–December.

Mathew, E. T. (1999), "Educated Unemployment In Kerala: Incidence, Causes, and Policy Implications," in B.A. Prakash (ed) *Kerala's Economic Development: Issues and Problems*, Sage Publications, New Delhi.

Mathew, E.T. (1997), *Employment and Unemployment in Kerala*, Sage Publications, New Delhi.

Martin Patrick (2005), "Labour Market and Employment,' in D.Rajasenan and Gerard de Groot (ed) *Kerala Economy*, Department of Applied Economics, Cochin University of Science and Technology, Cochin.

National Sample Survey Organization (2000), Employment and Unemployment Situation in India–1999-2000, Report No. 455, NSSO 55th round.

National Sample Survey Organization (2006), Employment and Unemployment Situation in India–2004-05, Report No. 515, NSSO 61st round.

Prakash, B.A. and Abraham, M. P. (2004), "Employment and Unemployment in Kerala," in B.A. Prakash (ed) *Kerala's Economic Development*, Sage Publications, New Delhi.

State Planning Board (2008), *Economic Review*, 2007, Kerala State Planning Board, Thiruvananthapuram.

Zacharia K. C. and Irudaya Rajan S. (2005), "Unemployment in Kerala at the Turn of the Century," Working Paper No.374, Centre for Development Studies, Thiruvananthapuram.

8

SOME ASPECTS OF POVERTY IN KERALA

P. Krishnakumar

Poverty is a concept that aggregates the situation of a number of people in a community. It involves an abstract definition of insufficiencies rendering a decent life impossible. As such, poverty cannot be defined in universal terms due to two reasons: firstly communities differ from each another and, secondly, 'a decent life' is interpreted in very different terms by them. Still poverty can be discussed in general since particular aspects of life, such as starvation and lack of shelter and clothing are always considered as instances of poverty, regardless of the specificities of context.

Apart from discussing the concepts of poverty is general, this paper mainly focuses on poverty in Kerala. Some methods used in Kerala to identify the poor, reasons for poverty in the state, and a brief discussion of the poverty profile of Kerala are included in this paper.

CONCEPT OF POVERTY

Inadequacy is considered as a reasonable proxy for the full set of poverty attributes. The economic interpretation of poverty considers it as a deprivation of resources related to needs. But wide divergences exist in the way in which needs are defined and resources are measured.

The conventional economic approach to the problem of poverty concentrates primarily on income. Poverty is here interpreted as a deprivation of income (resources) related to needs. Here the focus is on the objective attributes of an individual's economic status. In such measures per capita income is used as an index to assess poverty. This conceptualization of poverty suffers from several shortcomings.

Since income of a large proportion of the population varies from year to year and even low income people tend to under report their income, one cannot rely upon per capita income as a standard measure. Here markets are given priority as a major institutional mechanism for meeting the basic needs. Other institutional mechanisms for meeting this are ignored. Furthermore, institutional barriers which prevent certain sections of the poor (like women, tribals, dalits, minority groups etc.) from converting their enhanced income into enhanced access to basic needs are ignored. Carl Ruskin has demonstrated that income as conventionally measured clearly excludes or undervalues services that are crucial to human well being. Schultz has argued that poverty cannot be measured simply in terms of low levels of income, because there are families which have relatively low income, but own substantial amounts of wealth. Dreze and Sen have remarked that in many cases the link between income and important welfare outcomes such as longevity are weak.

Consumption has frequently been offered as an alternative to income in poverty estimates. It is considered a better proxy for permanent income than current income on the basis of which consumption decisions are made. Milton Friedman has also argued that consumption decisions are made not on the basis of current income alone, but on a variable he called permanent income which is a longer measure of resources available in the household.

Per capita food consumption is also considered as an index to estimate poverty. This approach focuses on food items alone and ignores non-food items such as housing and clothing.

Moreover this method directly depends on the household's propensity to consume food which may vary across households. Food consumption data can be used to focus directly on calorie intake. The objectivity of calorie based definition was challenged by VKRV Rao. According to him poverty has to be identified with deficiency in the total level of living rather than concentrating on calorie deficiency alone.

At present most of the poverty estimates are made on the basis of income (poverty line) or calorie norms. Since poverty is a social problem with several dimensions of its own, such measures cannot reveal a true picture of the existing scenario of poverty. Several factors such as literacy, wealth, health etc are left out of these measures. Moreover, poverty is not a static phenomenon. It changes over time. So the concept of poverty also changes with time and across regions. It also changes within individual economic groups and also at household level where there would be considerable differences in the perceptions of men and women. Further more, the poor are not a homogeneous group with common interests and views.

Dreze and Sen described poverty as a failure of capabilities. In their approach a distinction is made between 'ends' (capabilities) and 'means' (low income or other antecedents of failure of capabilities). Sen has identified several failures that lead to poverty. These failures have been classified by him as endowment failures, consumption failures, production failures and exchange failures. All these failures occur due to several reasons such as social inequality, structural problems, governmental and non-governmental policies and policies of global institutions.

Robert Chambers has observed poverty as a general condition of the people who are badly off and encompasses many aspects of wants and disadvantages. He suggests five clusters of disadvantages such as lack of assets, physical weakness, isolation, vulnerability and powerlessness as the characteristics of the poor in rural areas. According to him the poor themselves perceive that there are three priorities, namely, survival, security and self respect, the last being their highest priority.

WHO IS POOR?

Amartya Sen pointed out many years ago that the task of poverty assessment can be decomposed into two components, namely identification and aggregation. Identification means determining who is to be deemed poor and to what extent. Aggregation refers to forming a composite judgment concerning the extent of poverty in a society.

Macro level estimates of poverty undertaken in India have several limitations regarding identification of the poor as well as aggregation. Therefore such measures cannot bring out a true picture of poverty. Experiments made by different organizations and individuals at the micro level prove that such estimates can bring out the specific problems faced by the people.

Government of Kerala has evolved several steps to study poverty at a disaggregate level. In 1993, Government of Kerala formulated a Family Poverty Index (FPI). This measure permitted the local communities themselves to identify the poor households. FPI has been constructed by combining nine socio-economic variables (non-monetary factors), selected and approved by the members/representatives of the local community. This index was first applied in Alappuzha Town. Trained community volunteers in seven wards of Alappuzha conducted a survey of 5728 households. Following are the nine criteria used to identify the vulnerable/risk families.

(1) Kutcha House
(2) No access to safe drinking water
(3) No access to sanitary latrine
(4) Illiterate adult in the family
(5) Family having not more than one earning member
(6) Family getting barely two meals a day or less
(7) Presence of children below 5 years in the family
(8) Alcoholic or drug addict in the family
(9) Scheduled Caste or Scheduled Tribe family.

A family with four or more of the risk factors was classified as "high-risk poor". During 1998-1999 Prof. M.A. Oomman was appointed to look into the relevance of these factors in identifying the poor. Later on the poverty index was modified by incorporating his suggestions. State poverty eradication mission (Kudumbasree) is considering (2001 onwards) the following factors to identify the poor households.

RURAL AREAS

(1) Families without adequate shelter
(2) Families without access to safe water within 300 mtrs.
(3) Families without latrine
(4) Families without at least two meals a day
(5) Families which depend on the income of one individual alone
(6) Families belonging to scheduled caste and scheduled tribes
(7) Families with physically handicapped (more than 40%) and mentally retarded persons
(8) Families with unmarried mothers, widows, divorced women and unmarried women (above the age 18)
(9) Families without an adult male member.

URBAN AREAS

(1) Families without land to construct houses
(2) Families without houses
(3) Families without access to safe water within 150 mtrs.
(4) Families without sanitary latrine
(5) Families headed by women (who are widows, divorced women or unmarried mothers)
(6) Families with physically/mentally disabled persons and seriously diseased persons
(7) Families belonging to Scheduled Castes and Scheduled Tribes
(8) Families without steady income(employment for less than 10 days in a month)
(9) Families without colour television.

Kudumbashree estimates based on the above mentioned factors are helpful to understand the extent of poverty at the household level. A cut-off point of four out of nine factors is used to identify the poor. But families with more unfavourable factors are considered as more poor.

The State Planning Board has made a qualitative assessment of poverty in Kerala. Interactions with academic experts, local government leaders, representatives of the poor, and social activists were conducted as part of this process. These discussions reveal the following points about the prevalence of poverty in Kerala.

- There should be a prioritization of families below the poverty line, based on severity of poverty, enabling the formulation of separate strategies ranging from direct benefit support to facilitations of self help.
- There is persistent poverty among the outliers of the Kerala model such as tribals, traditional fishermen, people employed in declining traditional industries Scheduled Caste and Scheduled Tribe. They deserve special support.
- A large number of the poor have passed/completed high school education. Most of them are unskilled and lack entrepreneurial ability for self employment. Capacity building of this group is a major challenge.
- The falling job opportunities in agriculture and government service have worsened the poverty situation in the state.
- Since a large number of the poor have nothing more than their house plots the conventional strategy of improving land productivity cannot create a positive impact among the poor.

FACTORS AFFECTING POVERTY

The fortunes of the poor in Kerala are intrinsically linked to that of the agricultural sector. In Kerala the agriculture and forest sectors together account for over 83 per cent of the land area. It is observed that the net sown area is declining year after year. Moreover out of the total cropped area in 2005-06, food crops comprising rice, pulses, tapioca and minor millets occupy only 12.5 per cent. Kerala state which had a low base in food production is facing serious challenges in retaining even this meagre area. The reforms in the public distribution system have also resulted in a reduction of its significance as a substitute to this phenomenon. The decline in the quality of PDS has also affected the situation adversely. The undergoing structural transformation from subsistence crops to remunerative crops and the general negligence of the agricultural sector have increased the incidence of poverty and malnutrition in the state.

Agriculture impacts on the poor in more ways than one. A higher agricultural output helps lower food prices as well as improve food availability; both these are advantageous to the poor. Apart from creating employment opportunities in the sector through linkage effects, it encourages the growth of non-agricultural sectors also.

Another factor influencing the incidence of poverty is inflation. As Sen pointed out, inflation acts like a regressive tax hitting the poor hard and leading to deterioration in their entitlements and real incomes. Till recently it was the secondary and tertiary sectors which were the main locations for price rise. But drastic changes are observed and now the primary sector is leading the inflation figures. The main reason for this change is an excess of demand including for speculative purposes. Since food constitutes a predominant portion of the consumption basket of the poor, it is the food prices which cause most anxiety to the poor. Agricultural growth can solve this problem to a considerable extent.

Poverty and environment are closely connected. Poverty intertwined with population growth exercises intense pressure on scarce environmental resources resulting in environmental degradation. The overexploitation of resources has an adverse effect on poverty.

Another reason for poverty in the state is acute unemployment. Unemployed people in Kerala do not form a homogeneous group. With about 3.7 per cent of the country's population, Kerala accounts for nearly 16 per cent of the country's unemployed. The stagnation of the agricultural sector and the failure of traditional industries have made the problem of unemployment more severe. A paradox of Kerala's unemployment problem is that the state is facing a shortage of workers in agriculture and unorganized sectors, while the number of job seekers in the live register of employment exchanges keeps on increasing.

Educated unemployment also accentuates poverty in the state. Educated unemployment in Kerala has had several consequences. Firstly there has been an upgradation of the minimum educational qualifications prescribed for various posts; and secondly, even when the prescribed qualifications remain the same, the output of the educational system being in excess, highly qualified people will be appointed for jobs which require a lower qualification. This is referred to as the 'Cascade Model', according to which the highly trained currently unemployed replace the less qualified and the latter in turn replace people less qualified than them and so on. This situation also leads to an increasing incidence of poverty in Kerala.

The shortage of income-generating assets, the fragmentation of tiny homestead land acquired try virtue of land reforms, the failure of the public distribution system, the withdrawal of state from the key sectors such as health, education, housing etc, inequality in income and consumption levels, corrupt administration, and certain timely factors also contributes to increased poverty in Kerala.

POVERTY PROFILE

Even though several attempts were made and methods were used to estimate the extent of poverty in Kerala, a true picture of poverty has not yet been ascertained. As regards the extent of poverty wide variations are observed in different poverty estimates made in the state.

Dandekar and Rath were the first to present the relative magnitude of poverty in Kerala in relation to other states in India as well as the national average. One the basis of the evidences from NSSO private consumption expenditure data, they have identified Kerala as the state with high incidence of poverty in India in 1960-61. In a study undertaken by Rath in 1996, Kerala has been identified as the state with highest incidence of poverty during the period 1960-61 and 1987-88.

Estimates made by the Planning Commission in 1972-73 by fixing 2400 calorie for rural and 2100 calorie for urban as the requirements show that nearly 58% of the rural and 56% of the urban population in Kerala were poor in 1961-62. These figures have declined to 52% and 50.9% respectively in 1970-71. A sharp decline in poverty is witnessed since 1980. Planning Commission estimates show that in 1983, 26% of the rural and 30% of the urban population were poor whereas the rates have declined to 16.4% and 19.3% respectively in 1987-88. Since no dramatic change has occurred in the state after 1980, the sharp decline in the incidence of poverty in Kerala cited in the estimates of Planning Commission may be due to methodological and conceptual issues.

Poverty figures of the sample survey conducted by the NSSO in its 55th round amount to only 9.38% in rural and 20.27% in urban areas. The estimation of poverty based on NSS Consumer Expenditure data has several limitations in the Kerala context. Doubts have been raised by several researchers regarding the fact whether the calorie norms prescribed for this estimation is valid in the case of Kerala. In the studies made by Centre for Development Studies in 1975 also it is argued that Keralities need a lower calorie level than that recommended by ICMR. Low calorie requirements in Kerala are justified in several ways. The climatic conditions in Kerala are moderate when compared to other parts of India. The average weight of an Keralite is lower than that of people in North Indian States. The demographic structure also points to low calorie requirements (females exceed males).

In contrast to the findings NSSO, several other studies show that the incidence of poverty is much higher in Kerala. BPL survey conducted by the Ministry of Rural Development Department in 1997 show that 36.58% of the rural population in Kerala are below the poverty line. The Department of Urban

Affairs has observed that 27.8% of the urban population in Kerala is below the poverty line.

Kerala Sastra Sahitya Parishad (KSSP) conducted a state wide survey in 2004. This study has thrown light into how Kerala lives and thinks (Kerala Padanam 2006). The household was taken as the unit of study and a randomly selected set of 6000 households were surveyed. KSSP study observed that rural poverty in Kerala was 22.9% and it was more than double that of 9.4% given in the NSS data.

Kerala State Planning Board has observed that although poverty had reduced between 1993-94 and 2004-05 the pace of poverty reduction was lower than in the previous two decades. Taking the rural and urban areas together, the pace of poverty reduction fell from 1.1 per cent point per annum during 1973-88 to only 0.6 per cent point per annum during 1987-2005 and 0.7 per cent point per annum during 1993-2005.

CONCLUSION

As poverty is a multi-dimensional phenomenon, the pertinent question is how to eradicate it. The past experience of the State of Kerala shows that instead of trying to alleviate poverty by providing minimum purchasing power/income, the attempt has been to improve the quality of life of the people. For that objective, the State spent substantial amount on health, education, housing and other basic service, to make it accessible to the poor. Moreover, special attention was given to ensure food security and social security to the poor. But since late 1970s the State followed the national policy of attacking poverty directly. It was done by providing assistance to self employment schemes and wage employment programmes. The decentralised economic planning has to a greater extent enabled local bodies to identify specific problems in their localities and tackle them effectively. As a result of the developmental efforts made after the formation of the Kerala state and earlier, Kerala has maintained a very good human development index. The state's social development can be compared with that of the advanced nations. However, paradoxically, social development is not reflected in economic performance. Due to high social development, Keralites face a concealed type of poverty, which is remarkably different from that in other parts of India. It is important not to under-estimate the intensity of poverty in Kerala. Appropriate programmes need to be devised to improve the rural sector and to create workable and sustainable solutions to the problems related to poverty in the state.

REFERENCES

Amartya Sen (1981), *Poverty and Famines: An Essay on Entitlements and Deprivation*, Oxford University Press, New Delhi.

B.A. Prakash (1999), *Kerala's Economic Development: Issues and Problems*, Saga Publications, New Delhi.

Carl Ruskin (1993), 'Poverty in China Country side: Legacy and Change' in *Development and Change*, eds P.Bardan, Mrinal Datta Chaudhar and T.N.Krishnan, Oxford University Press, Delhi.

Jean Dreze and Amartya Sen (1990), *The Political Economy of Hunge,r* Clarendon Press, Oxford.

K.N. Ninan (1994), 'Poverty and Income Distribution in India, *Economic and Political Weekly*, June 18.

KSSP (2006), *Kerala Padanam*.

Milton Friedman (1957), *A Theory of Consumption Function*, Princeton University Press.

Roberty Chabers (1988), 'Poverty in India: Concepts, Research and Reality, *Discussion Paper 241*, Brighton, IDS.

Sanjay G. Reddy (2007), 'Poverty, Estimates: How Great is the Debate?, *Economic and Political Weekly*, February 10.

State Planning Board (2006), *Background Paper on Poverty, Labour and Employment*, Thiruvananthapuram.

State Planning Board: *Economic Review*, Various issues.

T. W. Schultz (1968), *Economic Growth and Agriculture*, Tata Mc Graw Hill Publishing Company Ltd., Bombay.

9

EDUCATION IN KERALA– BASIC FEATURES, PROGRESS, PROBLEMS AND POLICIES

Anitha S. Ramachandran

Education plays a pivotal role in empowering mankind. It provides exposure and access to new ideas and ways of thinking and triggers a demand for change. Kerala's remarkable progress in the field of social development and high quality of living are mainly attributed to the educational advancement the state has made over the past so many years. It has the dual distinction of achieving total literacy and quality of life which is comparable to that of the developed countries of the world. This success in spreading education is the natural continuation of a great past which goes back to the first few centuries of the Christian era.

Kerala has several features that distinguish it from the rest of India. Its efforts in improving the quality of life of its population reckoned in terms of life expectancy, sex ratio and literacy are well known. Further, Kerala is far ahead of other states in achieving the goal of universalizing elementary education. The state is ranked first in Educational Development Index (2005-06) and also first among major Indian states in the

Human Development Index (HDI) at the three times points of 1981, 1991 and 2001. This appears even more dazzling when we observe that these achievements occurred in the absence of high levels of income and economic development. To take stock of the achievements in the field of education, a peep into the various dimensions of educational development is essential and this paper attempts to focus on this aspect. The paper is divided into three sections. First section reflects on the literacy position and briefly touches on the evolution and educational policies of the state. Second part examines the structure and growth of education in Kerala. Progress of school education is examined in terms of accessibility, enrolment, attendance and drop out rates, teacher pupil ratio, physical facilities etc. Third section deals with the issues and concerns.

ACHIVEMENTS IN THE FIELD OF LITERACY

Literacy is a basic tool of self defense in a society where social interaction often involves the written media (Jean Dreze and Amartya Sen,).In the matter of literacy, Kerala stands at the apex as the most literate state in the country. According to 2001 census, the literacy rate for Kerala is 90.9 per cent as against the all India literacy rate of 65.2 per cent. Kerala's male literacy rate at 94.2 per cent and female literacy rate at 87.9 per cent are unique compared to the corresponding national figures of 75.6 per cent and 54.2 per cent respectively. Gender disparity in literacy rates is declining over the decades and is fast approaching a situation of gender equity. The gap between male and female literacy in Kerala is low at 6.3 percentage points against the 21.6 percentage point gap at the national level. This is as high as 32.12 percentage points in Rajastan.

In Kerala, the urban literacy rate stands at 91.1% and rural literacy rate is 89.2%. In every age group below 34, even the rural female literacy rate in Kerala is higher than the urban male literacy rate in India as a whole. Among the districts in Kerala, the highest literacy rate of 95.90% is in Kottayam and the lowest rate is in Palghat at 84.31%.

Table 1
Proportion of Literate Person and Literacy Gap

	Person		*Males*		*Females*	
Year	*Kerala*	*India*	*Kerala*	*India*	*Kerala*	*India*
1981	81.6	43.6	87.7	56.4	75.7	29.8
1991	89.8	52.2	93.6	64.1	86.1	39.3
2001	90.9	65.2	94.2	75.6	87.9	54.2

	Male Female Literacy Gap	
	Kerala	*India*
2001	6.3	21.6

Source: Economic Review, various issues.

EFFECTIVE GROWTH IN LITERACY

While the number of literates is bound to increase with the increase in population, it would be fallacious to assume that this is an absolute positive statistics. It is all the more important to consider the increase in number of literates in the context of increase in population. Effective growth in literacy (EGL) is defined as the increase in number of literates less the increase in population as a fraction of the population not classified as literate in the census. Accordingly the figure for the real growth rate in literacy in Kerala (0.61) is less than the all India figures (9.74). This is due to the fact that, the literacy rates are already way higher in Kerala compared to the rest of the states in India, even at the time of Independence. Hence, the scope for a substantial increase in EGL is much lower in Kerala compared to the other states. Also, Gender, spatial and community differences in literacy are narrower in Kerala compared to the all India pattern. (NIEPA, Tyagi).

EVOLUTION OF EDUCATION IN THE STATE

The education system of Kerala has evolved into its present form after a long and arduous historical process. This involves a series of long drawn socio-economic and educational planning initiated by the former enlightened rulers. It has an enviable record of achievements in reaching education to children from every strata of society

The Sangam literature suggests that education was popular and universal in ancient Kerala. The process of Aryanisation and the increasing hold of the caste system prohibited the backward classes from education. By the eighteenth century, education has come within the reach of all the socially and economically privileged sections of society. The distribution of educational opportunities was in those times determined by the pattern of distribution of ownership and control of land. (Nair, 1983). Kudipallikudams (village primary schools) and Ashan Pallikudams provided basic educational facilities. Attempts to introduce western education in Travancore began around 1800 AD. With the patronage of the enlightened rulers of the state, the Christian missionaries were encouraged in their efforts to promote educational activities.

The special importance the state gave to the spread of education is evident in the royal proclamation issued in 1817 in Travancore by Princess Rani Gouri Parvathi Bai. By this unique declaration the state undertook to "defray the entire cost of education of its people in order that there might be no backwardness in the spread of enlightenment among them." This was followed by an attempt to open vernacular schools in different parts of the state. The enthusiasm on the part of the government to promote english led to the establishment of Raja's Free School at Trivandrum in 1834. By 1900, Travancore had more than thousand schools of which, a little less than half were run by the government and the rest by private managements. Sincere attempts were also made by the government to improve the education of women and backward classes. The Temple Entry Proclamation of Travancore gave further fillip to the educational aspirations of lower castes.

The educational policies and developments adopted in Cochin were similar to those of Travancore in many respects. A land mark in the history of education in Cochin was the introduction of the Education Code of 1911 and its revision in 1921. By this, liberal grants were given to efficient private schools. The very many handicaps that Malabar experienced under direct British rule caused it to lag behind the two princely territories. One of the important reasons for Travancore pulling decisively ahead of Malabar in respect of literacy in the 20's was the spread of education among the backward communities.

Reform movements and social changes in the 20th century saw the emergence of several community associations which were guided by great visionaries like Mannath Padmanabhan (NSS), Sri Narayana Guru (SNDP), Aiyan Kali (SJPS) and Vakkom Abdul Khader Maulavi (MES)-who exhorted the people to educate them by starting their own schools. The untouchability Act of 1955 and the welfare measures provided by the government in the form of educational facilities and job reservations led to an improvement in the status and lifestyle of the marginalized groups.

As a result of the social intervention of the private agencies, the growth in the number of institutions and enrolment increased several fold during the 20th century. Kerala is also unique in the sense that at all stages (primary and secondary) of school education, the private sector dominated (Salim, Nair, 2002). After the formation of the state of Kerala in 1956, the government continued with the liberal policy of the earlier governments in matters of education. The Education Bill introduced and passed by education minister Joseph Mundassery in June 1957 is the one, which created revolution in the educational arena. The Act provided facility for education for all and introduced the practice of giving salary to the teachers directly by the government. These efforts brought about phenomenal progress in the education sector in later years culminating in universal literacy.

SCHOOL EDUCATION

The Directive Principles of state policy directs the state to provide free and compulsory education for all children under the age of 14. This far reaching directive was aimed at using literacy as a catalytic tool for social upliftment. The functioning of school education in Kerala is governed essentially by the Kerala Education Act of 1959 (KEA) and Kerala Education Rules (KER) whose provisions, in addition to free education, also assigns government the duty to see that mid day meal, clothing, books and writing materials are provided for pupils free of cost. The implementation of these provisions of the Act was a landmark in the efforts at universalizing primary education in Kerala.

School education in Kerala, in terms of quantity, has been consistently much higher than in any other state. As of 2006-07, there were 12,644 schools in Kerala. Out of this, 35.57% are in the government sector, 57.66% in private aided sector and 6.77% in private unaided sector. Kerala has one lower primary school for every sq.km, and one high school for every 4 sq.km. Facilities are more or less evenly distributed in both urban and rural areas (HRD Kerala, 2005).

Table 2 shows that at the lower and upper primary levels, there is a declining trend in the number of government and aided schools whereas the number of unaided schools shows an increasing trend. Even though private unaided schools are far more expensive than the government schools, their increasing popularity may be taken as indirect evidence of the quality deficiency.

Table 2
Trends in the Number Of Schools

	1980-81	*1990-91*	*2000-01*	*2006-07*
Higher Secondary				
Govt		31	416	996
Aided		0	508	1428
Unaided		0	8	366
Total		31	932	2790
High Schools				
Govt	789	961	985	996
Aided	1122	1380	1412	1428
Unaided	65	111	218	366
Total	1976	2452	2615	2790
UP Schools				
Govt	867	960	960	954
Aided	1866	1883	1873	1870
Unaided	20	72	124	213
Total	2753	2915	2957	3037
LP Schools				
Govt	2712	2565	2565	2548
Aided	4100	4068	4035	3992
Unaided	49	134	158	277
Total	6861	6767	6758	6817

Source: Economic Review, Relevant issues.

Enrolment at the school level which was 56 lakhs in 1980-81 fell to 47.19 lakh by 2006-07. The steady decline in the number of students enrolled at the lower primary stage is due to the fall in birth rate. Enrolment reached its peak during the early 90's and has been falling steadily since then. The gross enrolment ratio at the state level for 2004-05 for primary classes is 98.11 and for middle classes it is 97.07 whereas at the national level the figures are 95.39 and 60.99 respectively. Of the total students enrolled, only 30% are studying in government schools. During the 90's, enrolment in government schools fell by 25.6% whereas it increased by 79% in private unaided schools. This can be attributed mainly to the increase in the standard of living, pre monition about the quality of education in government schools, better infrastructure and educational facilities provided by private schools and the importance given to quality education in society.

Table 3
Trends in the Enrolment of Students-Kerala (Lakhs)

	1980-81	*1990-91*	*2002-03*
All Communities			
Boys	28.9	30.12	25.5
Girls	27.1	28.89	24.52
Total	56	59.01	50.02
SC			
Boys	3.2	3.4	2.75
Girls	3.1	3.2	2.59
Total	6.3	6.6	5.34
ST			
Boys	2.1	3.4	3.1
Girls	1.8	3.2	2.88
Total	3.9	6.6	5.98

Source: Educational Statistics since Independence.

At the all India level, school enrolment rates show great inter state variation in gender–disparity i.e. the male to female enrolment ratio. Again, Kerala is an exception as there is gender parity in the enrolment rates as can be seen from Table 3.

The total number of teachers too has been falling since the early 90's but not as fast as enrolment. The teacher pupil ratio, considered to be one of the indicators used for measuring the quality of school education works out to be 1:27 in Kerala as against the all India ratio of 1:36. In 1980-81, the number of teachers which stood at 1.75 lakhs increased to 1.91 lakhs by 1990 and later declined to 1.76 lakhs by 2006-07. Of the total school teachers in the state, nearly 68% are women.

Current attendance rates which are a more reliable indicator of schooling participation shows that in Kerala, school attendance is much higher than in the rest of the country. As per the NFHS study (92-93), 95% of the children in the age group 6-14 attended school while only 68% of children in the same age group in India attended school. The median number of completed years of schooling in Kerala is much higher than in the rest of India, and the difference between male and female achievement in this regard is much narrower than in the rest of India (Chandrasekhar, 2002)

Table 4
Drop Out Rates in Classes I-X (2004-05)

	Boys	*Girls*	*Total*
All Communities			
Kerala	10.64	3.52	7.15
India	60.41	63.88	61.92
SC			
Kerala	23.24	14.04	18.74
India	69.11	74.17	71.25
ST			
Kerala	55.4	50.18	52.87
India	77.75	80.66	78.97

Source: Annual Report 2006-7, MHRD.

Contradictory to the all India pattern, in Kerala, the drop out rates are lower for girls than for boys. This pattern is the same for all social groups, though the drop out rates are much higher for scheduled tribes.

National Sample Survey data for 1999-2000 shows a good deal of variation in the extent of inequality in accesses to secondary schooling as seen in Figure 1. The inequality which is measured as the difference in accesses to secondary

Figure 1: Differential Access (To Secondary Schooling) between the Top and Bottom Income Quartiles

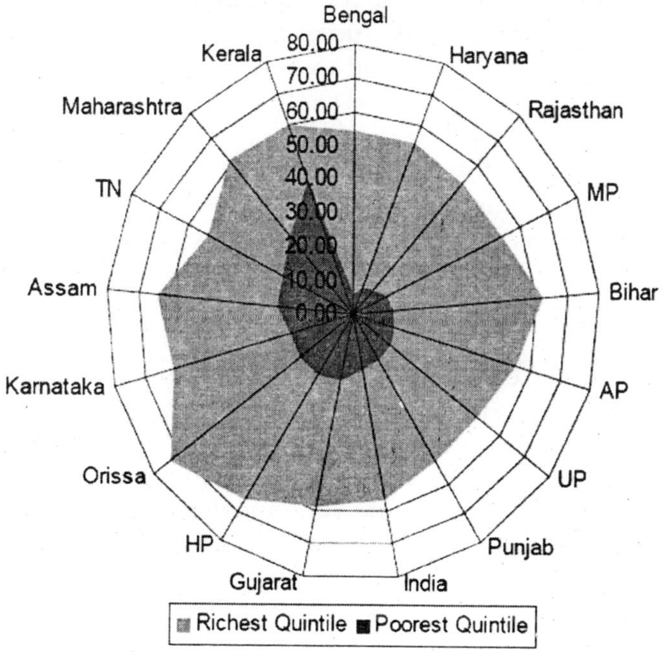

Source: World Bank (2006)

education among those in the top and bottom quartiles of the distribution of household per capita income, is greatest in Haryana, Andhra Pradesh and the 'BIMARU' (sick) states-Bihar, Madhya Pradesh, Rajastan and Uttar Pradesh–which lag behind in many other indicators of social development. The inequality is seen to be lowest in Kerala.

Another notable achievement is the increase in physical facilities. Sarva Shiksha Abhiyan implementation (the most ambitious educational project aims to provide useful and relevant elementary education for all children in the age group 6-14 by 2010) has given a big push in improving the school infrastructure and amenities. More than 97% of the government schools in Kerala have pucca building, access to drinking water and 95% have urinal and latrine facilities. Facilities provided by the government schools in Kerala are found to be much better than elsewhere in the country. All these indicators point to the fact that the state has succeeded in realizing the objective of universalizing primary education.

EXPENDITURE ON EDUCATION

A commendable feature of Kerala's education policy refers to the continued importance attached to school education. The multi pronged approaches adopted by the government for the educational development of the state such as provision of free school education, strengthening of mid-day meal programme, introduction of 'whole promotion' of pupils, reducing educational disparities by liberal financial support, introduction of parity in salary and service conditions between government and private institutes, maintenance of a group of protected teachers etc have brought about phenomenal growth in the expenditure on education by the state. The expenditure on education as a proportion of the total state government expenditure on revenue account reached its peak of 36.6% during 1990-91 and then declined to 18.8% in 2006-07. (Table 5).

Table 5
Share of Expenditure on Education (Kerala)

Year	*% of SDP*	*% of budget*
1980-81	5.7	33.9
1990-91	6.5	36.6
1995-96	6.3	27.2
2006-07	3.9	18.8

Source: Economic Review, Statistics for Planning, Relevant Issues.

Human Development Report (2005) notes that, in India, public expenditure on education as a percentage of total government expenditure was 12.7% and as a percentage of GDP was 4.1 (2000-02). Further the per capita expenditure on education in Kerala (Rs. 884 during 99-2000) stands well above the national average of Rs. 546. The role of the state in the education sector declined during the post liberalization period as is evident from Table 5. School education continues to get priority when compared with university and higher education (Table 6).

Table 6

Percentage Distribution of Education Expenditure by Levels in Kerala

Levels	*1970-71*	*1985-86*	*1995-96*	*2005-06*
University/higher	2.1	13.2	13.7	15.36
Secondary	66.2	50.8	40.9	36.71
Primary	24.1	30.2	40.9	41.3
Special/technical	0.9	4.9	4.1	5.05
Others	6.7	0.9	0.4	1.58
Total	100	100	100	100

Source: Economic Review, Relevant issues.

Out of the total expenditure, elementary education accounted for 41.31% and secondary education's share was 36.71%. University and higher education accounted for 15.36% during 2005-06.Yet, another feature, of funding education in the state is the large amount of government funds that goes to finance the private sector education. While costs at all levels of education are rising, revenues are not increasing in tune with the expenditure, thus perpetuating and widening the disparity.

No doubt, mass education and mass schooling is a laudable achievement. But the question now is whether we are able to transfer this to reasonably good returns. The results of an NCERT survey, ranks Kerala below 17 other states in respect of levels of learning achieved by school students (Nair, 1999). Its record in terms of student performance is not significantly different from other parts of the country. This may partly be due to the fact that primary education is near universal in Kerala and the drop out rates are very low. Another sample study conducted by Kerala Sastra Sahitya Parishad, a people's science movement, found that in Trivandrum district, 30-35% of students from standard VII have not attained the minimum level of language proficiency prescribed for standard II. (Tharakan P.K.M, 2003). The study also found that variation in performance between children in the state were greater within schools than between schools, the reverse was true of other states.

HIGHER SECONDARY AND VOCATIONAL HIGHER SECONDARY EDUCATION

The process of de linking the pre-degree course which was part of the higher education and attaching it to the school system was started during 1990-91 and completed within a decade. This has been carried out with the aim of reorganizing secondary level of education in accordance with the National Education Policy. With the objective of imparting skillful job oriented training to students, vocational higher secondary education was introduced in the state since 1983-84.

HIGHER EDUCATION

Higher education is of paramount importance for social and economic development as it contributes to self sustaining growth. Once primary education is universalized, focus is turned to the development of secondary and later to tertiary education as it is capable of yielding higher social returns and increase in labour productivity. In Kerala, it is gratifying to note that the development of higher education has taken place only after school education had reached fairly high levels of expansion. The rapid expansion in higher education in terms of the number of institutions and enrolment is evident from Table 7.

Table 7
Number of Colleges, Students and Teachers in Kerala (Higher Education)

	1980-81	*1990-91*	*2006-07*
No. of colleges			
Government	30	40	39
Private	104	132	150
Unaided			153
Total	134	172	342
Enrolment			
Degree	87467	129735	156029
PG	5866	10452	22748
Total	93333	140187	178777
No. of teachers	10154	13857	9697

Source: Economic Review, Relevant issues.

Educational policies adopted by the successive governments from time to time such as opening of more colleges, introduction of the shift system, allowing private registration and introduction of correspondence courses etc paved the way for this phenomenal growth. The University Bill of 1967 and 1974, the introduction of direct payment and unification of fees in 1972 are some noteworthy developments in the field of higher education.

Last two and a half decades witnessed more than 40% increase in the number of arts and science colleges followed by a 75% increase in enrolment at the degree level. Women now constitute 58.8% of all student enrolments in Kerala whereas it is 40% at the all India level and only 20% in Orissa. With the delinking of pre degree classes from colleges, the staff strength has come down.

The educational sector witnessed substantial expansion in professional educational institutions as a result of the government's policy decision in 2000 to allow private agencies to start unaided professional colleges. This evoked a huge response which culminated in the starting of a number of private educational institutions especially private professional colleges throughout the state. As a result, since 2001, the enrolment in engineering colleges in the state has gone up by more than 140%. The higher education sector in Kerala is dominated by arts and science colleges. At present Kerala has 7 universities, 2 deemed universities, 342 arts and science colleges, 84 engineering colleges,86 medical colleges including dental, pharmacy and nursing colleges and so on.

EDUCATIONAL LEVEL OF LITERATE POPULATION

On examining the educational qualification of people above 18 years in Kerala, it has been pointed out that majority of people are having education only up to the secondary stage or below that. Given the impressive performance of school education, one would expect more from higher education. It is surprising that Kerala should trail behind five major states–Maharashtra, Karnataka, Tamil Nadu, Gujarat and West Bengal–in higher education, even though all the five states lag far behind Kerala in terms of achievements in school education. (Human Development Report, Kerala).

Figure 2 : Educational Qualification of People Above 18 Years-Kerala (%)

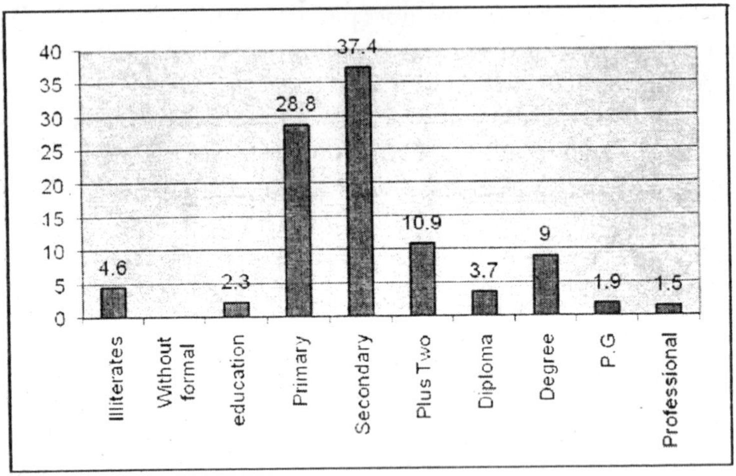

Source: Kerala Sastra Sahitya Parishad Report 2006.

ISSUES AND CONCERNS

It is ironical that even though Kerala has established itself as an exporter of human resources, the state has not been able to translate its high literacy into reasonably good performance in higher education. In the midst of quantitative expansion, quality of education seems to have suffered. It was being increasingly realized that public budgets cannot adequately fund higher education at the cost of mass education sectors that are already starved of basic needs. As an alternative, emphasis was shifted to self financing and private educational institutions. This paved the way for a mushrooming of private sector institutions, most of which are profit making.

With this 'explosion' of self financing institutions, a dual system of education exists–one segment offering high quality education that caters to the affluent group and the other the low quality institutions meant for the lower strata of society.

Another weakness plaguing our higher education system is a crisis of faculty. In this context, the observations of the U.R Committee are quite revealing- "One of the serious consequences of virtually unregulated growth of technical institutions is the extreme shortage of quality teachers at various levels". The dearth of qualified teachers impinges on the overall efficiency of the educational system.

Quality of education to a large extent is determined by the provision of adequate educational facilities. But many government educational institutions lag way behind as far as physical facilities are concerned.

Despite the enormous size of our educated labour markets, the pool of skilled labour is relatively shallow. It has been pointed out that the lack of suitability for job rather than unavailability of employment opportunities to be the major reason for educated unemployment in the state.

On analyzing the equity aspect, educational opportunities in the state are not evenly distributed among the population. The social and economic inequalities which are the legacy of the past get reflected in educational opportunities. In the race for educational advancement, the backward sections are invariably overtaken by the better off sections of society (Salim, Nair, 1999).

CONCLUSION

No doubt, Kerala's achievement in the field of literacy is laudable. We have unlimited scope for the development of human capital, the foundations of which have already been laid through a well developed system of primary and secondary education. But when it comes to higher education, our performance is not up to the mark. After successfully tackling the first generation problems, we are now dealing with the second generation problems. Hence, for a sustained development of the higher education sector, we have to maintain a proper balance between the immediate requirements of the job market and the need for research. Government's higher educational policy should also aim at fairness, transparency, equity and above all social justice.

REFERENCES

Abdul Salim, A and P.R.G Nair (2002), Educational Development in India, Anmol Publications, New Delhi.

Chandrasekhar, C. P., Ramachandran, V. K., and RamaKumar, R., (2001), Issues in School Education in Contemporary Kerala, Paper Prepared for UNICEF, New Delhi.

Dreje, J. and A. K. Sen (1995), India: Economic Development and Social Opportunity, Oxford University Press, New Delhi.

Joseph Thomas (1998), Education and Economic Development, Anmol Publications, New Delhi.

Government of Kerala, (2005), Human Development Report, State Planning Board, Trivandrum.

———(various years), Economic Review, State Planning Board, Trivandrum.

Human Development Report, Kerala (2005), State Planning Board, Trivandrum.

Kutty Krishnan, A. C. (1994), " Educational Development in Kerala", in Prakash B.A (ed), Kerala's Economy, Sage Publications, New Delhi.

Nair, P.R.G (1983), "Educational Reforms in India: Universalisation of Primary Education in Kerala, Working Paper No. 181, Centre for Development Studies, Trivandrum.

NIEPA (1990), Educational Data: A Compilation, New Delhi.

Ramachandran V. K. (1996), "On Kerala's Development Achievements", Jean Dreje and Amartya Sen (ed), Indian Development: Selected Regional Perspectives, Oxford University Press, New Delhi.

Tharakan, P.K.M. (2003), Community Participation in School Education: Experiments in the State of Kerala, in R.Govinda (Ed), Community Participation and Empowerment in Primary Education, sage publications, New Delhi.

Tyagi, P. N. (1991), Education for All-A Graphic Presentation, NIEPA, New Delhi.

World Bank (1997), Primary Education in India: Development in Practice, World Bank, Washington D.C.

10

HEALTH SERVICES IN KERALA FEATURES, PROBLEMS AND POLICIES

K. Gangadharan

INTRODUCTION

Health is considered as a fundamental human right and a worldwide social goal. It is essential for the satisfaction of basic human needs and to improve the quality of life. The development of any nation depends on the health of its people. The World Health Organization has defined health as "a complete state of physical, mental and social wellbeing, and not merely the absence of illness or disease". Among the several non-economic indicators of human welfare and national development, the health status of a nation's population requires prominent position. It is a fundamental factor affecting the quantity and quality of the population and thereby their productivity.

Conventional emphasis in public policy for economic growth and development has generally been on physical capital accumulation and technological progress for productivity improvements. There was little by way of recognition of the importance and role of human capital in promoting growth and poverty reduction. This is not to state that governments had little concern for these dual dimensions of human capital. In fact, the emphasis on health was largely based on welfare considerations rather than the perspective of human capital as a factor of production. Good health would enhance growth by:

(i) Reducing productivity losses due to illness

(ii) Permitting utilization of resources which otherwise would have remained in accessible or unutilized.

(iii) Promoting school enrollment of children and enabling them to learn.

(iv) Saving on resources required for treatment of illness (World Bank 1993).

Good health is not only an outcome of increase in income but is also a determinant of the latter. Apart from governing, the core of human well being, health itself promotes development via increase in productivity and hence income, which is known as health income linkages. The improvement in the health status of people is essential to sustain economic and social development.

The majority of the people living in India have yet to reach the utopian ideal of the health for all, despite many decades of planning and implementation programmes. Successive governments in India have over the past five decades, proposed and implemented many schemes for the provision of safe water, sanitation, and nutrition and vaccination coverage. Yet millions do not have access to these basic needs. The recent NFHS data (NFHS III 2005-06) reveals that 48% of Indian children are anemic and 40% of children are under weight. Vaccination coverage is inadequate and only 43.5% children below five years were undergone for all the basic vaccinations. The NFHS survey also reveals the differentials in health status across the country, and it clearly shows that the conditions of health is very deplorable in poor performing states like Orissa, Bihar, Rajasthan, Uttarpradesh and Madhyapradesh and also West Bengal and many North Eastern States including Assam and Tripura. Even after 6 decades of planned development health status of these states are very poor in terms of the basic indicators of health.

HEALTH SERVICES IN KERALA

Though Kerala has registered a significant improvement in key health care indicators, the health situation in the state reflects a paradox. It is a paradox of high morbidity and low mortality which resulted in the crucial social problem of ageing. Health is a fundamental human right emphasized in the Alma-Ata declaration of 1978. Since the Alma-Ata conference on health which focused on equitable and cost effective primary health care, health has became an important concern in most countries especially in the developing countries, where health status of large section of population is very low. Since 1960's the social development movement and from the beginning of the 1990's the human development reports of the United Nations Development Programme have emphasized the improvement in the health status of the population as one of the important goals of development.

Kerala has made significant progress in improving the key health statistics: death rates, birth rates, infant mortality rates and life expectancy at birth. The state performance in the health sector has been far better compared to the rests of the states in India and even at par with the health status of the advanced countries of the world. Still there is a long way to go in for improving the key health care indicators, new dimension of health status are emerging which need attention now. These are environmental issues causing for bad health, hike in chronic morbidity in urban and rural areas, shattered health status in urban slums, new contagious disease such as AIDS, and diseases of poverty and prosperity. Also much needs to be done to improve the health of the women and children especially among the dalits, marginal and deprived section of the community. Most of the children in the school going age group among the deprived sections and marginals in Kerala are suffering from nutritional anemia. Urbanization has brought in a new set of health problems including new generation diseases along with environmental hazards, new dimension of health along with the neglected aspects needs to be addressed simultaneously. Health is defined the World Health Organization (W.H.O) as "a state of complete physical, mental and social well being and not merely, absence of disease or infirmity". This definition was accepted by all the signatories to the Alma-Ata declaration on health. The purpose this definition was to bring the positive concept of general wellbeing into focus rather than a negative definition of absence of disease. Health is thus not only about diseases and medical care system, but also about the environment around us which influence the mental and physical state of a person. Thus the health has to be approached as a multi dimensional phenomenon (Hema and Muraleedharan, 1993). The National Council of Applied Economic Research (NCAER, 1992) considers health sector as an important indicator of the level of economic development and it includes mainly morbidity and mortality.

Health has importance in three distinct ways:

(a) Intrinsic importance

(b) Instrumental importance at personal and social level

(c) Empowerment importance (Mahadevia, 2000).

In intrinsic sense health is important because it is a direct measure of human well being. It is fulfillment of life and a valuable achievement in itself. In the instrumental sense, better health is important in many ways. It enables to reduce medical costs at the government and house hold level. Better health of the children leads to the decline in educational dropouts and higher level of knowledge attainment. Better education and knowledge leads to better paid jobs and larger benefits to posterity Kerala.

DATA BASE AND SIGNIFICANCE OF HEALTH SERVICES IN KERALA

The present chapter is based on the secondary data collected from the published records of National Research Institutions and from various Government departments of both Centre and State Government Thus the methodology of the study is based on the analysis of secondary data related to healthcare development in Kerala. The materials for the study is also developed on the basis of analysis and interpretation of secondary data collected from the published records of

National Research Institutions and from various Central and State Government Departments.

The health services sector has great relevance in the present socio-economic and environmental context. The State Kerala, which has been considered as a state with advanced human development index and better health status is now ailing from acute morbidity of different communicable and chronic illness. The State is trailing in sustaining the health status which retained in the last decade. It is very unfortunate that for a model State for better health status like, the Government of India was forced to provide a health package for protecting the state from the clutches of chikungunya and from other communicable illness. Coupled with this, the problem of drinking water and sanitation, low utilization of government health facilities, ageing of population etc also accounts for the changing health profile of Kerala which has vital significance at the national and international level.

HEALTH STATUS IN KERALA

Kerala has made remarkable advancement in the health status of its population. In India CDR has declined from 27.4 in 1951 to 8 in 2004 and the IMR has drastically reduced from the estimated 200-225 per 1000 live birth at the time of independence to 60 in 2004. The IMR has declined mainly due to decline in the neo-natal mortality in achievement of widespread immunization programme in the country. The performance of Kerala has been well in all these periods. The CBR and CDR are very low in Kerala (Table 1) compared to that in India and it is at par with the advanced countries of the world. The MMR, NNMR, PNMR, CMR etc. are three to five times lower in Kerala compared to national average and it is also at par with the advanced countries of the world.

The success indicators in this regard are the universalisation of immunization coverage. The CBR and CDR in Kerala for the last 12 years also reveals that situation in Kerala is far better compared to other Indian states. One particular fact revealed by the CBR and CDR in Kerala is that the urban rural difference is very meager or it is not at all significant compared to the national average.

Table 1
Health status in Kerala and India-2007

Health status indicators	*Kerala*	*India*
Crude Birth Rate per thousand population 2007 (CBR)	15.00	23.80
Crude Death Rate per thousand population (CDR)	6.40	7.60
Infant Mortality Rate (per 10000 population) (IMR)	14	58.00
Maternal Mortality Rate per lakh/live births 2007 (MMR)	110.0	300
Life expectancy at birth 2007		
Male	73.45	63.50
Female	70.90	39.00
NNM rate 2006	76.00	45
Perinatal mortality rate 2006 (PNMR)	11.5	18.00
Post neo-natal mortality rate 2006 (NNMR)	10.8	18.4
Child mortality rate 2006 (CMR)	3.8	2.90

Source: NFHS Survey 2005-06, Economic Review 2007.

The IMR in Kerala declined more rapidly than India during the last 25 years in both rural and urban areas The rate of decline in IMR was much speedier in Kerala and the state was able to reduce the rate to around ¼th of the rate in 1981 whereas at the all India level the rate of decline was much slower and it was able to reduce to·½ of the rate in 1981.This decline in infant mortality rate is mainly due to decline in the neo-natal mortality due to the wide spread coverage of immunization programme and also due to the better coverage and utilization of maternal and child health services in the state. Among the 28 states and 7 Union territories Kerala placed 11th with respect to CDR and 3rd with respect CBR in 2002. It is actually surprising that the tribal dominated Tripura, Arunachal Pradesh, Manipur, Nagaland and non urbanized state like Sikkim, Jammu and Kashmir where CDR an important indicator of health status is lower than that of Kerala. Similarly with regard to crude birth rate also the Kerala's position was only third next after Goa and Union territory of Chandigarh (Govt. of India 2003).

Kerala has shown best results with regard to most of the health status indicators, but the biggest paradox is that Kerala has been identified as the state with highest morbidity prevalence in India (Sheriff, 1995). It has been estimated that 181 out of every thousand people in Kerala are morbid due to any of the illness prevalence and urban Kerala records the highest male morbidity prevalence rate of 185 per thousand populations in India. Kerala has also been identified as a state with highest percentage non-infectious illness reported both from rural and urban India. The major reason for this hike in non-infectious or chronic illness in Kerala are the hike in aged population which has been estimated as 13.42% of the total population of Kerala. Ageing is an important stage in the demographic transition in the sense that people in the aged stage are succumbed to many illness and most of them are of chronic in nature which requires treatment for long period. The fast food habits of the people coupled with lack of exercise among the people also accounts for the hike in chronic illness in Kerala.

Recently Kerala also witnessed as an epitome of many communicable illness mainly dengue fever, leptosprirosis acute diarrhoeal diseases, acute respiratory infection ,chickenpox, Measles, enteric fever, chikungunya etc. The availability of safe drinking water and proper sanitation facility play a very important role in reducing the disease load of communicable illness. The recent statistics available reveals that only 42.8% of the Urban and 16.9% of the rural households in Kerala had access to safe drinking water(Govt of India, 2005) Similarly in the sanitation side also the performance of Kerala has been not sound since 26.6% of the rural and 10.2% of the urban household has no latrine facility (NSSO, 52nd round) the lack of safe drinking water and sanitation facility is responsible to a great extent hike in communicable illness in Kerala especially in the hot summer seasons.

Experts in the field of social and community medicines opine that high awareness among the people of Kerala was responsible for the hike in morbidity and it is also argued that high morbidity rates are due to decline in mortality rates (Rajan and James, 1993).

It is argued that with an increase in the level of development, the prevalence of communicable illness comes down, whereas that of chronic illness goes up. This seems to be true of the morbidity profile of Kerala. The morbidity analysis of Kerala reveals that the attack of acute diarrhoeal diseases, measles, pneumonia, pulmonary tuberculosis, dengue fever, leptorprosis etc. are the major diseases dominating the health profile of Kerala. Increasing pollution, increase in the use of fossil fuel, tobacco use, vehicle transport, increasing sedentary habits and ageing are the basic reasons for increasing respiratory infectious diseases.

Though Kerala succeeded to a great extent in reducing the vagaries of major public health diseases like small pox, filaria and malaria, but diseases like respiratory infections, acute diarrhoeal diseases is increasing. Among the chronic illness cardio vascular disease, cancer, hypertension and diabetes etc are emerging as the severe health problems of the state. Sedentary life styles, lack of physical activities and obesity increases the risk of chronic diseases. Cancer in fall forms is causing about 12% of deaths throughout the world. In the developed countries cancer is the second leading cause of death accounting for 21% of all mortality. In the developing countries cancer ranks third as a cause of death and accounts for 9.5% of all deaths (Govt. of Kerala, 2005).

In India cancer has become one of the ten leading causes of death. It is estimated that there are nearly 1.5 to 2 million cancer cases at any given point of time. Over 7 lakh new cases of cancer and 3 lakh deaths occur annually due to cancer. The contribution of Kerala towards this account seems to be of very high. In 2004 the Regional Cancer Centre at Thiruvanathapuram alone treated 10225 patients for different leading sites of cancer (Govt. of Kerala, 2005).

Though Kerala has achieved revolutionary progress in the health care development, recently the state is under the octopus hold of both communicable and chronic diseases. With the arrival of rainy season communicable diseases began to dominate both in the rural and urban slum areas of the state and in the pervasiveness of chronic diseases Kerala tops all the Indian states. The dominant chronic illness like diabetes, blood pressure, mental illness, cardiac illness etc.are common among all households in Kerala. Thus the paradox is that on the one side Kerala stands as the state with all indicators of better health care development in terms of IMR, MMR, PNMR, NNMR, birth rate, death rate etc. on the other it outstrips all other Indian states in terms of morbidity especially the chronic illness. Studies conducted in the pharmaceutical sector revealed that major chunk of the medicines manufactured in India are marketed in Kerala.

The attack and death due to chikungunya a vital illness affected by the people of Kerala reveals that within a short span of three months it affected around 42750 and resulted in the death of 75 persons. Since the illness has been spreading in a massive way the Govt. of India has been compelled to declare a health package for the state to liberate it from of this vital illness. The vagaries of the illness were most affected by the Alapuzha district. The bad living environment and lack of proper environmental sanitation has been identified as the root cause for the hike in morbidity of this illness.

Kerala spends fairly substantial amount on medical and public health compared to other Indian states which is evident from percapita Government health expenditure. In Kerala it was Rs. 238/- in 2001-2002 as against the all India average of Rs. 191/- including the investments of local governments. Percapita expenditure on health increased to Rs. 267/- in 2002-2003 and to Rs. 312/- in 2003-04. Expenditure on health including family welfare for the last four decade reveals the trends in this direction. (Table 2).

Table 2
Expenditure on Medical and Public Health 1956-2005
(Rupees in Lakhs)

Years	*Expenditure on medical and public health*[1]	*% of government expenditure*
1956	386	8.10
1960	541	8.24
1965	981	8.72
1970	943	8.02
1975	4627	7.71
1980	7879	6.82
1985	12681	6.56
1990	22199	5.01
1995	35590	4.02
2000	59800	1.2
2005	1,11,387.5	1.37

Source: Economic Review 2006.

Health status is generally measured in terms of mortality indicators like death rate IMR, expectation of life at birth among others. Mortality indicators show that health status of Kerala is far advanced and higher than the all India average (Table 1) and is even comparable with advanced countries of the world. The outstanding progress of health status is achieved through wide spread growth of three systems of medicine in public private and co-operative sectors coupled with health awareness of the people[2].

Similarly the growth of medical and paramedical personal in the health service department of government reveals a steady improvement in the health care delivery system. The medical officers increased to 26.9% over the 13 years period from 1992 to 2007. Other paramedical personal like nurses, JPH nurses, health inspectors etc also showed a steady increase over the same period indicating better and efficient delivery of health care services in Kerala. The distribution of medical and paramedical personnel among population in Kerala reveals that there exist only one doctor for 8244 people in Kerala and in the case of dentists it is more than forty one thousand. The Table also reveals the availability other paramedical staff among the populations.

Table 3
Growth of Medical and Para Medical Personnel in the Health Services Department 1992-2007

Category	*1992*	*1995*	*2000*	*2007*	*Distribution of medical and Para medical personnel*	*% change over1992 in 2007*
Medical officers	2905	3284	3421	3862	8244	32.94
Dentists	66	70	72	77	413484	16.6
Senior Nurses	1954	1954	1969	1605	19836	-17.86
Junior nurses	4137	4195	6067	7133	4463	72.41
Lady health inspector	894	923	942	962	33095	7.60
Pharmacists	1681	1681	1728	1650	19295	-1.844
Junior P H Nurses	5281	5911	5547	5583	5702	5.71
Junior Health Inspector	4505	4505	3642	3496	9107	-22.39
Health Inspector	845	845	915	857	37150	1.42

Source: Directorate of Health Services–Thiruvananthapuram
*population based on 2001 census.

In the developed countries quite a high proportion of the GDP is spend by the public sector on health. In all established market economies 5.6% of the DGP was spend by the public sector on health in 1990. In this countries another 3.5% GDP was spend by the private sector including the household sector taking the total expenditure on health to 9.2% of the GDP. Collectively as well as individually (except the US) the government burden in the health sector was higher than private burden. This was true for most sub Saharan African countries, Latin America, Caribbean and West Asia countries or former socialist block, whereas in Asian countries except China, private sector involvement was higher than the public sector in the health care system (World Bank, 1993).

In Kerala the budget allotment for the health sector for the last 4 years reveals that total expenditure on health and family welfare as a percentage of the GSDP of the state is very meager and it is steadily diminishing for the last few years. Though the percapita health expenditure[3] of Rs. 312 as (for the year 2002 to 2003) estimated for Kerala is comparatively better compared to other Indian states, but it is below the index of advanced countries.

As far as the utilization health facilities are concerned private sector has recorded 58.01%, public sector 28.57% and the remaining 4.76% utilized other facilities including co-operative and charitable institutions (Kunhikannan, 2000).

Kerala is now moving at higher rate of urbanization. It would therefore become a difficult task to deliver health care and other essential services to the unlimited and ever increasing population. Similarly the health budget of the government of Kerala is very fragile in the sense that the allocation for medicine and supplies has been very meager and the major chunk of the budget is meant for salary and allowances. Ageing is another area of concern of Kerala health. This also accounts for the hike in morbidity.

Another peculiarity of the state is that dependence on private health care is quite high even among the lower expenditure classes and rural areas especially for outpatient treatment. Public health centers are being utilized mostly for maternal and child health care programs especially for immunization schemes. In Kerala the utilization of maternal and child health services too is weak in tribal and hill areas where marginal, deprived and vulnerable sections of the communities are residing. The low utilization of public health centers is mainly due to lack of medicines and supplies in government hospitals which makes them as mere scarecrow. What the people can save from a government hospital or health center is the consultation fee of Rs. 20/- or Rs. 25/-, for the same they have to waste one whole day due to rush in the Government hospitals.

NUTRITION AND HEALTH TRANSITION

Conventional emphasis in public policy for economic growth and development has generally been on physical capital accumulation and technological progress for productivity improvements. There was little by way of recognition of the importance and role of human capital in promoting growth and poverty reduction. This is not to state that governments had little concern for these dual dimensions of human capital. In fact, the emphasis on health was largely based on welfare considerations rather than the perspective of human capital as a factor of production. Good health would enhance growth by:

(i) Reducing productivity losses due to illness

(ii) Permitting utilization of resources which otherwise would have remained in accessible or unutilized.

(iii) Promoting school enrollment of children and enabling them to learn.

(iv) Saving on resources required for treatment of illness (World Bank 1993).

WHAT IS UNDER NUTRITION?

The term under nutrition is defined as the outcome of insufficient food intake (hunger) and repeated infectious diseases. Under nutrition includes being underweight for one age too short for one's age (stunted) dangerously thin (wasted) and deficient in vitamins and minerals (micronutrient and nutrition). When individuals are under nourished they can no longer maintain natural bodily capacities such a growth, resisting infections and recovery from disease, learning and physical work, pregnancy and lactation in women. Poor feeding of infants and young children, especially the lack of optimal breast feeding and responsible complementary feeding along with such illness as diarrhea, pneumonia, malaria and HIV/AIDS are major cause of under nutrition.

Nutritional deficiencies and poor health of children are major public health concerns in developing countries, where they present both a cause and a reflection of poverty. After the Independence the elected Governments in India has undertaken a lot of steps for the improvement of the health and well being of the population especially the health of the children. But still malnutrition is a severe problem in India, according to NRHS-3, 46 per cent of the India's children under the age of three are suffering from underweight and 79% of them are categorized anemic. This malnutrition is a severe hurdle in the way of proper health care development at the global level and the developing countries are the greatest victims of this nutritional deprivation.

NUTRITION AND ITS DETERMINANTS

Nutrition is an integral part of the health and well being of all individuals. Good nutrition is determined by the consumption of an adequate diet and also a person's ability to resist disease and infections that interface with digestive and absorption process of the biological system. On the one hand, good nutrition enables us to lead a socially and economically active life whereas malnutrition has an adverse impact on morbidity. It hinders physical growth; lead to functional impairment, disability diminishes productivity and reduces resistance to diseases.

The important determinants of nutritional status are educational facilities for all the members of the society and also facilities for continuing informal education. Similarly the living environment like good sanitation, safe drinking water, proper facility for travel and communication, electrification, proper health care facilities, family income, members in the family, proper spacing among children, housing set up, occupation of the household members etc influence a lot in the nutritional enrichment of the society. Chart 1 provides how poverty and education are connected with nutritional deprivation:

Chart 1: Ecology of Malnutrition

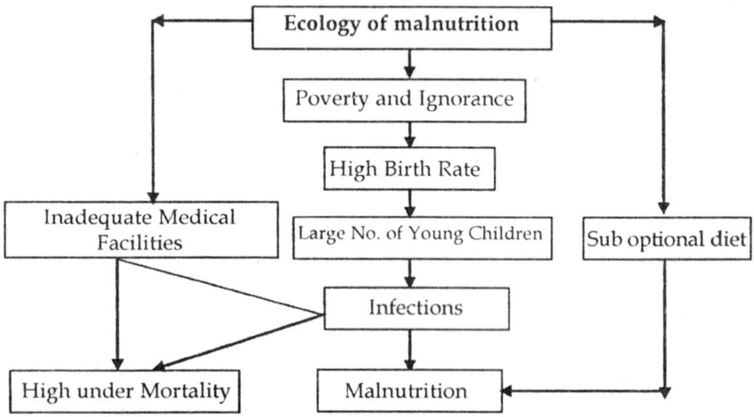

NUTRITIONAL DEPRIVATIONS IN KERALA

Kerala has been recognized as a state with better health care indices which is even comparable with most advanced nations of the world. This achievement has been stated as the culmination of great stress on social development, better social justice (Ratcliff 1978) or a combination of greater stress on education and improved health delivery system (Nair, 1974). Table 19 provides a summary of key health indices of Kerala in comparison with India and some other countries. These figures indicate the advancement the State has gained in many spheres of health. The gains are all the more impressive since the income of the State falls below the national average.

The state of Kerala within India has received international attention and acclaim for its conscious policy intervention for high levels of human development. Contrary to the previous apprehension about the sustainability of the Kerala model, recent evidence seems to show that high levels of human development have also been instrumental in registering sustained economic growth. However the recent trends related to morbidity, nutrition etc. reveals that Kerala is passing through a stage of health care transition in which the advancement gained in health care in the initial stages of development in 1960's and 1970's and 1980's is now eroding fastly due to the hike in the morbidity load on the one side and gaining momentum of the nutritional deprivation among the under five children. The Human Development Report 2005 for Kerala and NFHS 3 report also shows trends in this direction.

NUTRITIONAL DEFICIENCY AND CALORIE CONSUMPTION

Clearly India is eating less. People are increasingly becoming poor and marginalized which directly tells upon their food intake and so the nutrition their bodies receive. Its nutritional deficiency adversely affects the health and working potential of all.

What is shocking is that, the state like Kerala also witnessed a slight improvement in increasing the population of people with caloric intake less than 90% of the recommended norms. Still in Kerala around 52% of the people are getting less than 90% of the recommended calorie intake which reveals the extent of nutritional deprivation and vagaries of malnutrition in Kerala. The class wise calorie consumption also reveals that the BPL categories and poverty line categories in Kerala have respectively obtained only 1100 and 1389 calories per day (rural) instead of the basic minimum of 2738.6 calories recommended by the Indian Council of Medical research (ICMR)

MATERNAL AND CHILD HEALTH

Though the state of Kerala has witnessed rapid strides in the health sector, the recent NFHS data related to child health, nutritional standards among women and children reveals that

Kerala is now in the reverse trend in the health care advancement or in other words Kerala now finds it very difficult to sustain the tempo of advancement that gained in the health sector for the last three decades and it is passing through a health transition in all its spheres. The data related to overweight of women steadily increased over 14% during the short span of 1998-99 to 2005-06. Similarly though infant mortality was reduced to a considerable extent in Kerala compared to all India level they are celebrating their birthday with acute health problems. The proportion of children in the age group of 6 to 35 months with anaemia actually increased from 43.9 in 1998-99 (NFHS I) to 55.7% in 2005.Similarly anaemia among the women also increased from 22.7% to 32.3% over the same period The problem of anemia has been also severe among the pregnant women and the same has increased from 20.3% in 1998-99 to 33.1% in 2005-06. The children's nutritional status at the Inter State level reveals that though the states of Kerala is far better compared to other Indian states, the reduction in nutritional problem like underweight, wasting and stunting over the time period is far better in other Indian states compared to Kerala.

The population of children who are having under weight and wasted also recorded a hike in the last two NFHS reports indicating that over the time period the health status of the children in Kerala deteriorated heavily (Table 4). This transition in the child health may be due to the change in the dietary habit of mothers and the involvement of mothers in the active labour force. Even during pregnancy period the employed women are not able to eat properly due to the stress and strain of the work and the nature of food consumption also changed a lot. A sort of fast food culture has also emerged in urban Kerala which culminated in breeding diseases like diabetics, blood pressure and hike in cholesterol even among youngsters. The urbanization and migration to urban centres in Kerala also accounts for the change in dietary style and health transition of the people hectic life cycle from morning to evening. Faty foods and lack of any sort of exercise or body movement on the part of urban dwellers and overall negligence of

Table 4
Children's nutritional status Interstate Trends

	Percentage of children							
	Stunting		*Wasting*		*Underweight*		*Children age 6-35 months who are Anemic*	
States	*NFHS-2 1998-99*	*NFHS-3 2005-06*	*NFHS-2 1998-99*	*NFHS-3 2005-06*	*NFHS-2 1998-99*	*NFHS-3 2005-06*	*NFHS-2 1998-99*	*NFHS-3 2005-06*
Andhra Pradesh	39	34	9	13	38	37	72.3	79
Assam	50	35	13	13	36	40	63.2	76.7
Bihar	55	42	20	28	54	58	81.1	87.6
Chattisgarth	58	45	19	18	61	52	87.7	81
Delhi	37	35	13	16	35	33	69	63.2
Goa	18	21	13	12	29	29	53.4	49.3
Gujarat	44	42	16	17	45	47	74.5	80.1
Haryana	50	36	5	17	35	42	83.9	82.5
Himachal Pradesh	41	27	17	19	44	36	69.9	58.8
Jharkhad	49	41	25	31	54	59	82.4	77.7
Jammu & Kashmir	39	28	12	15	35	29	71.1	68.1
Karnataka	37	38	20	18	44	41	70.6	82.7
Kerala	22	21	11	16	27	29	43.9	55.7
Madhya Pradesh	49	40	20	33	54	60	71.3	82.6
Manipur	31	25	8	8	28	24	45.2	52.8
Meghalaya	45	42	13	28	38	46	67.6	68.7
Mizoram	35	30	10	9	28	22	57.2	51.7

Contd...

	Percentage of children							
	Stunting		*Wasting*		*Underweight*		*Children age 6-35 months who are Anemic*	
States	*NFHS-2 1998-99*	*NFHS-3 2005-06*	*NFHS-2 1998-99*	*NFHS-3 2005-06*	*NFHS-2 1998-99*	*NFHS-3 2005-06*	*NFHS-2 1998-99*	*NFHS-3 2005-06*
Maharashtra	40	38	21	15	50	40	76	71.9
Nagaland	33	30	10	15	24	30	43.7	na
Orissa	44	38	24	19	54	44	72.3	74.2
Punjab	39	28	7	9	29	27	80	80.2
Rajasthan	52	34	12	20	51	44	82.3	79.6
Sikkim	32	29	5	13	21	23	76.5	56.9
Tamilnadu	29	25	20	22	37	33	69	72.5
Tripura	40	30	13	20	43	39	61.8	67.9
Uttaranchal	47	32	8	16	42	38	77.4	61.5
West Bengal	42	33	14	19	49	44	78.3	69.4
INDIA	46	38	16	19	47	46	74.2	79.2

environmental hygiene caused for the morbidity hike in Kerala. Incidence of morbidity is higher in Kerala than in India as a whole for the population as a whole. It is 25.11% for Kerala as against 9.11% for All India, for both men and women. It is higher, though marginally in the rural sector than in urban Kerala and the reverse at the all India level. Similarly though life expectancy has improved a lot in Kerala, compared to other Indian States the 60 + categories are experiencing a bitter life due to hike in morbidity among them. Arthrities, blood pressure, asthma, pain in joints, mental illness, hypertension, urinary complaints, cardiological, paralysis etc. are the important ailments faced by the 60 + categories. The better and advanced health care facilities provided by the high-tech private hospitals in Kerala is one important factor responsible for hike in life expectancy in Kerala. Though they are morbid due to chronic illness, the advancement of modern medical care facility and regular and continuous treatment enabled , majority of them to succeed better in extending their life and this can be noticed as an important health care transition that occurred recently in Kerala.

In the case of treatment also majority of the aged prefers allopathic care from private (409/1000) followed by Govt. (288/1000). Moreover 32 out of 1000 prefers self treatment and on the other extreme 38 out of 1000 prefers no treatment at all. The ranking of states in terms of life expectancy at birth has always put Kerala on the top. However in terms of absolute improvement in life expectancy at birth between 1970 and the 1990's Kerala ranked in the 9th position among the states in India indicating the deteriorating quality of life of the people.

FERTILITY, MORTALITY AND MORBIDITY

With regard to total fertility rate in Kerala, it can be seen that it is declining from the 1960s. Total Fertility Rate (TFR) which was 5.6 per woman in the 1950s declined to 3.7 in the 1970s and reached to 1.8, which is below the replacement level in the 1990s. The fertility rate declined in both rural and urban areas and there is virtually no difference between the two. By contrast in India, the TFR was 6.3 in the 1950s and declined to 3.3 in the 1990s. Though Kerala and India had a difference of 0.7 children during 1950s, the difference has widened to 1.5 children 1990s indicating a faster decline in Kerala than in India as a whole. Among the numerous indicators available to measure health status of a population, the most dominant among them one are mortality, fertility and morbidity. It can be seen that (Table 21) IMR in Kerala declined steadily for the last 6 decades and now records the lowest rate of 14 per thousand live births. At the beginning of the century the IMR of the state was very high and did not differ much from the all India average. While in Kerala the IMR declined steadily throughout this century to the present level of 14 per thousand live birth. It can be seen that IMR also began to increase recently and it was 11 for the year 2001 now in 2005. This has reached to 15 indicating a sort of transition which is a bad signal to the health status of Kerala. The Crude Birth Rate (CBR) which remained at 17.7/1000 in 1992 has declined to the present level of 15.3 per thousand population and the Crude Death Rate remained the same at the rate of 6.4 for the same period. A unique feature of Kerala's population profile is that, unlike in the rest of India, the gender ratio favours women (1058:1000). The projection of birth rate and death for Kerala for the next 10 years revealed that constant birth rate will reduce to 13.47 per thousand population and death rate will come down to 7.04 per thousand Population. This indicates that the demographic transition in Kerala is moving in such a way that natural growth rate will be declined from 9.75 in 1996-2001 to 6.42 in 2011-2016.

In spite of many short falls in the nutritional intake and health care spending, the state has been successful in managing the mortality, and fertility and gender equality to a great extent compared to other Indian states. The secret behind this management lies in the Cost Rican development path followed by the successive Governments in Kerala. The domination of adult literacy and universalisation of primary education acted as the lubricant force in creating better health awareness among the people.

The enrollment of children in the age group of 6-11 in the lowest annual income groups (less than 20,000 per annuam) household is 96.9% (HDR, 2007) whereas at the all India level this was only 60.6%. A unique feature of the educational system in Kerala is the high enrollment of girls in schools and college education. The gross enrollment ratio for females in Kerala is 96.7% and literacy rate among the female is 94.2% compared to 87.9% among men. Female literacy has been treated as a very important determinant for affecting decline in mortality (Cald Well, 1986) This indomitant linkage is responsible for fall in Infant mortality Rate (IMR) and rise in female literacy in Kerala.

An examination of the growth of health services in Kerala reveals, the rapid expansion and spread of health care facilities. The number of PHCs functioning in the state at the end of the 6th plan was only 199 and this has reached to 944 by the middle of the Tenth Plan. (Govt. of India, 2007). Similarly the number of sub centres also increased from 2270, in 1981 to 5094 in 2004. The availability of number of beds, doctors etc. also increased abundantly during this period. The number of rural and urban hospitals identified in 2004 was 189 with a bed capacity of 25839. It is often suggested that improved health status of Kerala is also the result of Kerala's egalitarian policies dating back to last century. This is particularly true of the Travancore-Cochin region where the former rulers pursued progressive health policies which were continued by the democratically elected Governments after Independence (Soman 1992).

The most dominant factor related to health transition in Kerala is the low nutritional status due to low in take of food, cereals, proteins etc. The calorie consumption of Below Poverty Line categories in rural Kerala was 1100 and for poverty line group, it was 1389 The percapita cereal consumption of poverty line classes in rural Kerala was 9.2 kgms per month in 1993-94 which has declined to 8.18kgm in 1999-2000. Similarly for urban areas also, it declined from 9.24 kgm to 8.67 kgms for the same period.

This sharp decline in cereal consumption by the poor classes is due to the fact that cereals no longer occupy the same space in the consumption choice of the poor as they had in earlier times on the one side and also reduction in the availability of cereals and its price hike also contributed for decline in consumption. The utilization of health care services and maternal and child health services is far better in Kerala compared to other Indian States, though slight reduction in utilization is seen recently. The reduction in M.C.H. services is mainly due to domination of private health centers in Kerala and also due to the increase in the proportion working woman in Kerala. For the working women timely utilization of health care services will be a problem since they loss income of the day in which they have to go for the checkup. The predominant form of malnutrition in Kerala is growth retardation, stunting and wasting and under weight problem among children is also severe in Kerala. Compared to NFHSI the data released by NFHS III is really a shock for Kerala in the sense that Kerala represents 28.8% of underweight children, 16.1 wasted children and 21.1% stunted children. By considering the sound human development base that existed in Kerala for the last few decades the present the nutritional picture of Kerala is not attractive compared to the rest of the country except for a slight decrease in the severely malnourished children. In the consumption basket the proportion of protein is comparatively higher than the ICMR norms of balanced diet.

What the Kerala health demonstrates is that though the calorie intake is comparatively less compared to other Indian states especially among the BPL and poverty line categories, higher rate of education among females and the cent per cent educational enrollment etc. influenced considerably the improved health status. Along with this the massive spread of private health care centers in different parts of the state augmented the health expenditure of even the lowest socio-economic classes in Kerala. What actually needed for the state is more income generating outlets and activities supported by proper infrastructural facilities including good drinking water, sanitation, drainage and proper solid waste management system for the urban and rural folks. A proper nutrient package with good living environment and proper supportive infrastructure along with a change in the life style of the people will certainly bring a hike in the nutritional status, improvement in health status and health care development in Kerala.

TOWARDS HEALTH FOR ALL

Having analyzed the over all trends in health status and public health care intervention in Kerala, is it possible to conclude that whether health for all is achievable in the immediate future? To answer this we have to address two major issues. What ails Kerala? Secondly what needs attention?

WHAT AILS IN KERALA?

Though the health status of Kerala is comparatively far better compared to other Indian states, Kerala still ails in the health front. First and foremost event is the issue of high morbidity reported both from urban and rural Kerala. As discussed earlier the communicable and chronic illness are equally disturbing the state causing for the hike in morbidity. Lack of basic infrastructural facilities in the interior rural, urban and slum areas are responsible for the hike in illness prevalence rate.

WHAT NEEDS ATTENTION?

Though we have retained better health care indicators, massive effort is still needed to attain health for all. Since high morbidity prevalence is the basic issue of Kerala's health sector, greater attention is needed to reduce the intensity of communicable and non-communicable morbidity prevalence. Better provision of safe drinking water and sanitation is to be provided to the urban and rural community and thrust should be provided to better drainage and environmental facilities in the urban areas. If antibiotics have helped to save millions from dying from typhoid, cholera and dysentery, hundreds of millions have been saved from contracting these diseases through improved water supply, hygiene, sanitation and safe waste disposal. If thousands of cancer patients are given an extended lease of life through radiation and chemotherapy, millions and millions can be saved from cancer through measures to reduce air pollution and clean up the environment.

To improve the utilization of government hospitals more medicines and supplies is to be provided to the government hospitals and health centers and for this budget allocation should be augmented to the medicines and supplies in the health budget of the government. Private health care can only be complementary to public institutions and not as a substitute to achieve health for all at least in the near future. To attain the status of health for all, the aged population has to be properly rehabilitated and measures have to be devised for their health and happiness since majority of them are under acute loneliness and in the stage of negligence. Efforts should be made to increase the utilization of maternal and child health services among the marginal, deprived and vulnerable sections in the country.

Health is a broad concept and health status is a function of large number of factors. The major issues discussed above are to be sorted out with support and co-operation from all the authorities and people connected directly or indirectly with the health care development of the State. It is high time that the paradox of high morbidity and low mortality is to be viewed very seriously in relation to the overall social sector advancement of Kerala to make health for all a reality in the near future.

NOTES

1. Expenditure on medical and public health as a percentage of total government expenditure was 8.10% in 1956 then steadily declined year after year and in 2005 it was 1.37%.
2. There exist 396 beds per one lakh population in Kerala (ie including government, private,and Co-operative sectors). There exist a total of 1,26, 245 beds as on 2004 based on the population of 2001 Census. Similarly the growth of the medical and paramedical personal in the health service department of the government reveals a steady improvement in the health care delivery system (Table 13).
3. The plan outlay for medical and public health increased 62 times from the first five year plan to 10th plan. Percapita expenditure

on public health in 1985 was Rs46.27 which increased to 232.68 in 2000.

REFERENCES

Caldwel, J. C. (1986), "Routes to Low Mortality in Poor Countries", *Population and Development Review,* Vol. 12.

Govt. of India (2001), Preliminary Tables–Kerala, Director of Census Operations, New Delhi.

Gangadharan, K. (2005), "Life After Sixty. Problems of Ageing and Ill Health", *Kerala Calling,* Vol. 25.

Gangadharan, K. (2006), "Deteriorating Health of Mothers and Children. A Study on Urban Kerala", *Asian Economic Review,* Vol. 48, No. 2.

Gangadharan, K. (2006), "Emerging Issues in Urban Health Care with Special Reference to Kerala", *Indian Journal of Social Development,* Vol. 6, No. 1.

Gangadharan, K. (2007), "Changing Health Profile of Kerala", *Economic Affairs,* April-June.

Gangadharan, K. (2007), "Health for all in Kerala", *Kerala Calling,* June.

Govt. of India (1995), *Nutritional intake in India 1994-95.* National Sample Survey Organization, Ministry of Statistics and Programme Implementation, New Delhi.

Govt. of India (2001), *Nutritional intake in India. 1999-2000.* National Sample Survey Organization, Ministry of Statistics and Programme Implementation.

Government of India (2003), *Health Information of India,* New Delhi, Director General of Health Services.

Govt. of India (2004), *Health Information of India,* Ministry of Health and Family Welfare, New Delhi.

Government of Kerala (2003), *Economic Review,* Thiruvanathapurm: State Planning Board.

Govt. of Kerala (2005), *Economic Review,* State Planning Board, Thiruvananthapuram.

Govt. of India (2006), *National Family Health Survey, NFHS-3, Fact Sheet, India,* International Institute for Population Science, Mumbai.

Govt. of Kerala (2005), *Report on Survey of Aged in Kerala,* Dept. of Economics and Statistics, Thiruvananthapuram.

Govt. of Kerala (2006), *Human Development Report 2005*, Centre for Development Studies, State Planning Board, Thiruvananthapuram.

Hema, R. and Muraleedharan, U. R. (1993), "Health and Human Resources Development", *Economic and Political Weekly*, 28(43), pp. 2328-30.

Keralas Sastra Sahithya Parished (2006), *How Kerala Thinks and Acts*, Sastra Sahitya Parisheth, TVM. Kunhikannan, T.P., and Aravindan , K. P. (2000), *Changes in Health Status of Kerala 1987-1997*, Discussion Paper No. 20, Thiruvanathapuram: Centre for Development Studies.

Mathrubhoomi, October 5, 2006, p. 1 (Kozhikode edition).

Mahadevi, Dharshini (2000), "Health for all in Gujarat, Is it Achievable", *Economic and Political Weekly*, 25(35/36).

Nair, P. R. G. (1974), "Decline in Birth Rate in Kerala. An Explanatory Hypothesis About the Relationship between Demographic Variables, Health Service and Education", *Economic ad Political Weekly*, Vol. 9.

National Council for Applied Economic Research, NCAER (1992), *Household Survey of Medical Care*, New Delhi, NCAER..

Prakash, B. A. (2004), *Kerala's Economic Development, Performance and Problems in the Post Liberalization Period*, Sage Publications, New Delhi.

Panicker P. G. K and Soman C. R. (1984), *Health Status of Kerala Economic Backwardness and Health Development*, Centre for Development Studies, Thiruvananthapuram.

Ratcliffe, J. (1978), " Social Justice and Demographic Transition. Lessons from India's Kerala State", *International Journal of Health Services*, Vol. 8.

Ramalingaswamy, V., Jonsson U. and Rhode J. (1996), *The Asian Enigma, The Progress of Nations*, UNICEF Rajan Irudaya, and James, K. S. (1993), "Kerala's Health Status: Some Issues", *Economic and Political Weekly*, 28(36), pp. 1889-1992.

Rajendran, R. (2006), " Dengipani", Vijhana Kairali ,Kerala Language Institute, Vol. 37, No. 4.

Registrar General of India (2004), *Sample Registration System, Statistical Report 2003* New Delhi, Office of the Registrar General of India.

Seckler D. (1982), *Small but Health; A Basic Hypothesis in the Theory Management and Policy in Nutrition* in P. V. Sukhatme (ed), Newer

Concepts and their Implication for Policy, Pune, Maharashtra, Association for Cultivation of Science.

Sharief (1995), *Health Transition in India. Differentials and Determinants of Morbidity in India by Disaggregated Analysis* Working Paper No. 57, NCAER, New Delhi, Sundar Ramamani (1995), *Household Survey of Health Care Utilization and Expenditure,* New Delhi:NCAER.

Shariff, Abusalesh (1995), *Health Transition in India, Differential and Determinants of Morbnidity in India, Disaggregated analysis,* Working Paper No. 57, New Delhi, NCAER.

Soman C. R. (1992), *Nutrition and Health Development Lessons From Kerala,* Proceedings of the Nutrition Society, Vol. 51.

World Bank (1993), *World Development Report 1993, Investing in Health,* Oxford University Press, New York.

World Bank (1993), *World Development Report 1993,* Newyork: Oxford University Press.

WHO (1999), *Report on Health Research 1999,* Switzerland: Global Forum for Health Research.

11

THE KERALA MODEL OF PUBLIC HEALTH SYSTEM: YESTERDAY AND TODAY

B. N. Ghosh

The much-vaunted Kerala model of development is basically related to the development of social reproduction, particularly health and education. The Kerala model of economic development is indeed a misnomer. It is *per se* neither a model of economic development nor a model of economic growth. Broadly interpreted, it is a model of socioeconomic development that envisages a people-centred rather than growth-centred approach to development. The basic message of the model is very clear and profound: the objective of development should not merely be economic growth, but the expansion of people's capabilities and freedom. The end product of the model is a conflation of two contradictory situations—low economic growth rate with high index of human development [Panikar, 1999, Kutty *et al.*, 1993]. In Kerala, evidently, development is given precedence over economic growth and the model is embedded in an egalitarian and progressive distribution system of public goods at affordable cost and on a broader scale catering to all sections of population. The underlying philosophy is: development does not mean what you have but that what you are. This essentially implies the development of capability expansion of human beings along with the improvement in human contestability. Both these critical qualities of human beings are directly related to education and health.

The model was designed to work like the Marxian paradigm that aims at conspicuous deliverance of people from the realm of necessity to the realm of freedom. The same idea was also entertained by Mao Tse Tung. But it is fundamentally different from the principle of transformational growth pursued in capitalism which is essentially based on excessive materialism where human beings are reduced to mere cogs in the wheel, without equity and freedom. These are contrary to the principles of human development. Since the hoary past, Kerala has tried to give development a human face, and in so doing, it has relegated to the background the philosophy of the western notion of economic growth and has opted for human development.

The human development index prepared by the UNDP takes into account three critical variables including literacy rate (knowledge and education), life expectancy and per capita income adjusted for purchasing power parity. In fact, life expectancy is an offshoot of the achievement in the medical sphere over a period of time but it does not capture the impact of public health system at a point in time. So, many will like to take infant mortality as a more critical indicator than life expectancy. However, as an indicator of qualitative development, the UNDP upholds that for gaining the developed status, the human development index value must be above 0.80, which is high HDI.

THE PRE-LIBERALISATION SCENARIO

An important indicator of the qualitative nature of economic development is the degree of structural change achieved by a country. It is a critical dimension of development and indirectly related to healthcare problems, though the apparent nexus is apocryphal to some. Let me give it a special margin in order to appreciate the achievement of Kerala in this direction.

Occupation structure is a critical reflection of the degree of economic development that a country has achieved. We can classify a country on the basis of its occupation structure. In a developed country, primary occupation is a negligible proportion of the total employment in all sectors and generally, labour employment in the non-agricultural sector is the highest. The opposite is the situation in a backward country. The rate of economic development may be described by the rate at which the 70: 30 occupation ratio in underdeveloped countries is changed to 20:80 approximately [Singer, 1952]. Structural changes in the realm of occupations are very conspicuous in the case of Kerala compared to India as a whole. This bespeaks of a more dynamic nature of the economy of Kerala. Within a period of nearly two decades, Kerala's occupation structure has changed tremendously. The primary sector, which used to absorb 53 per cent of the labour force in 1981, had been able to work only with 32 per cent in the year 2001. The 32:68 ratio of agricultural *vis-à-vis* non-agricultural occupations is *per se* a great accomplishment. Whereas the agricultural sector in Kerala is undergoing the process of structural slimming, the secondary and tertiary sectors have started gaining weight. In the case of Kerala, the structural transformation in the area of occupation and also in the performance indicators of health went hand in hand. In the area of human health, Kerala has done much better than India (Table 1) in spite of low per capita income and GSDP. This is perhaps the basic accomplishment of the so-called Kerala model of development. But why this rigmarole? Does the discussion on the occupational distribution of population have anything to do with the performance in health? Let me pursue the Heffalump a bit farther.

With higher income and productivity in the non-agricultural sector, the ability to pay for the healthcare services goes up, and it is indeed possible to spend more on family health and welfare. The shift of more and more people in the non-agricultural sector implies an expansion of the urban sector where the incidence of pathological problems is comparatively low. It is a well-known fact that urban people remain better protected by many types of social safety nets. People in the urban areas can also avail of the services of more experienced medical personnel and well-established hospitals which are conspicuous by their absence in rural areas in general. Moreover, the cost of the same quality medical services, even if available, will be exorbitant in rural areas. The state policy of Kerala could ensure better public health by structural shifts of people from the rural to the urban sector. To a discerning researcher, changes in the occupational distribution of people have been a contributing factor to public health in Kerala.

However, the Kerala model of development is a path dependent model and not a model of path creation. It is the legacy of the erstwhile princely states in Kerala. A bit of historicity is associated with the genesis of the Kerala model of development. The healthcare paradigm followed by the rulers of the princely states of Travancore, Cochin and Malabar has been adopted more or less in the same way by Kerala. In the past, these three princely states of Kerala visualised, and to some extent developed, and systematically and institutionally integrated the structure of public healthcare services that could ensure a simultaneous protocol of preventive, promotive, curative and rehabilitative medicare to the people of Kerala. The healthcare paradigm in those days also gave active encouragement to the development of alternative medicines such as ayurvedic, homeopathic, allopathic and traditional medicines. All these provisions made the healthcare system very broad-based. The model that was working in the days of princely states was retained in principle in the post-independence period, and due to the untiring efforts of the state, significant results in the area of healthcare indicators could be achieved over time. The Kerala model of healthcare is well comparable to that of many developed countries, and is appreciated by many world organisations such as the Asian Development Bank and the United Nations. The Kerala model of healthcare system (KMHS) worked so well for many years, till the period of liberalisation in the 1990s. Two crucial proximate reasons can be adduced for the success of the KMHS . First, at every stage of healthcare development, namely, policy formulation, allocation, implementation and repair of the fault-line in the system, the government worked as friend, philosopher and guide, like the Wordsworthian state of nature as both being an impulse and a part of deontic duty. Second, all through those initial years, the healthcare system was institutionally embedded. The creation of institutions as such cannot take the process of development too far unless it is properly embedded in the system. For instance, a market is an institution but sometimes it fails to deliver goods because it is not in many cases properly embedded in the socioeconomic milieu of a particular country.

The Kerala model remains a paradox to economists in the sense that in spite of low income and low growth rate, the state is able to provide the best healthcare to the people in contradistinction to the rest of the Indian states and most of the developing countries with the same growth rate and per capita income. The message of the Table *infra* is revealing in this context.

Table 1
Health Parameters of India and Kerala

Health Parameters	*India*	*Kerala*
Infant Mortality Rate	58	14
Neo-natal Mortality	43.4	34.8
Child Mortality	29.3	2.6
Under Five Mortality	94.09	63.3
Not Immunised	57%	5%
Birth Not Attended by Medical Professionals	57.5	5.1
Life Expectancy	65	73
Crude Birth Rate	26.1	15.0
Crude Death Rate	8.7	6.4
Total Fertility Rate	3.0	1.8
Maternal Mortality Rate	407	136
Real Per Capita Health expenditure (Rs.)	101.59	145.89
Health Expenditure as% of GDP/GSDP	1.03	1.04
Dependency Load	63	42
Morbidity Rate	9.11	25.11

Sources: Economic Survey, 2002-03; NSS, 60th Round, SRS, NFHS, IIPS (Mumbai), All data are for 2005/2006.

The model is basically distribution-centric and not production-centric. Kerala has been able to achieve a human health index whose value (0.80) is much higher than that of many developing countries and of Indian states (Table 2).

Table 2
Health Development Indices of Indian States

States	*Index value*	*Sates*	*Index value*
Andhra Pradesh	0.64	Assam	0.58
Bihar	0.67	Gujarat	0.64
Haryana	0.70	Karnataka	0.65
Kerala	0.80	Madya Pradesh	0.56
Maharashtra	0.72	Orissa	0.58
Punjab	0.76	Rajasthan	0.62
Tamil Nadu	0.72	Uttar Pradesh	0.64
West Bengal	0.71		

Note: Calculated on the basis of the UNDP formula
Source: Annapoorani (2008, p. 5)

Kerala is still ahead of the Indian union with respect to almost all critical health indicators. For instance, the dependency load for India was 63, but 42.34 in Kerala; the toilet coverage was much wider in Kerala than that in India, and immunisation percentage was 44 in India and 74 in Kerala in the recent past. It is gratifying to note that for serious diseases, the immunisation coverage has gone up to around 80 per cent in Kerala. The life expectancy at birth is much higher in Kerala compared to other Indian states (Table 3) and is well-comparable to developed countries.

It appears to be paradoxical that, in spite of Kerala's much lower per capita income as compared to the Indian average and for that matter many of the rich Indian states, Kerala's health indicators are all much better than the national indicators. As a matter of fact, it is still now the best in the area of public health. There are many explanations to resolve this apparent paradox. Let me take up a few critical factors that often go unnoticed by experts who may not be so intimately acquainted with the Keralian economy, polity and society.

It is a hard fact that although Kerala is a rather poor state in terms of per capita income or GDP growth rate (around 6%

Table 3
Life Expectancy at Birth by Sex in India (1996-2002)

(Average for Four Years)

Life Expectancy				
	1996-2000		*1998-2002*	
States in India	*Male*	*Female*	*Male*	*Female*
India	61	62.7	61.6	63.3
Andhra Pradesh	61.7	64.3	62	64.6
Arunachal Pradesh	-	-	-	-
Assam	57.4	57.7	57.7	58.1
Bihar	60.9	59.1	61.4	59.5+
Goa	-	-	-	-
Gujarat	62.1	64	62.4	64.4
Haryana	64.4	65.1	64.7	65.4
Himachal Pradesh	65.4	66	65.7	66.3
Jammu & Kashmir	-	-	-	-
Karnataka	62.5	65.8	62.8	66.2
Kerala	70.7	76.7	70.8	75.9
Madhya Pradesh	56.6	56.3	57	56.7
Maharashtra	64.7	67.2	65	67.4
Manipur	-	-	-	-
Meghalaya	-	-	-	-
Mizoram	-	-	-	-
Nagaland	-	-	-	-
Orissa	57.8	58	58.4	58.5
Punjab	67.1	69.2	67.4	69.5
Rajasthan	60.1	61.1	60.5	61.6
Sikkim	-	-	-	-
Tamil Nadu	63.9	65.9	64.2	66.3
Uttar Pradesh	59.1	57.9	59.4	58.5
West Bengal	63	64.5	63.3	64.8

Source: SRS, Govt. of India.

per year), it gets a large inflow of remittances from the non-resident Keralites from various parts of the world, especially from the Gulf countries. The amount is a whopping $4000 million evey year at the exchange rate of Rs. 50 = $1. This is equivalent to about 23 per cent of the state GDP. This more than compensates for the meagre domestic income. The amount remitted is increasing every year as more and more Keralites are trying their luck in foreign countries. This is so because of two basic reasons. First, unemployment rate in Kerala is more than 20 per cent and 36 per cent of the people are below the poverty line income. Thus, most of the Keralites have the outward-looking proclivity for making themselves established in life. This propensity is further encouraged and sustained by a strong demonstration effect from the fact that the next-door neighbour or a known fellow who started his career in the similar situation has been able to turn the clock of life simply by going abroad. People are not only trying to keep up with the Joneses but some of them are also trying literally to go ahead of Smith.

The concentration of Keralites in the Gulf imparts some real lessons to the new aspirants in the form of gathering costless information, possibility of staying together in the Gulf and favourable push and pull factors and other externalities. Most of the migrants from Kerala are from the middle class and lower middle class families without much of formal education. Their real opportunity cost in their own country is indeed very low. They are working as drivers, foremen, machine operators, welders, electricians and so on. These semi or low skilled workers are much in demand in the Middle East. The outflow of these types of workers does not constitute the real brain drain but is simply a kind of brain overflow, which is not harmful for a labour-surplus state like Kerala; rather, it makes the employment situation at home more comfortable and manageable. The remittances sent by these emigrant workers are utilised by their families for improving their health and education status which is important for the next generation to join the bandwagon of non-resident Keralities (NRK), which is how the private health expenditure gets spurted up in Kerala. It is a common knowledge that body capital is more important than human capital as the former embodies the latter. For a large section of the Keralian people, expenditure on health and education is basically an investment expenditure which is much more important than simply a consumption expenditure. Even common people by and large prefer to resort to private hospitals and clinics. My first hand information as a resident of Kerala gives me the impression that in many ways, health gets a top priority in the list of individual family expenditure and there are many facilities existing in the state. The demand creates its supply in the majority of situations

The Success Story of Healthcare Development

The state is full of health care resorts, ayurvedic dispensaries as well as allopathic clinics. Never before I have seen before a state in India as Kerala where almost every village has either a private or a government hospital, a government-run health centre or a primary health centre. If a village does not have a hospital in Kerala, it is conveniently linked with a hospital nearby within five minutes' drive. *Panchayats* hold regular meetings and run courses on health and family problems. There are also *angan baris* to tackle children's education and health problems. Food and medicines are distributed free of cost through these centres. People are immensely health conscious in Kerala. Every household in Kerala is habituated to drinking boiled water. The sanitation and toilet coverage is far wider across the state. Regular immunisation of children is a very common routine work for parents. One of the reasons why the health of children is well looked after and cared for is perhaps the fact that mothers are fairly educated in Kerala. It does not always have to be a higher level of formal education but is mostly experiential in nature, and is handed over from generation to generation on various types of healthcare provisions and possibilities. It is a well-established conventional wisdom that mother's education is directly related to better health of children in general and family health in particular.

Ubiquitous presence of hospitals and health clinics ensures that healthcare services are available nearby and these are easily accessible not only in terms of distance but also in terms of costs. The hospitals are more or less clean and less crowded, the fees are affordable and available facilities are more or less satisfactory. A person belonging to another Indian state will be astonished to see that even a patient with ordinary means can afford to visit a specialist for his/her ailments in Kerala.

One of the critical factors for the success of any healthcare system is the low dependency load. Kerala has been able to achieve the lowest rate of total fertility rate (and also birth rate) amongst all the Indian states. This has been possible without the use of forced family planning methods. There is ample empirical evidence to show that coercive family planning practices such as sterilisation, sanctions and restrictions, besides being morally objectionable, have proved to be least effective and anti-democratic as in India during Indira Gandhi's regime. In Kerala, the reduction in the fertility rate has been more successful as public policies have stressed people making their own decisions and capitalised on strategies such as empowerment of young women, awareness campaign, and easy access to healthcare and education. Kerala's achievement of nearly cent per cent literacy in the recent past helped the expansion of health programmes with considerable success. There is a definite complementarity between education and health. Educated people are in a much better position to appreciate the value of health and the cost of sickness to take proper actions to maintain good health and chalk out their own action programmes. People who cannot read and write and are unable to critically participate in what is going on around them, remain impoverished, unhealthy and vulnerable to infectious and contagious diseases. In Kerala, the health sector has done well partly because the education sector has done pretty well.

Significant contribution to longevity and sustainable wellness paradigm is made possible in Kerala by its sharing and caring culture. Cohesive familial bonds and cooperative community feelings have gone a long way in the formation of what is termed as *social capital* in Kerala. Studies on social capital in Kerala point out that the success of the Kerala model of development can be attributed to a significant extent to the prevalence of enormous amount of social capital.

Social capital is often conceptualised as the sum of social goods and relations that a society generates in the course of its development. Social capital depends on social institutions and their interactions and relations. The whole concept of social capital is based on the notion of availability and needs of social cooperation among inter-family groups, inter-corporate groups, inter-institutions, and the overall relations among all these. Sometimes coordination by the state becomes essential to lay down the contours of such relationships. Social capital includes various types of organisations, institutions, and NGOs. It is a critical dimension of non-human wealth and can positively contribute to raising the quality of life and standard of living of the people in a society [O' Hara, 2001, p. 112].

Health-conscious as they are, people are engaged with neighbours and known families through different types of meetings and organisations like *Ayalkoottam* and *Kudambasree* to deliberate on many household problems of day-to-day importance, and the exchange of information on health and health-related matters is on the regular agenda. The state agencies are also engaged in distributing pamphlets and announcing through loudspeakers the latest health hazards and how to tackle them. This considerably reduces the information asymmetry in the area of health.

THE POST-LIBERALISATION SCENARIO

The health scenario in Kerala was hunky dory during the pre-liberalisation days. However, during the post-liberalisation period many a problem cropped up in the health care system, and unfortunately, the health indicators gradually started showing an unfavourable trend, and in many cases, they are getting worse than the average all-India indicators over time. The morbidity rate is now all-time high, malnutrition and under-nutrition alarming, various types of capitalist diseases are predominant, calorie intake going down and infant mortality has started rising. In the meantime, the state expenditure has been declining, the government-run institutions stand outdated due to lack of modern health infrastructure and shortage of properly skilled manpower. The globalisation game has reduced the health sector into a shambles and prepared the stage for a victory of the private sector, which now demarcates the configuration of a new history. The emergence of the private sector in a big way has created a tale-tell situation with the imposition of user fees, escalation of costs of life-saving drugs, unnecessary (in many cases) pathological tests, intensification of iatrogenic illness and other similar phenomena that are so very common to a private sector-dominated market economy where the main players are a few drug multinationals. As news reports reveal, very often physicians forge an unholy alliance with MNC drug companies to prescribe expensive branded drugs. This badly hits the poor and the needy who occupy the lowest rung of the ladder in terms of percentile position in the scale of income distribution. A message that is clear from the contemporary healthcare scenario of Kerala is that, health is no longer a public good but is becoming increasingly a private good. The implication of this conceptual metamorphosis of health is explosively damaging to the poor and the down-trodden masses of the world, let alone Kerala. The Kerala model, which was known in the past as the dispenser of a high degree of distributional equity, is now marked by rampant inequalities that grossly violate the difference principle of justice *a la* Rawls.

It is interesting to note that, usually, government intervention follows market failure, but in the case of Kerala's healthcare system, the market has been working with gusto in the wake of apparent government failure in this direction. A post-facto analysis of some of the inter-temporally sliding critical factors affecting the health scenario is presented in the discussion that follows.

PARADIGM CHANGES AND POLICY SHIFTS

The deteriorating position of Kerala in the realm of healthcare system in the post- liberalisation period is due to several factors but policy shift and paradigm changes at the governmental level are the prominent ones. Interestingly, in many ways, while the public healthcare scenario is improving at the all-India level, it is taking a 180 degree turn in the case of Kerala. There is a perceptible change in public expenditure on healthcare in Kerala. If the present trend continues, Kerala's percentile position is likely to fall further in the foreseeable future unless some checks and balances are placed in order, and Kerala will no longer hold its title as the best state in India as a healthcare provider. At present, the healthcare system in Kerala is passing through a period of crisis. The policy of the government may be a benevolent one but there may be at some stage some type of implementation failure. It has to be accepted that since the state sector is no longer doing well in providing good quality healthcare services in public hospitals and dispensaries, people are looking towards the private outlets. The enormous growth of private sector hospitals and clinics is an indication that the state sector is lagging far behind in the field of social reproduction.

The government expenditure is falling in Kerala unlike the national expenditure on healthcare services, which is on the rise since 2005 under the auspices of the National Rural Health Mission (NRHM). However, it is not often the absolute amount of money spent that matters in healthcare services; the more important fact is how the amount is spent, who spends it, on which items and who are the beneficiaries ? In general, many modern facilities and technology are lacking in government-run hospitals. The equipments is old, houses dilapidated and so is the working environment. People are therefore turning to private healthcare hospitals even if they are pretty more expensive. The growth of private hospitals and clinics has not reduced the healthcare cost but has rather accentuated it in Kerala. The cartels created by doctors and private-run hospitals are able to create a situation of collusive oligopolistic health market where prices are high and sticky (in many cases, they may go up but cannot come down so easily). This type of ratchet inflation is working in full swing in the health market in less developed countries, particularly in India where the healthcare services are controlled mainly by the private sector. The private sector does not encourage collision or competition but thrives on the basis of collusion and a bit of product differentiation. For instance, a vitamin preparation prescribed by one hospital doctor may not contain selenium but another hospital does prescribe a product with selenium and PABA even for the same disease. In the same way, the cost variations for different types of pathological tests are shown to be due to the age of the machine, the type of technology, the experience and the qualifications of technicians and so on. The private hospitals are thriving mainly because of modern and more versatile technology and equipments, more skilled manpower, attractive ambience and cleaner and spacious lobbies. In the private sector, allocation of funds is not much of a problem in the sense that money rolls on and a part of the profit is ploughed back into the business.

In contradistinction to this, money allocated to government hospitals is never adequate, and a large portion of the allocated funds (about 50 per cent) is spent on salaries of the staff. However, higher salary to the staff may not be indicative of high absolute amount going to the health personnel but remarkably low spending on health [Rao, 2007, p. 31]. Government's indifference or inability to improve the health sector is apparent from many instances. It is not surprising that there are unfilled vacancies in different district hospitals in Kerala (Table 5).

A decline in health spending in recent years is another blow to the public health services in Kerala. The following Table (Table 4) clearly brings out the fact that the share of Kerala's health spending in GSDP declined between (2000-2001) and (2004 and 2005), and the share of health spending in total state spending also plummeted between (1999-20000 and (2004-2005).

Table 4
Kerala's Health Spending as % of GSDP

2000-2001	*2001-2002*	*2002-2003*	*2003-2004*	*2004 2005*
0.99	1.04	0.99	0.96	0.92

Share of Kerala's Health Spending as % of Total Spending

1999-2000	*2000-2001*	*2001-2002*	*2002-2003*	*2003-2004*	*2004-2005*
5.74	5.52	6.17	5.15	4.92	5.13

Source: RBI Bulletin: Various Issues.

As against the Keralian scenario, the share of health spending in many states in India is found to be higher. These states are: Bihar (1.10), Jharkhand (1.0), Orissa (1.06), Uttarkhand (1.23). Kerala's position is neither too low nor too high. However, Kerala's status with respect to the share of health spending in total spending is somewhat better. Only one state, Jharkhand, spent more than Kerala in 2005. The relative position of Kerala for the later years in both these areas is not yet reliably known. Low spending aside, there are many other problems that include the inefficiency of the public sector healthcare delivery system, increasing private healthcare costs, mushrooming of the private healthcare clinics and decreased spending on preventive medicines [Ekbal, 1997].

The treatment costs which were very low in the past in Kerala because of its good infrastructure and liberal subsidies are now looking up. It appears that of late the hospitals are not only lacking in the modern infrastructure but are also suffering from the shortage of effective skilled manpower such as physicians and surgeons, and many approved vacancies throughout the state are not filled (Table 5). This may be due to paucity of funds or partly because of a lack of effective supply of qualified manpower. It does not seem to be due to

Table 5
Unfilled Vacancies of Govt. Doctors in Kerala (2007)

District	*Assistant Surgeon*	*Civil Surgeon*	*Total*
Kasargod	36	12	48
Kannur	98	4	102
Wayanad	21	12	33
Kozhikode	2	10	12
Malappuram	36	21	57
Palaghat	73	11	84
Trichur	39	29	68
Ernakulam	58	1	59
Idukki	41	9	50
Kottayam	43	7	50
Alappuzha	34	10	44
Pathanamthitta	50	0	50
Kollam	26	0	26
Trivandrum	0	12	12
Total	567	138	705

Source: Directorate of Health Services (2007) Thriuvanathapuram.

an austerity drive at the government level. There are two basic reasons for the unfilled vacancies of physicians at the district levels in Kerala. First, the pay in the government health sector is much lower and not competitive. Second, the young medical practitioners at the first instance try to migrate to foreign countries where the pay and perks are much better and the scope of further research and education is almost unlimited. The government, then, usually appoints comparatively greenhorn specialists and generalists to run the show.

The implication is obvious: Kerala's comparative advantage as the provider of the best health care services is at a stake now. Let me provide some concrete evidence.

The Paradox of High Morbidity and Low Mortality

The current morbidity rate in Kerala is the highest among the major Indian states although its mortality rate is the lowest (6.4). The total morbidity rate was around 25 per 1000 population in 2005. A conflux of high morbidity and low mortality rate is the most confounding health conundrum in modern Kerala. A similar view was expressed by Panikar and Soman in 1984. Mortality rate as an historical actuality evolves over a period of time but morbidity rate is a temporal reality that reveals at a point in time. A change in mortality rate is essentially a long-term phenomenon, but morbidity is rather a short-term epiphenomenon that captures various temporary syndromes of aberrations in the body economy. Whilst the long-term indicator like mortality is changing at a very slow rate, the syndromes of morbidity are all rampant and are cognisable through simple eye-ball testing. A high rate of morbidity speaks of and results from inadequate or complete absence of treatment due to paucity of resources at the micro individual level and macro state level. A high rate of unemployment, lower expenditure on health, and escalating cost in the private sector force people to be satisfied with temporary palliatives rather than searching for the permanent panacea. The incidence of morbidity rate in Kerala *vis-à-vis* India among various classes of people is shown in the following Table 6.

Table 6
The Incidence of Morbidity in Kerala *vis-à-vis* India

Household Type	*Kerala*	*India*
Self Employed (Non. Agricultural)	21.91	9.31
Regular Wage Salary	25.95	9.86
Casual Labour	22.59	9.58
Others	30.58	15.60
All India	24.06	9.95

Source: NSS 60th Round (2004).

The morbidity rate is on the rise in Kerala in both urban and rural areas and among males and females. The rural sector is more adversely affected by this pernicious condition, and in terms of gender impact, women have greater incidence of morbidity. Besides morbidity, Kerala's health sector now is facing many critical challenges and the overall performance is going downhill.

Kerala's comparative long-term supremacy in human life expectancy and its unique position in India is incrementally deteriorating although it is still the best in the country in many respects. Similar is the situation with respect to infant mortality rate in Kerala, which went up to 14 in 2005 from 11 in 2001 [Kannan, *et al.* 1991]. The calorie intake for the urban population in Kerala came down from 55.9 per cent in 1983 to 52.5 per cent in 1999-2000, although the calorie intake in the rural sector marginally increased (Table 7).

As for the people below the poverty line, it is disquieting that the consumption of cereals for this class of people went down over time (vide Table 8). However, in many instances, Kerala's relative health performance in India is not adversely affected so much, but its record of achievement is going to be tarnished.

The nutritional status of women and the intensity of anaemia among children perceptibly deteriorated during the period 1998-2006 (vide Table 9). There were more underweight children and obese women in Kerala in 2005-6 compared to 1998-99. The scenario is getting more saturnine in recent years.

Table 7
Per Capita Cereal Consumption of Poverty Line Class (Kgs Per Month)

	Kerala		*Urban*	
State	*1993-94*	*1999-2000*	*1993-94*	*1999-2000*
A.P	11.40	10.95	11.25	10.62
Assam	12.98	12.11	10.96	10.33
Bihar	15.11	13.32	12.74	12.79
Gujarat	9.87	9.88	8.97	8.07
Haryana	11.33	9.79	9.98	7.91
Himachal Pradesh	12.37	11.48	11.89	9.80
Karnataka	11.84	10.18	10.69	9.71
Kerala	9.21	8.18	9.24	8.67
M.P	14.11	12.48	12.08	11.28
Maharashtra	11.25	20.89	9.80	9.46
Orrssa	16.96	15.44	14.20	17.18
Punjab	9.09	9.24	8.10	8.37
Rajasthan	13.71	12.84	11.80	11.61
Tamil Nadu	10.86	9.79	10.32	9.14
Uttar Pradesh	13.82	12.89	11.4	20.34
West Bengal	14.57	13.03	11.92	10.97
All India	13.19	12.27	20.89	10.75

Source: Govt. of India (1995) and (2001).

Table 8
Indian Population with Calorie-intake (%)

	Urban		*Rural*	
State	*1983*	*1999-2000*	*1983*	*1999-2000*
Andhra Pradesh	53.8	50.8	39.3	51.0
Assam	49.9	46.6	48.8	61.5
Bihar	44.4	43.5	39.6	45.9
Gujarat	52.1	51.3	46.7	53.6
Haryana	43.5	46.2	27.5	30.2
Karnataka	48.8	51.2	42.3	54
Kerala	55.9	52.5	61.2	61.6
Madhya Pradesh	44.6	49.1	33.7	50.7
Maharashtra	57.1	52.7	44.4	52.4
Orissa	35.7	31	46.2	42.1
Punjab	48.1	44.6	24.1	31
Rajasthan	42.6	34.5	28.8	24.3
Tamil Nadu	65.6	55	62.9	65.2
Uttar Pradesh	52.1	46.5	31	32.9
West Bengal	53.1	49	53.6	47.8

Source: Shekhar & Ghosh (2003). The data relate to less than 90% of the Recommended Norms.

Table 9
Nutritional Status and Anemia among Children and Adults

	NFHS I	*NFHS II*		*NFH3*	
		All		*2005-06*	
Particulars	*All*	*1998-99*	*All*	*Urban*	*Rural*
Women whose Body Mass Index is below normal in %	NA	18.7	12.5	9.1	14.3
Women whose Body Mass Index is below normal in %	NA	-	11.9	11.2	12.3
Women who are over weight or obese n %	NA	20.6	34	40.1	30.9
Men who are over weight or obese in %	NA	-	24.3	28	21.9
Children in the age of 6 to 35 months who are anemic in %	NA	43.9	55.7	51.3	57.9
Married women in the age of 15 to 49 who are anemic in %	-	22.7	32.3	32.3	32.4
Pregnant women in the age of 15 to 49 who are anemic in %	-	20.3	33.1	27.7	35.8
Children under 3 years who are stunted in %	25.2	21.9	21.1	21.3	21.1
Children under 3 years who are wasted in %	12.8	11.1	16.1	10.1	19.1
Children under 3 years who are underweight in %	27	26.9	28.8	22.5	31.9

Source: NFHS,IIPS Mumbai.

A CRITIQUE OF THE DECENTRALISED MODEL OF HEALTHCARE SERVICES

The triadic system of a decentralised model of healthcare services (including districts, blocks and village *panchayats*) that Kerala has been following since 1996 is not doing well now [Varghese *et al.* 2007]. There are some misgivings that the *Panchayats* which are flooded with funds to be spent within a given period of time, might not have been able to properly allocate the money [Nair, 2000]. These *Panchayats* do not have the necessary expertise to prioritise and evaluate the best possible way in which the resources have to be allocated. There are some health experts in some *Panchayats* but they often remain aloof from the decision-making process [Varghese *et al.* 2007]. A full-scale public participation is indeed very vital for the health programmes to be appropriate and implementation to be successful. Indeed, remarkable progress can be made in democratising health when there is a concerted action by both the government and the public to redress the situation. Development is not just a script written by some experts to be faithfully enacted by others. Participation at all levels is both the end and means of development. It is the responsibility of a just society that all types of people, particularly the poor and the needy will have the necessary opportunities, contestability and institutions to exercise and develop their capabilities. These may either be in the realm of education or in health. Public cooperation and participation is the key to success everywhere. There may be a conflict at times but that should be a sort of cooperative conflict and not a conflict *qua* conflict.

Interestingly, the study by Varghese *et al.* has found a priority conflict between the State Planning Board and the *Panchayats*. The conflict arises because the State and the local bodies have different sets of priorities, and a compromise or trade off is often necessary. The allocation of resources for health development in Kerala is not based on a set of objective criteria but on the whims and caprices of *Panchayat* members. Moreover, the technical experts generally put pressure on *Panchayat* members to allocate resources to those areas which are familiar to them. In such a situation, it is indeed difficult to say whether the resources are allocated efficiently or inefficiently.

In the healthcare sector, the government has to operate under many convoluted constraints and the problematics are indeed innumerable. But what one strongly feels is that the target setting in the arena of healthcare is often done without much empirical verification of the needs of the people, and there is indeed no fool-proof mechanism to achieve the target. No cost-benefit study, cost effectiveness study or programming is done seriously at the state level, or even at the national level. The possibility of trade-offs between healthcare expenditure and education or development expenditure is just assumed away. The fixation of targets is very arbitrary and is done in a slip-shod manner simply on the strength of political leverage. In fact, fiscal targets for health spending should be based on goals for outcomes and the resources needed to achieve them, which are basically lacking in India [Berman and Ahuja, 2008, p. 209]. Kerala does not seem to be an exception in this regard. Sometimes economists are hired for soliciting advice but they are not free from political pride and prejudices. I have discussed elsewhere how macroeconomic policy making is influenced by politics in developing countries; Kerala does not qualify to be an exception [Ghosh, 2007]. While contextualising the Keralian perspective, it needs to be emphasised that the decentralised healthcare model has failed to achieve the desideratum, as unflinching and effective cooperation and active participation in the decision-making stage at the grass-root level are palpably lacking. The whole attempt is indeed like playing Hamlet without the prince of Denmark.

REFERENCES

Annapoorani, R. (2008), "Emerging Health Scenario in India: Challenges and Strategies", paper presented in the International Conference on Health and Development, Kannur University, Kerala, India (22-23 October).

Berman, Peter and Ahuja, Rajiv (2008), "Government Health Spending In India", *Economic and Political Weekly,* June 28.

Ekbal, B. (1997), *People's Campaign for Decentralised Planning and Health Sector,* Kerala State Planning Board.

Ghosh, B. N. (2007), "Politics of Macroeconomic Policy", *Man and Development,* March.

Govt. of India (1995 & 2001), *National Calorie-intake in India*, NSS, New Delhi.

Kannan, K. P. *et al.* (1991), *Health and Development in Rural Kerala*, KSSP, p. 06.

Kutty, V. R. *et al.* (1993), " How Socioeconomic Status Affects Birth Rates and Death Rates in Rural Kerala, India: Results of a Health Study", *International Journal of Health Services*, Vol. 23.

Nair, Gopinath (2000), *People's Planning in Kerala A Case Study of Two Village Panchayats*, KRPLLD Discussion Paper No. 16, Centre for Development Studies, Trivandrum.

O, Hara, P. A. (2001), " Wealth Distribution and Global Inequality in the Multiple Capital Paradigm", *International Journal of Human Development*, Vol. 1, No. 1, September.

Panikar, P. G. K. (1999), *Health Transition in Kerala*, KRPLLD Discussion Paper No. 10, centre for Development Studies, Trivandrum.

Panikar, P.G. K. and Soman, C. R. (1984), *Health Status of Kerala: The Paradox of Economic Backwardness and Health Development*, Centre for Development Studies, Trivandrum.

Rao, Mohan (2007), " Roshomon's Truth: Public Health and NGOs in India", *Journal of Health and Development*", Vol. 3, Nos. 1&2, January-July.

Shekhar, Chandra and Ghosh Jayati (2003), "The Calorie Consumption Puzzles", *Business Line*, Feb. 11.

Singer, H. W. (1952), " The Mechanics of Economic Development", *Indian Economic Review*, August.

Varghese, Joe *et al.* (2007), "Local Factors Influencing Resource Allocation to Health Under the Decentralised Planning Process in Kerala, India", *Journal of Health and Development*", Vol. 3, Nos. 1&2, January-July.

PART–FOUR

The Influential Externalities

12

MIGRATION FROM KERALA TO THE GULF COUNTRIES– PATTERN, PROBLEM AND POLICIES

L. R. Usha

INTRODUCTION

The international migration of workers from India during the post independence period may be broadly divided into three phases. During the first phase in the 1950s and 1960s, persons with administrative, technical and professional qualifications as well as experience migrated in search of better jobs and prospects. The principal destinations were the United Kingdom, the United States, Canada and, on a smaller scale, Western Europe, Australia and the African countries. The migrants included among others, teachers, nurses, engineers, doctors, scientists and technicians and a majority of them settled in the host countries. This is a traditional type of migration where people from developing countries migrate to developed countries to secure better jobs, opportunities, living facilities and to settle there. It is often associated with the concept of brain drain and is essentially voluntary and individual in nature. The volume of this movement however declined during the 1970s (ILO, 1989).

The second phase of migration began in the mid 1970s towards the oil rich Middle East countries. The price hike of oil in 1973 and the consequent earnings of large revenue accelerated a process of industrialisation and social change in the Middle East Countries. This phenomenon was characterised by massive investment in social and economic infrastructure which in turn necessitated the service of large number of foreign workers. The major destinations of the Indian workers in the Middle East were the United Arab Emirates, Saudi Arabia, Oman, Bahrain, Kuwait, Qatar, Yemen and Iraq. Compared to the earlier migration this type of migration and the category of migrants were different. Labour was recruited for work in the Gulf strictly on limited contract terms and was expected to return home at the end of the contract period. This type of migration is referred to as 'contract migration'. The Majority of emigrants to the Middle East belonged to the category of unskilled workers, semi skilled or skilled workers in manual or construction related occupations. The migration which started with a few thousands per year during the mid 1970s assumed large proportions during the 1980s. From the second half of the 1980s the rates of annual outflow showed fluctuations due to low economic growth in the Gulf countries, competition from workers from other Asian countries, the Kuwait war and unfavorable changes in the labour policies of the Gulf Countries.

The third phase of migration was characterised by young professionals, mostly software engineers and managers, migrating to developed countries, the United States of America and the United Kingdom in particular. The Y2K software problem, rapid growth of computer networks, shortage of computer professionals and opening up of world economies have drawn Indian engineers and technicians into the world computer industry. The movement of such highly educated people began in the second half of the 1990s and its volume has increased considerably in the past few years.

PATTERN OF EMIGRATION FROM KERALA

The process of migration from Kerala gathered momentum at the time of the Second World War. The war provided an impetus to the manufacture of artillery and other armaments. Consequently, there was a hike in transportation and shipping. The increased tempo of productivity which triggered industrial growth in and around many cities of India attracted a new segment of Kerala migrants to those places. Migrants from Kerala flocked to those cities and industrial centres of India. But the nativist opposition to the immigrants began to be felt in all the states from 1970 (Weiner, Myron 1978). Almost all state governments issued orders reserving 80% of the jobs to local candidates styled as "sons of the soil" to put constraints on out migration. A significant change in the pattern of migration from Kerala has taken place since 1973 following the oil price hike. Keralites began to migrate in large numbers to the Gulf countries. The outflow continued unabated till the middle of the 1980s. The number of Keralites who migrated to the Gulf countries was estimated to be around 5.5 lakhs in 1985. During the second half of 1980s there was a decline in the rate of annual outflow due to low economic growth of the Middle East countries. The worst year in the history of Indian migration to the Middle East was 1990 when about 1.80 lakh Indians were repatriated from Kuwait and Iraq as a result of the Gulf crisis that followed the conquest of Kuwait in August that year. But with the recovery of Middle East economies from the fall in oil prices and Gulf war, the migration revived in 1991. Though there had been a rapid growth in emigration to the Gulf during the first half of the 1990s, the situation changed drastically in 1996 due to the changes in labour policies adopted by the host countries. Return migration began to assume large dimensions. The annual outflow of migrants remained stagnant for a brief period. The recent construction boom in Gulf and increased oil revenue has again created a great demand for workforce. The majority of the migrants from India nowadays are skilled and professional personnel.

Factors that Contributed to Large Scale Migration from Kerala

In view of the high density of population, stagnant and less productive agricultural sector, low level of industrialisation, rising unemployment, failure of economic organisation to expand employment in secondary and tertiary sectors, low per capita income and high levels of education, Kerala has become a manpower exporter to other parts of India as well as other countries. These can be referred to as the push factors for migration from Kerala. High wages, better employment opportunities in the Gulf, the absence of restrictions on remittances and tax relief on foreign earnings are the pull factors attracting Kerala migrants to the Middle East countries. The devaluation of the Indian rupee in 1991 also encouraged fresh emigration.

MAGNITUDE, TREND AND CHARACTERISTICS OF EMIGRANTS

Regarding the stock of Indian emigrants in West Asia we do not have an accurate estimate based on sample surveys or systematic collection of data. Different agencies have conducted surveys for specific purposes in various periods and published their study results. However on the basis of the data provided by the Ministry of External Affairs, surveys of the State Department of Economics and Statistics, Govt. of India Reports, World Bank Publications and micro level studies conducted by various researchers, a picture about the magnitude of migrants to the Middle East can be developed. The migration of Keralites which started with a few thousands in 1973 assumed larger proportions in later years. The number of Keralites in the Gulf region increased from 1.33 lakhs in 1975 to 2.65 lakhs in 1979 and 4.58 lakhs in 1983 (Table 1). The latest CDS survey conducted in 2007 estimates the number of Keralites working abroad as 18.48 lakhs of which about 16.43 lakhs are in the Middle East countries.

Distribution of Emigrants by Districts

The statewide surveys on emigration conducted by K. C. Zachariah *et al.* (1998, 2004 and 2007) provide more reliable estimates about the emigration from the various districts of Kerala.

Table 1
Stock of Indian Emigrants in the Gulf Region

Year	*No. of. Indian Migrants (in lakhs)*	*No. of Migrants from Kerala (in lakhs)*
1975	2.66	1.33
1979	5.31	2.65
1983	9.16	4.58
1987	10.96	5.48
1991	15.05	7.52
1999	30.00	15.00
2003	-	18.38*
2007	-	18.48*

Source: Govt. of India (2002), Report on High level committee on the Indian Diaspora and Zachariah *et. al.* (2004, 2007) Migration Survey, CDS, Thiruvananthapuram.

Table 2
Number of Emigrants by Districts, 1998–2007

	Number of Emigrants (EMI)			*Emigrants per 100 households*		
District	*2007*	*2003*	*1998*	*2007*	*2003*	*1998*
Thiruvananthapuram	189361	168046	13705	22.0	21.5	19.9
Kollam	146892	148457	102977	22.1	24.4	18.4
Pathanamthitta	53936	133720	97505	16.8	44.3	33.1
Alappuzha	114020	75036	62870	21.1	15.2	13.2
Kottayam	75610	106569	35494	15.6	24.0	9.1
Idukki	1989	7880	7390	0.7	2.9	2.9
Ernakulam	142785	121237	103750	18.1	16.9	17.0
Thrissur	170308	178867	161102	23.5	27.2	25.6
Palakkad	89655	177876	116062	15.2	32.6	21.8
Malappuram	336251	271787	296710	49.8	45.0	49.2
Kozhikode	158430	167436	116026	24.4	28.6	22.0
Wayanad	15409	7704	4552	8.1	4.4	2.9
Kannur	254453	202414	88065	48.3	43.2	19.0
Kasargod	98803	71449	38747	38.5	30.6	19.1
Kerala	1847902	1838478	1361955	24.5	26.7	21.4

Source: Zachariah K. C. and S. Irudaya Rajan (2007), Migration, Remittances and Employment, W.P. No. 395 CDS, Thiruvananthapuram.

Malappuram is the leading district in terms of the number of emigrants followed by Kannur, Thiruvananthapuram, Thrissur and Kozhikkode as per the 2007 estimates. In terms of emigrants per hundred households Malappuram, Kannur and Kasargod are far ahead than other districts and the state average.

The hilly districts of Wayanad and Idukki are the lowest in sending emigrants. It is observed that the northern districts of Kerala have gained dominance in this matter.

Distribution of Emigrants according to Destination

The major destinations of Kerala emigrants to the Middle East are the United Arab Emirates (UAE), Saudi Arabia, Oman, Kuwait, Bahrain and Qatar. The UAE, Bahrain, Kuwait have preferred Indian workers since the 1970's. Indians constitute about 50% of the migrant workforce in those countries. Large scale migration to Saudi Arabia and Qatar started in 1978. The number of Keralites in the Gulf during the period 1998-2007 is shown in the table given below.

Table 3
Country of Residence of Keralite Emigrants

Country	*Year 1998 (in lakhs)*	*Year 2003 (in lakhs)*	*Year 2007 (in lakhs)*
UAE	4.20	6.70	7.74
Saudi Arabia	5.11	4.90	4.47
Oman	1.40	1.53	1.35
Kuwait	0.68	1.14	1.35
Bahrain	0.75	1.09	0.58
Qatar	0.63	0.99	0.94
Others (including USA, UK etc.)	0.85	2.03	2.05
Total	13.62	18.38	18.48

Source: Zacharia *et. al.* (2007), Migration Survey CDS, Thiruvananthapuram.

The table shows that the number of emigrants to the UAE and Kuwait increased steadily between 1998 and 2007 whereas it showed a declining trend in the case of Saudi Arabia. A notable development in the international migration from Kerala during the present decade is the increase in emigrants towards other countries like the USA, the UK, Canada and the European nations. Despite these changes the Gulf countries account for 89% of the total emigrants from Kerala in 2007.

Characteristics of the Emigrants

The migration survey conducted by K.C. Zachariah *et. al.* in 2007 arrives at the following conclusions regarding the characteristics of the emigrants. Nearly 48 per ecent of the emigrants are Muslims. The corresponding proportions of Hindus and Christians are about 33 per cent and 19 per cent. More emigrants belonging to the Muslím community have gone for employment in Arab countries (98 per cent) than Hindus and Christians (89 per cent). Most of the emigrants are men in their prime working age group of 15 to 59 years. Women account for less than 15 per cent. The proportion of female emigrants is found to be the highest among Christians. The majority of emigrants, both men and women, belong to the age group of 20-29 years at the time of their first emigration. Most of the emigrants have less than secondary level education. Nearly 60 per cent of the emigrants had some employment or other; prior to emigration. The unemployed among them constitute only less than 25 per cent.

REMITTANCES TO KERALA

Kerala began to receive large amounts of remittance from the emigrants to the Middle East in the second half of 1970s. Gulf emigration and remittances from the Gulf had its impact on Kerala's economy. It contributed much more to poverty alleviation and reduction of unemployment in Kerala than any other factor including agrarian reforms, trade union activities and soçial welfare legislations during the last quarter of the 20th century (Zachariah K.C. *et. al*, 1999). The remittances increased from Rs. 337 crores in 1981 to Rs. 2428 crores in 1991 and Rs. 18465 crores in 2003 (Table 4).

The infusion of Rs 18465 crores in the year 2003 to Kerala had a significant impact on the Kerala economy. This amount was about 22% of the Net State Domestic Product (NSDP). It helped raise the per capita annual income of the state (Rs. 31442 in 2003) by Rs. 5678. The remittances were 1.74 times the revenue receipts of the state, 7 times the amount the state received from the central government and sufficient enough to wipe out 60% of the state's debt in 2003. The survey conducted by K. C. Zachariah *et. al.* in 2007 estimated the total remittances received in Kerala from emigrants as Rs. 24525 crores.

Table 4
Remittances to Kerala 1981–2003

Year	*Amount (Rupees in Crores)*
1981	337
1983	568
1985	523
1987	891
1989	1156
1991	2428
93	3882
95	7069
97	10761
99	13652
2001	15732
2003	18465

Source: Govt of India (2007) Kerala Development Report, Planning Commission, New Delhi.

IMPACT OF MIGRATION

The impact of migration can be analysed from two points of view–the financial inflow effects and the human outflow effects.

Financial Inflow Effects

The increased remittances by the migrants have augmented the foreign exchange reserves of India. The growth of remittances has helped arrest the increase in trade deficit to a large extent. In other words, it has helped in mitigating the balance of payment problem to some degree.

Parameters for Assessing the Impact of Remittances on the Economy of Kerala–Consumption, Savings and Investment

Remittances are essentially transfers of personal income. A part of them is utilised for consumption by the family of the migrants. The remaining portion is used for savings and investment. Does the amount spent on consumption lead to an increased demand for consumption goods and consequent inflation? How much of the savings are channelled into productive investment in tune with the country's priorities? These questions are to be investigated for assessing the over all impact of remittances on the economy of Kerala. A few surveys were conducted by different researchers at different points of time (Govt. of Kerala, 1987; Prakash B.A, 1978 & 1998; Mathew E. T. and Nair P.R.G, 1978 and Zachariah K. C. *et. al.*, 2007).

Based on these studies, it was found that the migrant households had higher income, better consumption levels and asset position compared to non-migrant households. The migrants invested a major share of their savings in land and houses. Their investment in business was small and in productive activities it was almost nil. Investment in savings and financial assets were also small. According to the study conducted by the CDS (Zachariah K. C. *et. al*, 2007), remittances per emigrant household increased during 2003-2007 by about 20 per cent, partly due to structural changes including taking up of work in the advanced countries of the west. About 17 per cent of the households in the state received remittances in cash or kind. The major part of the remittances (nearly 94 per cent) was used by recipient households to meet their substantial requirements. The other uses to which the amounts were spent were the education of children, repayment of debts and construction of houses. Only 2% of the recipient households utilized remittances for investment and business. In a nutshell, the migrant households were not investing in productive activities.

Human Outflow Effects

The migration of large numbers of unskilled and the unemployed has decreased unemployment and under-employment to some extent.

The migration survey (Zacharia *et. al.* 2007) reported that during 2003-2007, the magnitude of unemployment decreased dramatically. Employment, including self-employment, increased impressively. The unemployment rate in the state registered a steep fall from 19% of the labour force in 2003 to a little over 12% in 2007. The decrease during the period came to about 40%. The emigration of skilled workers like carpenters, masons, etc. had a positive effect on the wages of construction workers. This led to an increase of wages in other sectors too. It also promoted the mobility of non construction workers into the construction sector and large scale migration of Tamil workers to Kerala. The shortages of construction workers and increase in wages have led to the introduction of capital intensive technique on a large scale during the 1990s. Another change that occurred in the labour market due to the Gulf opportunities was the introduction of vocational education and training for skills. It was found that the majority of returned emigrants got some employment on their return (Govt. of Kerala, 2000).

Impact on Poverty and Income Distribution

Available evidences (Nair P.R.G., 1986) suggest that the poor households receiving remittances from the West Asia attained substantial increase in their income levels. The hike in the price of land, commodities and services due to the inflow of remittances has affected the distribution of income in favour of some sections of people while adversely affecting others.

Another impact was the increase in the price of construction materials, consumer goods, food products, rent rates and increase in charges of health, education, transportation etc. The flow of remittances and the consequent increase in demand pushed up the prices of all the above items. Here also the sections which were adversely affected were the poor, the middle class and the fixed income groups.

RETURN EMIGRATION

When people return to their countries of origin after significant periods of sojourn abroad, it is called return emigration. This is the essential final stage of the migration process of overseas contract workers. Return emigration was scarcely referred to by researchers before the 1960s. The reason is that very little data existed on the phenomenon. Return emigration studies swelled since the early 1970s. The earliest source of information regarding return emigration is the survey of about 700 returned migrants' households conducted by Nair in 1985 (Nair P.R.G, 1986). The surveys made by the Government of Kerala in 1987 and 1992-93 also give some information. The survey conducted by the Govt. of Kerala in 1992-93 estimated that 124000 workers had returned to Kerala from the Middle East till 1992 (Govt. of Kerala, 1994). Nair estimated that returnees till 1997 was likely to be about 5 lakhs (Nair P.R.G., 1997). Another study estimated that in 1998 there were about 739000 return emigrants in Kerala. Between 1998 and 2000, some more emigrants came back to Kerala while some of the earlier return emigrants went back to the Gulf countries. The number of return emigrants in Kerala in 2001 was estimated to be about, 5 lakhs (Zachariah, K. C., Nair P. R. Gopinathan and S. Irudayarajan, 2001). These authors reported that the years 1998-2000 witnessed a decrease in the number of emigrants returning to Kerala. The fluctuations in oil price and the consequent changes in money supply were factors that attributed to it. According to the migration surveys conducted by K. C. Zachariah *et al.*, in 2004 and 2007, there was a marginal fall again in the number of return emigrants between 2003 and 2007. It is shown in the table given below (Table 5). The table also gives a district-wise distribution of the return migrants.

Return emigrants were a selected group among the emigrants. They were unevenly distributed among the various districts. Their intensity was high in the three districts namely Thiruvananthapuram, Malappuram and Trissur. They had relatively lower levels of education than the emigrants working abroad. Nearly two-thirds of them had worked in the Gulf for a period of less than five years. The largest proportion of returnees was from Saudi Arabia. A majority of them were employed in the post-return phase. Self-employment particularly in trade, transport and other services was a means by which many of Kerala's unemployed were able to become engaged in gainful occupations. Emigration tuned out to be a successful venture for seventy per cent of the returnees. For one-fifth of the returnees, emigration was a misadventure resulting in loss of wealth, wastage of energy and time and loss of health (Usha L. R., 2002).

Table 5
Number of Emigrants by Districts, 1998–2007

	Number of Return Emigrants			Return emigrants per 100 house holds		
Districts	*2007*	*2003*	*1998*	*2007*	*2003*	*1998*
Thiruvananthapuram	161441	103059	118878	18.8	13.2	18.1
Kollam	85236	69314	74106	12.8	11.4	13.2
Pathanamthitta	25534	83502	54537	7.9	27.7	18.5
Alappuzha	60630	43109	34572	11.2	8.7	7.2
Kottayam	28571	28368	18164	5.9	6.4	4.6
Idukki	8436	3766	5017	2.9	1.4	2.0
Ernakulam	61063	74435	45028	7.7	10.4	7.4
Thrissur	104391	86029	116788	14.4	13.1	18.6
Palakkad	51521	55008	89238	8.8	10.1	7.4
Malappuram	143419	141537	123750	21.2	23.5	20.5
Kozhikode	56845	109101	60910	8.8	18.6	11.5
Wayanad	9127	3852	3327	4.8	2.2	2.1
Kannur	53957	45394	28263	10.4	9.7	6.1
Kasargod	36132	47468	16667	14.1	20.3	8.2
Kerala	886303	893942	739245	11.7	13.0	11.6

Source: Zachariah K. C. and S. Irudayarajan (2007), Remittances and Employment, Working Paper No. 395, CDS, Thiruvananthapuram.

Factors that Contributed to Large Scale Return

Developments in the Gulf region since 1980 brought about significant changes in the size and composition of flows of return migrants. The year 1996 was a turning point in the history of Indian migration to the Middle East. There was tightening of emigration laws in many of the Gulf countries.

The policies followed in the destination countries to reduce the size of foreign workers, to promote native workers in job placements, to reduce wage rates of expatriates and to impose strict restrictions on the immigration of expatriates resulted in the repatriation of a large number of immigrant workers. The fall in oil prices, recession and stiff competition from migrants belonging to other countries also caused the return of migrants on a significant scale.

MAJOR OBSTACLES TO DEVELOPMENT IN KERALA

The Kerala economy is Janus-faced; it is forward looking and developed in its social sectors. But it is backward-looking and stagnant in its materially productive sectors. The major obstacles to development in the state are to be evaluated in respect of each other as this affects the return migrants in a significant way.

Land and Agriculture

Kerala's is land-scarce economy. The average size of agricultural holding is about 0.30 hectares. Almost the entire cultivable area has been brought under cultivation. Even forest lands have been encroached upon for human settlement and cultivation. The proportion of forest lands has reportedly come down from 33.33% to 10%. Owing to the ever-increasing demand for land for non-agricultural uses, the area under cultivation is steadily on the decrease. The increase in the demand for land has raised land prices to a prohibitive level. This trend was reversed to some extent after 1996. Rice cultivation has become non-profitable. The reason is the high labour cost disproportionate to the value of the produce. So land is increasingly being shifted to perennial tree crops such as coconut, arecanut and rubber.

Capital, Technology and Entrepreneurship

Industrial investment and capital accumulation is low in Kerala, even by Indian standards. It is not the lack of resources which hinders investments in the state. The banking sector in Kerala has a surfeit of deposits compared to the demand for credit. The banks are of the view that adequate numbers of bankable projects are not received by them from entrepreneurs in the state. According to the banking circles in the state, the difficulties encountered by them in raising the credit-deposit ratio are:

(1) absence of proper industrial infrastructure and power supply
(2) problems in acquiring large areas of land in suitable locations at reasonable prices for setting up medium/large scale industries
(3) shifting of the traditional industries such as cashew and coir processing to tax and wage haven states in the neighbourhood

(4) sickness of industries and
(5) lack of entrepreneurial initiative in the state (Nair, P. R. Gopinathan, 1998).

These factors act as constraints in utilizing the skills and remittances of the returnees for the development of Kerala.

CONCLUSIONS

The three phases of international migration are identified as: the brain-drain of the 1950s and1960s to western countries like the UK, the USA and Canada; 'contract migration' to the Gulf region since the 1970s and the recent emigration of software professionals to developed countries since the second half of the 1990s. Following the oil price hike of 1973, Keralites began to emigrate in large numbers to the Middle East countries. This outflow of unskilled, semiskilled and skilled workers continued unabated till 1985. The leading districts of emigrants were Malappuram, Trissur and Thiruvananthapuram. Wayanad and Idukki were the lowest in the list of emigrants. Muslims constituted almost half of the emigrants. Kerala received large amount of remittances and this had its impact on the economy. With economic recession in the Gulf region in the second half of the 1980s, there was a return flow of emigrants to Kerala. The Kuwait war and subsequent wage cut and competition from low-paid workers from other Asian countries resulted in large scale return of migrants in the 1990s. About 16.5 lakh Keralites are now working in the Middle East countries, constituting about 89% of the total emigrants from Kerala. The remittances account to Rs. 24525 crores in 2007 which was about 21.6% of the Net State Domestic Product. Though there was a large inflow of remittances, it could not be effectively utilized for the development of the state. The industrial backwardness, lack of entrepreneurship initiatives, absence of industrial infrastructure and shortage of power, etc. acted as constraints in utilizing the skills acquired by the returnee emigrants.

REFERENCES

Department of Economics and Statistics (DES) (2000), '*Survey on Activity Status and Rehabilitation of Migrants from Kerala*', Thiruvananthapuram.

Government of Kerala (1987), *Report on the Utilization of Gulf Remittances in Kerala,* Directorate of Economics and Statistics, Thiruvananthapuram.

Government of Kerala (1994), *Report on Migration Survey, 1992-93,* Department of Economics and Statistics, Thiruvananthapuram.

Government of Kerala (2000), *Survey on Activity Status and Rehabilitation of Migrants from Kerala,* Directorate of Economics and Statistics, Thiruvananthapuram.

Govt. of India (2002), *Report on High Level Committee on the Indian Diaspora.*

Govt. of India (2007), *Kerala Development Report,* Planning Commission, New Delhi.

International Labour Organisation (ILO) (1989), *World Labour Report,* International Labour Office, Geneva.

Mathew, E.T. and Nair, P.R. Gopinathan (1978), Socio-Economic Charactristics of Emigration and Emigrants Households: A Case Study of Two Villages in Kerala, *Economic and Political Weekly,* Vol. 13, No. 28.

Nair, P. R. Gopinathan (1986), *Asian Migration to the Arab World: Migration from Kerala (India),* Centre for Development Studies, Thiruvananthapuram.

Nair, P.R. Gopinathan (1997), Return Migration, Rehabilitation and Development: Problems, Dilemmas and Options in Kerala, Paper presented at the *Regional Workshop on Return Migration and Long-term Economic Development in South Asia,* Islamabad, Pakistan, 26-29 May.

Nair, P. R. Gopinathan (1998), Dynamics of Emigration from Kerala: Factors, Trends, Patterns and Policies, in Appleyard, Reginald (ed.) *Emigration Dynamics in Developing Countries,* Vol. 2, South Asia, UNPFA/IOM, Ashgate Publishing Ltd., England.

Nair, P. R. Gopinathan (1998B), Releasing the Development of Potential of Return Migration, The Case of Kerala (India), *Paper Presented in the Technical Symposium on International Migration and the Development,* The Hague, Netherlands, 29 June-3 July.

Ogden, P. (1984), *Migration and Geographical Change,* Press Syndicate of the University of Cambridge, London.

Prakash, B. A. (1978), Impact of Foreign Remittances: A Case Study of Chavakkad Village in Kerala, *Economic and Political Weekly,* Vol. 16, No. 27.

Prakash, B. A. (1998), Gulf Migration and its Economic Impacts: The Kerala Experience, *Economic and Political Weekly*, Vol. 33, No. 50.

Usha, L. R. (2002), *Socio-Economic Transition of Return Emigrant Households: An Enquiry into Factors and Dimensions of Success and Failure* (Unpublished Ph.D thesis), University of Kerala, Thiruvananthapuram.

Weiner, Myron (1978), *Sons of the Soil*, Princeton University Press, Princeton, New Jersey, UK.

Zachariah, K. C., Mathew E.T. and S. Irudayarajan (1999), "Migration in Kerala State (India): Dimensions Determinants and Consequences", *Working Paper*, Centre for Development Studies, Thiruvananthapuram.

Zachariah, K. C. and S. Irudayarajan (2001), Migration Mosaic in Kerala: Trends and Determinants, *Demography India*, Vol. 30, No. 1.

Zachariah, K. C. and S. Irudayarajan (2004), "Emigration Moving into a Higher Orbit", *Passline*, Vol. 8 (7&8), August 15-31.

Zachariah, K. C. and S. Irudayarajan (2007), Migration, Remittances and Employment, *Working Paper* No. 395, Centre for Development Studies, Thiruvananthapuram.

13

TOURISM IN KERALA: PAST AND PRESENT

BAIJU K. C.

Tourism has become one of the largest and rapidly growing sectors of the world economy. Tourism does not have a unique base as an industry, but encompasses widely disparate firms and organizations from many industries which serve with a variety of incomes, tastes and objectives. The consumers, the suppliers and the government agencies are the major actors and elements that shape the tourism industry. The tourism industry employs 10.6%of the global work force, contributes 10.2% to world's GDP, generates tax revenues of $3.4 trillion gross output and accounts for 10.9% of all consumer's spending(Swain, 2006). It is reflected that the level of prosperity of the world has reached where leisure has been a key priority, (WTO, 1997).

TOURISM: MEANING AND SCOPE

The tourism concept dates back to about 4000 years ago, which speaks the truth for trade and travel. The Sumerian and Harappan civilization provide evidence about the nomad's trend of life. The world has become very small on account of the increased rate of nomadation of people from one country to another. The International Association of Scientific Experts in Tourism (AIEST) defined tourism in terms of: involvement in travel by non residents, stay of temporary nature in the area visited and stay not connected with any activity involving earnings. OECD Countries' definition. states that a foreign tourist is "any person visiting a country other than that in which he usually resides for a period of at least 24 hours" (Sharma;1996) Within the given explanations what one can conclude is that the movement is for the sake of pleasure, knowledge, meeting new people, visiting new places without any profit motive.

The importance of tourism was duly recognized in the OSARA Tourism meet-2001 as:

- Tourism is the greatest producer of world's gross domestic products and employment , accounting for one-tenth of each.
- The growth of international tourism contributes to the promotion of the mutual understanding among countries and people
- Tourism is an effective means of income redistribution between countries and thus contributes to a balanced de elopement of world economies.
- Tourism is essentially an act of being in touch with appreciating and learning from bountiful nature and foreign societies and cultures.
- The adverse effect of tourism is cited in the destruction of traditional cultures and life styles. And exploitation of vulnerable groups can lead to serious consequences.

The world tourism grows in its leaps and bounds as it envisages different concepts in different situations, locations and time. Different forms of tourisms live across the world. They are mass/circuit tourism, nature based tourism, eco-tourism, sustainable tourism, heritage tourism , health tourism, responsible tourism etc.

TOURISM–INDIAN SCENARIO

The National Tourism policy of 1982 gave new ethos and values to tourism in its purpose, direction and development. It aims "to promote tourism as a means to ensure a more meaningful and wider understanding of India and its people amongst all sections of the societies within the country and abroad and to achieve sustained economic development and positive social change through development of tourism while preserving and protecting the environment and heritage". The National Policy emphasized that by and large, the schemes to promote international tourism, will be mainly the responsibility of central sector and that of domestic tourism primarily of the state sector.

The Indian scenario presents some emerging trends in the tourist sector as a catalyst for its development. The contribution of tourism services in the GDP for 2002-03 is estimated 9.83% including its direct and indirect effect. (Approach paper XI F.Y.P). It is the third largest net earner of foreign exchange $6billion in 2005 and contributes to 8.27% of the total employment in the country. The Approach paper XI F.Y.P itself claims that there is potential to generate 27million additional jobs due to tourism. It states that India should tap fully benefit from natural, cultural, business, spiritual religious, ecological, adventure and medical tourism. In this context it is quite interesting and revealing to look into the past and present tourism scenario of Kerala, the most sought after tourist destinations in the world.

TOURISM IN KERALA: A HISTORICAL LEGACY

Kerala, known as 'God's own country' having beautiful hills, valleys, lakes, backwaters, lagoons, seashore associated with rich heritage of art, culture, indigenous medicines coupled with ideal climatic conditions creates a paradise for tourists (Economic Review, 2007). The historical tracking of this most popular upscale destinations connected with its trade relations with Greek and Roman traders, looking for its exotic spices, ever since 1st century BC (Pushpanath, 2004). Later, in 3rd century BC, relations had expanded with Egyptians, Phoenicians, Chinese and Babylonians. During the regime of Chera Empire, ie; 800AD to 1102AD, the local kings divided the state amongst themselves as the Zamorins of Calicut, the

Rajah of Cochin, the Kolathiris of Canannore and the King of Travancore.

The European rediscovery of the 'spice kinds' of Kerala through Vasco da Gama's voyage to Calicut in Kerala from Europe made a break through in the history of Kerala's trade and tourism connections with the rest of the world. The Dutch invasion in1663, helped them to establish supremacy over Cochin and Canannore and thereby their monopoly of trade with this region. The first trade agreement between East India Company and the Zamorin of Calicut was made in 1625 helped to open a British base in Malabar Region. However, the 17th century witnessed royal rivalries between Zamorin of Calicut and Raja of Cochin. By this time many major developments were initiated including construction of water ways for transportation under the rule of Raja Marthanda Varma, 1729-58. With the emergence of Madras Presidency in 1800, British control over royal kingdoms in Kerala became strong and led to the predominance of British monopoly in the princely states. After the decades of struggle India was pronounced independent in August 1947. The present state of Kerala was established in November, 1956 integrating the erstwhile princely states: Malabar, Cochin and Travancore.

EXPERIENCES OF KERALA IN TOURISM

The region of Kerala had a prolonged legacy of patronizing religions from ancient ages. Tourism in this region dates back to the past ages, mainly flourished through trade, religious and cultural movements. The cultural heritage of the people created a sense of 'athithi devo bhava' (treat the guest like God) and 'vasudhaiva kutumbakam' (the world is one family).

Buddhism, 200 B.C to 800 AD and Jainism 300BC to 500 AD fiourished in Kerala before the revival of Hinduism. Similarly India's first Christians, Muslims and Jews found a home here. Christianity reached Kerala when St. Thomas landed here in AD 52. Europeans' presence in Kerala can be well documented by the oldest European built St. Francis Church, 1503 AD. The Cheraman Juma Masjid in Kodungalloor, 629 AD, the oldest Mosque in the Indian sub continent, depicts the real pieces of art and represents deep rooted legacy of Islam faith as well. The Mattancherry Jewish Synagogue 1568 AD is the oldest in the Commonwealth. (Mohanlal, 2006) Its interior is one of the finest of any synagogue in the world. Beautifully decorated with Chinese hand-painted blue and differing slightly in design.

The Kerala region was a major player in India's trade glory in the past. It had a flourishing trade and travel with Phoenicians, Arabs, Egyptians, Greeks, Chinese. Muziris, the ancient port city, presently 'Kodungalloor, was one of the busiest in Asia and was known as "primum emporium Indiae"(Mohanlal, 2006) The well known spice route, the trade route to the Malabar costs for spices and other treasures is famous all over the world attracted tourists at large.

The Portuguese connection of Kerala also helped in flourishing trade and travel. Vasco da Gama was the first European to land in India arrived in Kerala in 1498. Cochin was the seat of Portuguese in India till 1530. This period gave wide spread influence on language, religion, cusain and gifted some architectural heritages like Pallippuram Fort, Muttancherry palace, St, Francis of Assissi Church etc.

MAJOR TOURIST ATTRACTIONS IN KERALA

Backwaters

It refers to the large inland lakes of Kerala, consisting of an entire net works of lakes, canals, estuaries and curious water formations. The back waters of Kerala stretch over 900 km of water world which constitutes the expansive back waters extending inland, right into the heart of beautiful green Kerala. It mainly covers four districts of the state namely Kollam, Alappuzha, Kottayam and Eranakulam. The largest back water body , the Vembanadu lake stretches through Alappuzha and Kottayam districts and opens out into the sea at Kochi port. The second largest back water stretch is the Ashtamudi lake in Kollam, hailed as the gate way to the majestic back waters of Kerala. The eight hour cruise from the magnificent Ashtamudi Lake to Alappuzha, the Venice of the East provides the longest and the most enchanting backwater experience to the tourists. Other major backwater spots in Kerala are Thiruvallam, Veli, Akkulam, Kappil, Kollam, Alumkadavu, Kuttanadu, Pathiramanal, Kumarakom, Kochi, Kozhikkodu-Valiaparamba and Kottappuram etc.

The traditional house boat of Kerala is the most enduring images of the backwaters. These are converted forms of the 'Kuttanadan kettuvallams'–a boat made by tying together pieces of wood. They were once the primary means of transporting cargo, mainly Kerala's staple crops of rice and coconut and even the mail and morning newspapers. Today these sturdy vessels have been converted into luxury house boats equipped with all modern amenities for the tourists. A cruise between Allappuzha and Kottayam would be an unforgettable experience to them. Back waters host many special events during the months of August/September. The electrifying races by carved wooden boats set the backwaters literally on fire. The 'Nehru Boat Race' is the most exciting of all the boat races. During the Onam festival season many boat races, including the spectacular Aranmula boat race are conducted in the Alappuzha region.

Beaches

Most of India's finest beaches are in Kerala. The entire 600 k.m length of Kerala coast is lined with sandy beaches, rocky promontories and coconut palms. Each year an impressive number of visitors arrive here in search of tranquil, palm fringed beaches. Along with the internationally renowned Kovalam beach, there exist at least thirty well reckoned beaches like Fort Kochi, Thankasseri, Nattika, Sanghumukam, Varkala, Payyoli, Kozhikkodu, Payyambalam, Beypore, Kappil, Ezhimala, Dharmadam, Thikkoti etc.

Kovalam, a sheltered natural bay is one of India's most spectacular beach resorts. It is located just 16k.m from Thiruvananthapuram, the capital city of Kerala. The unwinding miles of fine sanded beaches washed by the surf, which roars and hisses at the feet of the swishing palms. This sea side destination comprises three adjacent crescent-shaped beaches, of which the southern most, known as the light house beach is the most attractive spot.

Hill Stations

Lying on the windward side of Western Ghats, Kerala has a long chain of lush mist-clad hill stations that are home to exotic wild life. The hill resorts in Kerala offer the most magical experience of nature in all its virgin beauty. The high ranges of Kerala have some exotic spice plantations, cardamom, black pepper; cinnamon and ginger grow in abundance. Many higher destinations have mesmerizing greens of the tea estates and coffee plantations which could enthrall the tourists. A ride through the winding roads along rubber plantations, where the small and friendly towns form stopovers for a cup of steaming coffee or tea, gives an unforgettable experience to any traveller. The major hill stations of Kerala are: Ponmudi, Munnar, Vagamon, Nelliampathy.

Wild Life Sancturies

Kerala boasts of more than a dozen wild life sanctuaries. The Periyar Wild life Sanctury is one of the major wild life sanctuaries in India. Set amidst dense and evergreen forests, marshes and valleys, is the Parambikkulam sanctury which is home to the Bisons. The other important destinations are: Eravikulam National Park, Neyyar sanctuary, Peppara Wild life Sanctury, Senduruney wild life sanctuary, Idukki wild life sanctuary.

Performing Arts

Blessed as it is by nature and a vibrant people, Kerala also has a rich repertoire of music, dance and arts. Most of these are unique for the land and reflect the love for life of its people. The renowned Kathakali is considered to be a complete art form as it synthesizes all that is best in the fields of drama, music and dance. The folk dances, on the other hand, are reflections of rhythmic impulses. Both the art forms replicate the life of the sensitive people of this state. Like wise, 'Theyyam' in Kerala is a ritual dance form and one of the oldest forms of dances. Many tourists within and outside Kerala are being attracted by the performing art forms like koodiyattam, Mohiniattam, Krishnanattam, Ottanthullal etc.

Health Tourism

Kerala is treated as the abode of Ayurveda system of Health care. People all over the world express their curiosity and interest to this system of medicine. The term 'Ayurveda'- 'the knowledge of life' as it denotes, is not only a system to cure disease but a system teaching us how to achieve 'perfect health from disease or abnormal conditions' and how to maintain both physical and Mental health to enjoy the bliss of real life. It is reported that special Kerala treatments like 'pizhichil', ie; oil bath; 'ela kizhi'ie; leaf bundle massage, which are widely and effectively used in curing the chronic and severe ailment such as rheumatoid arthritis, facial palsy, motor neuron disease, peptic ulcers, various spinal problems etc. Kerala is the only place in the world where Ayurveda, the ancient form of science and the holistic system of medicine based on nature is practised to perfection. The state's equable climate, natural abundance of forests and the cool Monsoon season are best suited to Ayurveda's curative and restorative programme and thereon, in the promotion of health tourism.

Monuments

Kerala has an impressive array of historic and cultural monuments. In regions like Fort Kochi, which was the trade centre for centuries, the architecture is a typical Kerala, European, Chinese, Jewish and Arabic styles. But the most prevalent architectural style is the traditional Kerala style- 'nalukettu' or 'ettukettu'. The important monuments which remain as tourist destinations are Padmanabha Swamy Temple, Kuthira Malika Palace Museum, the Napier Museum, Padmanabhapuram Palace, Krishnapuram Palace, St. Francis Church, Santa Cruz Basilica, Mattanchery Palace, Mattancherry Synagogue, Bolgatty Palace, Hill Palace Museum, Vasco da Gama Square, Palakkad Fort, Thalassery Fort, Bekal Fort etc.

PERFORMANCE OF KERALA TOURISM

Over the decades, Kerala Tourism remains one of the strongest growth sectors of the region. The consistent and successful performance of Kerala tourism is quite evident as it continued to win world wide awards and recognitions. For instance, the state bagged five times 'Best Tourism State' award from the Government of India including the year 2006-07, Kerala was selected as the third best tourist destination in Asia by 'Smart Travel Asia' by one of the three finalists in International destinations in WTTCS "Tourism for Tomorrow Awards-2006, UNESCO Asia Pacific Heritage Awards for heritage conservation, 'Most Eco Friendly Destination' Award from Government of India-2003. (Economic Review, 2007).

The phenomenal growth of Kerala Tourism at a rate of 13.3% is quite visible as one looks into the growth rate of domestic and foreign tourist arrivals in this region. There is an increase of 23.7% in the number of foreign tourists arrived in Kerala in the year 2006. (See Table 1) the average annual growth rate of foreign tourist arrivals in Kerala from 1991 to 2006 is 25%. (Economic Review, 2007).

Table 1
Growth of Foreign and Domestic Tourists to Kerala (2002-2006)

Year	*Foreign tourists*	*% change*	*Domestic tourists*	*% change*	*Kerala's share in Indian Tourism (%)*
2002	232564	11.37	5568256	6.27	9.75
2003	294621	26.68	5871228	5.11	10.81
2004	345546	17.28	5972182	1.72	9.99
2005	346499	0.28	5946423	-0.43	8.85
2006	428534	23.68	6271724	5.47	9.67

Source: Department of Tourism-Kerala.

Among the districts in Kerala, Thiruvanathapuram and Eranakulam are continuing as the leading districts for the last few years on the basis of foreign tourists arrivals to Kerala. Whereas Eranakulam and Thrissur are the leading districts with regard to the domestic tourists arrival to Kerala (Economic Review, 2007).

ECONOMIC IMPACT OF TOURISM

Tourism becomes an economic tool for the development process of developing economies. Kerala, the regional economy always acclaimed the apparent development paradox- high human development and low economic development, successfully found an alternate development space in tourism in respect of generation of income and job opportunities. Growing at a rate of 13.31% the tourism industry becomes a major contributor to the state's economy. The direct and indirect economic benefits of tourism resulted in income multiplier effect for a tourist area. For instance, a cost benefit study of the Kovalam Beach Resort Project, one of the key tourist destinations in Kerala, the multiplier effect was found to be 2.5 (Sinha, 2006) It is found that foreign earning during the year 2006 is Rs. 1988.40 crore, which recorded a growth of 28.09% over the previous year. (See Table 2) Tourism contribution to State's Domestic Product is 7.7%. the total employment generated from tourism is around Rs. 10 lacs including skilled semi skilled and unskilled employmen (Economic Review-2007).

Table 2
Earnings from Tourism (2002-06) in crores

Year	*Foreign exchange earning*	*% change over previous year*	*Earning from domestic tourism*	*% change over previous year*	*Total revenue generated from tourism (direct & indirect)*	*% change over previous year*
2002	705.67	-	3011.31	-	4931	-
2003	983.37	39.36	3492.6	11.14	5938	20.42
2004	1266.77	28.81	3887.32	10.29	6829	15.00
2005	1552.31	22.55	4281.42	15.54	7738	13.31
2006	1988.40	28.09	4891.94	14.25	9126	17.93

Source: Dept. of Tourism, Kerala.

INFRASTRUCTURE DEVELOPMENT

Effective and efficient tourism sector requires proper infrastructure services. Facilities to enable the tourists to come to our shores, mountain resorts, game sanctuaries, and cultural monuments are to be created. A tourist needs a comfortable hotel to stay, dainty, delicious and choice food he is used to, and efficient and comfortable transport to take him around. Department of Tourism in Kerala has undertaken some steps in the following areas (Economic Review 2007):

- boat club at Thanneermukkam
- sarovaram project at Kozhikkode
- conservation of Kottuli wetlands at Kozhikkode
- implementation of first phase of responsible tourism at Kovalam Kumarakom, thekkady and wyanadu
- 'my village , tourism friendly village'-scheme launched to identify and develop unknown tourist destinations with participation of local bodies.
- schemes like 'wakeup to Malabar' , Vazhiyoram, farm tourism etc.
- international Convention centre at Trivandrum
- Bekal Tourism Project under BRDC.

Similarly DTPC activities involve improvement in hygiene at Tourist destinations, coordination of tourism clubs for creation of tourism awareness and preparation of host community, promotion of home, stay home, development of ports etc. the government is also offering various incentives to private sector for the development of infrastructure to facilitate the growth of tourism. *Eg*:- The joint ventures of tourist resort Kerala limited with taj and Oberoy hotel groups. Tourist accommodation remains the core sector of tourism industry. Kerala has to its credit 8510 rooms in classified hotels, the maximum number of rooms being three-star categories. (Economic Review 2007) KTDC actively participates in building up basic infrastructure needed for the development of tourism in the state.

NEW INITIATIVES AND POLICIES

Tourism has been granted industry status in 1986 Kerala tourism subsequently adopted the tag line "God's own country" in its advertisement campaigns. Aggressive promotion in print and electronic media were able to invite a sizable investment in the hospitality industry. Early 2000s' witnessed a plethora of innovative and market focused campaigns in Kerala tourism industry such as:

- -innovative, focused and sustained marketing select markets
- -a healthy private-public partnership-synergy which facilitates
- joint promotion and marketing initiatives between the tourism-trade and government
- -Conscious focus on the up market, quality conscious tourist vital in terns of sustaining and developing the destinations.
- -Aggressive media and PR (public relations)
- -Innovative promotion o fall expenses paid familiarization tours for trade
- -First state to initiate a dedicated investor guidance cell.
- -Brand building exercises with celebrities like M.F Hussain, Yusuf Arakkal and so on
- -First destination to resort to electronic media and the internet (www.kerala tourism.org.) aggressively for promotion.
- -New initiative for the promotion of Monsoon tourism
- -Kerala as the best health tourism destinations in the world.

ECO TOURISM IN KERALA

Tourism, the multi faceted industry was initially promoted as an industry with little problem. But later on, it was experienced that tourism is creating a variety of impacts on social cultural and environmental areas. Eco tourism emerged as one form of tourism that evolved as an option to minimize negative impacts due to tourism development and aimed at sustainability. Eco tourism is often considered to be a potential strategy to support conservation of natural ecosystems while at the same time, promoting sustainable development. The government of Kerala ensures that eco tourism is promoted on the basis of ecological sustainability and the guiding principles of eco tourism in Kerala are:

- to convert entire tourism industry in Kerala into eco-friendly mode
- to strengthen eco-tourism development initiatives in the state
- to ensure local community involvement in tourism initiatives leading to employment and income generation
- to create public awareness and involvement in responsible tourism development.

The state's eco tourism potential is exhaustive and has been used by the government to draw tourists to the state. The Western Ghats of Kerala with its tropical forest eco system provides a natural advantage for development of Eco Tourism. The state's major eco tourism resources are broadly classified as hill stations, forests and wild life sanctuaries where there is immense scope for a variety of eco tourism activities such as mountaineering, trekking, bird watching, etc.

THENMALA ECO TOURISM PROJECT

This is India's first planned eco Tourism destination inaugurated in 1999 with the commencement of boating in Shendurney Wild life Sanctuary reservoir and the Deer rehabilitation Centre. The second phase of the project was inaugurated during 2001 with the commencement of eco friendly general tourism activities involving Leisure Zone, Mass Tourism zone, Adventure Zone, Deep woods comprising of the 75 hectares of forest, environmental education activities, local community involvement, Biological diversity of the project area etc.

Number of tourists and the revenue generated out of the project are increasing over the years. (Economic Review, 2007) this project becomes a model to other segments of tourism to strengthen the scope for public–private and local community partner- ship in tourism and be a tool for sustainable livelihood and poverty alleviation for the fringe area communities of the protected area.

Another case of eco tourism eco tourism which upholds the biodiversity retention is the Kumbalangi village tourism. The Kumbalangi village offers the tourists with a unique island ecosystem , bird watching, special local cuisines , backwater cruise around islands, heritage structures, traditional local knowledge, study of mangrove conservation and rehabilitation. Thus, Kumbalangi is unique with its dynamic eco system, traditional crafts, ethnic touch, biodiversity, art and culture. What else we need to make this island an ideal locality for village tourism.

HUMAN RESOURCE DEVELOPMENT IN KERALA TOURISM SECTOR

Human resource development is of vital importance in a service industry like tourism. It is imperative to have a right selection, training and development of the personnel engaged in tourism services. Being service industry, the tremendous potential for employment to the vast cross section of the youth without any caste and religious bias can be generated in accommodation, hospitality and travel trade.(Swain, 2006) Successful human resource needs to identify skills, knowledge and attitude for their effective performance. The Kerala Institute of Travel and Tourism Studies (KITTS) established in 1988, caters to the man power requirement of the tourism industry by offering various courses in tourism, training programmes, seminars and publications on tourism in Kerala. KITTS developed various projects initiated for the development of human resources.

CHALLENGES AND ISSUES

Tourism in Kerala made tremendous strides since 1950's and this trend is expected to move on higher ladders. History cites tourism in Kerala had close association with limited areas such as trade, religions and cultural movements, whereas in due course it extended itself towards large spectrums assuming different forms in different situations, locations and time. However, the haphazard development of tourism has created unsavory impacts on the sector in many areas such as society, environment and culture. In addition, the basic infrastructure development of the region remains the main bottleneck. Some other national level challenges/issues like terrorism and violence, language barriers, diplomatic relations, lack of awareness, customs, immigration and health are also to be addressed. Too much effective emphasis is required to tap the employment and income potential of local tourism like better human resource management in man power planning , value addition , job specialization, multi-skill and multi-functioning, competencies in hospitality industry, off the job training, performance management system etc. Moreover, the regional economy has to make perspective planning in tourism in its employability and income potential at the global level.

Tourism has become the buzz word in the 21st century. It has lured today into a normal and dispensable consumer product due to higher income, increased leisure, extending mobility and higher standard of living. Kerala by virtue of its rich historical and cultural legacy, green nature and eco diversity, tourism becomes an ideal product to the region for its prospective income, employment and global recognition. The region's high quality of life becomes an added asset to its future prospect. With a clear perspective, efficient management of resources, active involvement of the private sector and local community, pro active support of the government and imaginative widening of the range of products, tourism industry in Kerala can make impressive strides in the years to come despite regional and global set backs.

REFERENCES

Swain, Sampad Kumar (2006), Human Resource Development in Tourism, New Delhi, Abhijeet Publications.

WTO(1997), Compendium of Tourism Statistics and Tourism Organization, Madrid, Spain.

Sharma, K. C. (1996), Tourism, Policy, Planning and Strategy Jaipur, Pointer Publishers.

Pushpanath, Salim (2004), Kerala Tourist's Handbook Kottayam, Dee Bee INFO Publications.

Govt. of India (2007), Approach Paper Five Year Plan X1: Planning Commission, New Delhi, India.

Mohanlal, K. G. (2000), *Experiences of Kerala in Eco / Tourism Initiatives* in "Issues and Trends in Eco Tourism Development in India" National Seminar Proceedings Organised by KITTS, Trivandrum.

Government of Kerala (2007), Economic Review, State Planning Board, Kerala, Trivandrum.

Sinha, P. C. (2003), Encyclopedia of Eco Tourism, Vol. 3, New Delhi, Anmol Publications.

Government of Kerala (2007), The Kerala Companion, Kerala Tourism Trivandrum.

Bhatt, Harish & Badan B. S. (2006), Sustainable Tourism, New Delhi, Crescent Publishing Corporation.

Eadington, William R. & Red-man, Milton (1991), Economics and Tourism, USA Perganson Press.

Bull, Adrian (1991) The Economics of Travel and Tourism, Melbourne: Longman.

kerala tourism.org-Tourist Statistics, (2006) *http//www. kerala tourism.org*

14

THE ENVIRONMENTAL STATUS OF KERALA

JOSE J. NADUTHOTTY

The economy environment interface is a well accepted fact in modern development economics[1]. This awareness has, however, not generated enough enthusiasm among policy makers inviting action towards protection of environmental resources. The degree of response has been better in MDC's, but not sufficient enough to cover the global issues such as warming and ozone hole." The quick and dirty rule seems to be that if you can't see it or smell it in your local urban neighborhood, then, no matter how rich you are, you aren't going to do much about it"[2].

Governments of the LDC's take cover behind the 'development' bandwagon and clamor for very long deadlines for implementing global agenda. There was no dearth of international efforts at breaking the deadlock but precious little has come out of them. Nations that account for the bulk of pollution are adamant in the virtual challenge of the 'differentiated responsibility' principle. The South nations, especially countries like China and India with healthy growth in recent past, are in no mood to strengthen their environmental control system (ECS), in the apprehension that such a step environmental problems. In Kerala's case the pertinent question to ask is whether it is doing enough to keep the house in order? Obviously, the State and non-governmental sector have to move hand in glove in containing problems and improving the situation. Being at the top in literacy among states for a long period, one would naturally expect the existence, in Kerala, of a vibrant people's movement for environmental protection. However, apart from assorted local initiatives, a consistently strong people's movement is sorely missing. As an observer has commented, "the present environmental consciousness in the state in terms of its ideational underpinnings is essentially heterogeneous. While some view it purely as an esthetic question some others perceive it from a cultural and religious perspective...they tend to underplay if not overlook the relation between man and nature"[6]. The moral of the story is that general literacy and environmental literacy are not directly related. The record of governments–left and right alike–in furthering the cause of a healthy environment is not at all enviable. It is the favorite past time of Kerala politicians, in general, to take a dig at environmental activists by branding them anti-developmental, anti-people and agents of the CIA, or some other conspirators from outside.

The situation, though, was much different in the past. Kerala boasts of a unique tradition that attached great importance to the preservation of environment in its various dimensions. The art, culture and architecture that developed in this part of India extolled the positive role that nature plays in furthering the welfare of the individual and society. It was a normal practice for families having large area of land, to use a portion of it to maintain a lush mini forest (Kavu or sacred groves), which played a major role in maintaining the ecological system of the adjoining area by being an abode for numerous endemic species of plants and animals and by helping to recharge the water sources of the locality.[7] While there were thousands of such kaavu at the turn of the 20th century, at the start of the new millennium their number dwindled to just 175. This is a true indication of the changing scenario of environmental 'priority' of Keralites in general.

As it happened elsewhere, the urge for economic growth, in the post- independence period- has overshadowed the desire for a healthy environment, in the case of Kerala too. The first two decades of the above period witnessed extension of farming to hitherto uncultivated areas through felling of virgin forests, a process which was 'justified' by mainstream political parties and major social groups alike as a 'natural reaction' to the severe food shortage that prevailed at that period. However the process continued unabated even after the attainment of relative food security (in terms of purchasing power) .Such brazen violation of law would not have taken place without the connivance of influential political parties, which occupied commanding position in the coalition arrangement that set up successive governments. Administrators had to bow to the demand for legitimizing encroachments from time to time. The Government at crucial junctures looked the other way when concerned environmental groups warned of the serious environmental repercussions of its actions. On numerous occasions the government had to suffer the ignominy of being at the receiving end of strictures of the judiciary in litigations involving violations of environmental regulations by its departments.

However, it may be an exaggeration to state that Kerala has already reached a crisis point with respect to the health of the environment. Yet there are clear indications of deterioration in environmental quality. We shall discuss the present state environment of Kerala state with special reference to: (a) Industrial growth, (b) Land use pattern, (c) Agricultural practices, (d) Deforestation, and (e) Pollution.

INDUSTRIAL GROWTH AND ENVIRONMENT

The low profile of the industrial sector in the state's economy, a major cause of its economic backwardness, is a blessing in disguise as far as environment is concerned. Lately, there is a perceptible enthusiasm, at the government level, to push up industrial growth so as to close the gap in growth between

Kerala and other states. [8]This would require a rate of growth exceeding 10 per cent per annum whereas the current level is below 4 per cent. [9]A scenario where industry grows at more than double the present rate, if realized, does not auger well for the environment if the process takes place in the business-as-usual mode. The record of the state's industry with respect to environmental upkeep is not at all enviable. Giving a candid account of the lethargic approach of Industry to environmental issues, the government funded Kerala State Council for Environment and Development, in it's latest report on environmental state, notes the following: of a total of 117 industries, which were approached for information on their environmental management practices only 34 (merely 29%) were willing to provide any data. Those who responded failed to answer all questions. Only 26 per cent of this group had an environmental policy department. Environmental benchmarking was practiced only in case of 41 per cent of the respondents. Among public sector concerns, in only 29 per cent cases, environmental matters were reported direct to the MD/CEO.[10] In the rest, 3rd or 4th rung officials with little power looked after this crucial portfolio.

A glance at the 'industry category' list of Kerala reveals that nearly 43% belongs to the highly polluting type.[11] Available industries are not evenly distributed. The concentration of industries in some pockets is a factor that raises the potential for pollution. About 35 per cent of all large and medium industries are situated in the Ernakulam Dt.[12] and naturally, Kochi reports maximum level of air pollution. The first major people's uprising, in Kerala, for the environment that took place in 1972 was related to the growing pollution in the Kochi- Kalamassery industrial belt. In the 1980's there was a concerted action by masses led by the Kerala Sastra Sahitya Parishad to force the eventual close down of the Grasim Industries that polluted the Chaliyar River. The firm's activity involved processing of 18 million tons of timber per annum for which it drew from the river 6800 cu. mtr of water every day. "The enormous discharge of untreated effluents,...was a source of untold misery to the people living in the adjoining basin"[13]. The latest in the list of such environmental activism is the fight against the Hindustan Cococola's plant at Plachimada in the Palghat Dt. Though the Perumatty Panchayath, in which the plant is situated, was officially declared one of the four water scarce Panchayaths in Palghat, [14]the unit was allowed to draw one million liters of groundwater per day. Within a short span of time water table in the adjoining area began to recede. Scientific study of water samples showed carcinogenic waste contamination and excess salinity, in open wells in the two km radius of the soft drink plant[15]. Environmental activists could inspire the local people, including tribals, to put up a stiff resistance to further exploitation of remaining ground water. The issue was brought to the attention of courts and, at least for the time being, people-power has the advantage. Production has been temporally suspended under court order.

Unorganized mining in various parts of the state causes considerable land and air pollution. Though the mining industry of Kerala is not very large in size, its activity is not properly monitored and controlled resulting in indiscriminate mining without considering the environmental repercussions.[16] Unauthorized and unorganized clay mining for brick making, and sand mining for construction activities have serious implications. According to a recent estimate, excessive rate of sand mining results in the lowering of river beds by 11 c.m. on the average per annum. In case of the larger rivers, the problem is most acute in Periyar (18 cm p.a.) and Pampa (15 cm p.a.).[17] The process destroys many micro organisms living in the river bed besides leading to a lowering of the water table.

IMPACT OF CHANGING LAND USE PATTERN

Kerala supports 3.1 per cent of India's population with just 1.18 per cent of the nation's land area. In response to population pressure, life style changes and changes in agricultural practices, the pattern of land use has changed to a notable extent. Such changes, by and large, have added to the problems facing the environment. The table given below summarizes the transformation in land use.

Table 1
Changing Land Use Pattern in Kerala

Category	*1975-1976*	*1980-1981*	*1990-1991*	*2000-2001*	*2003-2004*
Net sown area	56.34%	56.1%	57.83%	56.74%	56.45 %
Forest	27.84%	27.84%	27.83%	27.83%	27.83 %
Land used for non-agricultural purposes	6.67%	6.94%	7.65%	9.70%	9.98 %
Barren and uncultivated area	2.02%	2.21%	1.50%	0.77%	0.76 %
Others	7.13%	6.91%	5.19%	4.96%	4.98 %

Source: Planning Commission (2008), Kerala Development Report, Tab 1.1, p. 49, (adapted).

A cursory glance at the table brings out some pertinent information which is highly relevant for our discussion. The state has one of the largest proportions of area devoted to non-agricultural use, and it grew over the years: from 6.67 per cent of total geographical area in 1975-76 to 9.98 in 2003-04. Relatively higher size of service sector–close to 65 per cent in 2003-04- which demand large built up area to house required facilities and the peculiar type of urbanization that took place–large number of small towns-explain the disproportionate extent of land used for non-agricultural use. What is relevant for our discussion is that land for such development was often generated through filling of wet lands, modification of slopes and leveling of hills- all having some adverse environmental effects.[18] The large scale soil erosion witnessed in Kerala is another land-related issue which has considerable environmental implications. Certain peculiar features of geography, unscientific changes in land use and defective farming practices explain the enormity of the problem. An estimated 15-20 tons of top soil is lost in erosion on average plots every year, which render land less fertile.[19] Soil erosion impacts on environment indirectly, by impoverishing farmers and forcing them to live at the expense of nature. Besides, it has got a significant role in air and water pollution. Also, it restricts water availability by silting up of reservoirs, and reducing their storage potential by two per cent per annum.[20]

SHIFT IN AGRICULTURAL PRACTICES AND ENVIRONMENT

When we turn to the trends in cultivation and cropping pattern a few things attract attention. First, the long term decline in area available per head and diversion of more land for non-agricultural purposes. Between 1901 and 2001, land area per head declined from 0.61 ha to 0.12 ha. This forced farmers to resort to intensive farming resulting in a secular rise in cropping intensity (estimated recently to be 140 %).[21] As per well accepted norms, in case of most of the small and medium farms of Kerala, cropping intensity is excessive. The 2008 edition of the World Development Report explains how 'high intensity cultivation' can harm environment:" in intensive cropping systems, the excessive and inappropriate use of agrochemicals pollutes waterways, poisons people, and upsets ecosystems."[22]

The second disturbing trend is the shift from food crops to cash crops which not only endangered food security but also harmed environmental health. Between 1980-81 and 2000-01, area under rice and tapioca declined by 58% and 57% respectively. In the same period area devoted to rubber went up by nearly 93%[23]. Most other cash crops also gained in area. With cash crops the system of monoculture gained acceptance, at the cost of the rich biodiversity of the respective areas. Several native species of trees that occupied farmlands in the rubber growing areas have almost disappeared since subsidy to cultivators, distributed by the Rubber Board, was made conditional to cutting down of other trees. Farmers reacted by cutting down 'uneconomic' species.

A third undesirable development was the shift of agriculture from short maturity crops to perennial crops. There were some environmental trade off's when farmers shifted from annual crops to perennial crops-a tendency which has been quite notable in Kerala from 1970's onwards. This was the era of so called gulf-boom in migration. Migration predominantly involved male members of cultivator families and obviously the lower labor demand of perennial crops was an attraction. Added to this was the relative shortage of casual workers and consequent rise in their wages. In response to such developments, farmers increasingly moved away from crops like rice that demand constant attention to others like rubber, which can be looked after without the help of substantial number of hired labor. But this process had its downside. The cultivation of perennial crops- tea and coffee in particular under plantation system- involved clearing of other species of plants. The tea plantations in the past displaced the unique southern west temperate forests of the shoals of Western Ghats, which contained "several endemic and phytogeographically important species like Rhododendrons".[24] Besides, raising of tree crops such as rubber and teak dried up local water sources.

Further, cultivation of plantation crops involved heavy application of diverse kind of pesticides and insecticides- which have to be sprayed from considerable height by pumps or helicopters-leading to sharp increase in pollution of various sort, raising the mortality and morbidity rates in the nearby areas. The fact is that no one in the area can really protect his family, land, water sources etc against the side effects of aerial spraying. Thousands of people in the Kannur district have fallen prey to the highly poisonous pesticide endosulfan, over a period of about 30 years. What is particularly disturbing, in this case, is that it was the state-owned Kerala Plantation Corporation that engaged in spraying of this pesticide, which is a banned item in most developed countries, in its plantation extending 450 hectares. By the time public outcry became audible, the irresponsible act caused the death of hundreds of people and widespread incidence of physical deformities (among new born) and disorders of the nervous system. Only after a prolonged legal battle did the state consent to pay a paltry sum of Rs. 50000 each to the next of kin of 135 victims who died.[25] Excess trace of copper was detected in portions of Manimalayar, which has been attributed to frequent spraying of copper sulphate in rubber plantations lining the river in the Kottayam district.[26]

Though Kerala is yet to witness a genuine green revolution, the chemical intensive farming popularized by the central government, since mid-1960's, has been adopted by farmers of the state. They widely use chemicals in the form of fertilizers and pesticides. The practice of rearing cattle has ceased in many farm households which foreclosed the option of environment-friendly organic farming. Subsequently the application of chemical fertilizers increased substantially which led to higher levels of land and water pollution. The instability of prices for agricultural products led to much disenchantment among cultivators–particularly those raising commercial crops-resulting in inadequate maintenance of land and farmer suicides.[27] The remittance from NRI's had a rather negative effect on upkeep of land quality. Their families know that they have an alternative to fall back upon in case of reverses from cultivation. Agricultural failures did not cut the supply lines and one could afford to be lethargic.

DEFORESTATION

The exact proportion of area under forest in Kerala is a debated subject. Official data adds to one's confusion. As per forest survey of India, Kerala had a forest area of 15577 sq. km in 2002. According to forest survey of Kerala, done in 2003-04, there was just 11266 sq.km of forests.[28] It does not make sense to assume that in a single year there was a 27% fall in area under forest. Difference in methodology may explain the gap. Another source put the total at 9561 sq km, which includes 1862 sq km of plantations.[29] Yet another account is that over a 40 year period from 1960-61, the extent of forests declined from 27.35% of land area to 22%.[30] A disturbing fact about available forest area is that most of it is in a degraded condition. Nandakumar has calculated the extent of degradation to be as high as 62 per cent. Of the different sub groups, moist deciduous forests are degraded to the extent of 78 per cent.[31] In another recent evaluation of forest quality, Sathish Chandra found that 'the actual forest area that sustains forest biodiversity and functioning of forest ecosystem is only less than 8% of the total area.[32]

Various causes can be pointed out for declining forest cover and forest degradation. We have referred earlier to the migration of cultivators to forest land in an attempt to expand food production. No serious attempt was made by the government to curb this undesirable tendency. Second in the list of causes is the commissioning of several hydro-eclectic projects in and around forests. The proposal to construct a dam in the environmentally sensitive Silent Valley forest, with large number of rare and endangered species, was shelved in 1980 under all round protest including that of inter national environmental activists. The extent of evergreen forest saved in the process was 830 ha. A watered down scheme was mooted a few years back by the KSEB in the form of the Pathrakkadavu Hydroelectric Project, across the Kunthipuzha, at a spot just on the boundary of Silent Valley National Park, which once again brought the environmental activists on the war path.[33] A few wood based industrial units in the state were permitted to collect forest produce at rock bottom prices which led to an excess demand situation. The changes in weather pattern over the geographical area of the state also played a role. In recent years the state had to cope with abrupt changes in weather, which is attributed to global warming [34] and changes in land use pattern in the state, particularly the contraction in forest cover.

The adverse impacts of deforestation are well known. It can trigger undesirable changes in the pattern of rainfall and cause a secular rise in temperature. Mean maximum temperature in majority of observation stations of Kerala has risen by about one degree celsius in 9 years from 1994. There was considerable variation in average monthly rainfall too.[35] The rise in temperature is said to have played a role in the increased occurrence, in recent years, of some diseases in Kerala. Problems related to air pollution turn more acute with a reduction in tree cover, as plants absorb carbon dioxide in sizable quantity. Perhaps the most worrisome outcome of deforestation is the extinction/reduction of large number of species of different kinds. The ICUN Red List for 2004 gave the following figures regarding flora and fauna of Kerala.

Table 2
Threat to Biodiversity.

Category	*Extinct*	*Endangered*	*Vulnerable*
Flora	3	68	48
Fauna	1	24	48

Source: KSCST, State of Environment Report-2007, Tab. 1.16, p. 21, (adapted)

POLLUTION RECORD

The extent of pollution is widely regarded as a proxy for overall environmental quality of a country or region. Space constraint does not permit a detailed consideration of all kinds of pollution. We will concentrate on pollution of air and water. A brief mention is made of problems of inadequate disposal of waste.

(i) *Water pollution:* Kerala which was once a water rich territory is currently having a deficit situation with respect to this vital ingredient of life. While total demand is estimated at 49.7 billion cubic meters (BCM), utilizable supply is only 42 BCM.[36] Under such condition people are forced to depend on insecure sources like ponds for drinking purpose. Majority of rivers, lakes and ponds suffer from serious levels of pollution. A recent paper on land and water management in Kerala makes the startling revelation that "there are river sections which do not support living organisms".[37] Reference was made earlier to high rate of soil erosion. Such soil, mostly from farms, where chemical intensive cultivation is practiced, transports poisonous or otherwise dangerous elements into water streams. No area in the state is more affected than Kuttanad, famous for its rice fields that lie below sea level. According to reports, "the concentration of cadmium, iron, manganese, nickel, lead, zinc, chromium and copper in water in kuttanad region... indicates heavy metal pollution"[38] In spite of agricultural growth being very small, there was an increase of nearly 11 per cent in fertilizer use between 2000-01 and 2003-04.[39] Pollution has seeped down to ground water sources in many places. Kerala Development Report-2008, of the Planning commission, traces the causes for this serious situation: "over exploitation of ground water, deep infiltration of surface water from irrigated fields using chemical fertilizers and pesticides, infiltration of saline soils and effluents from industries affect the quality of ground water".[40] A number of cases have been reported of industries callously violating regulations banning the pumping of effluents in to water bodies. The Hindustan Insecticides Ltd, for eg., lets out about 100 chemical compounds to nearby river; none of which are found in upstream sections in detectable concentration.[41] After agriculture and industry it is the inflow of municipal waste that accounts for water pollution. Inadequate collection of waste and unsafe disposal-land fill being the widespread practice-adds to water pollution.

Air Pollution

Though most parts of Kerala are free of serious air pollution, larger cities are exceptions. As it is true with the country in general, the exponential growth in automobile population is the dominant cause for air pollution. The following table gives the number and growth rate of motor cars and two wheelers in Kerala (1970-2003).

Table 3
Growth in Automobile Population

Type	*1970*	*1993*	*2003*	*Rate of growth 2003 Over 1970*
Motor car	33294	205564	336583	911%
Two wheelers	15117	369000	1450407	9495%

Source: Sooryanarayanamurthy (1997), p. 117, KSCSTE (2005), p. 323.

The total number of registered vehicles was 25.53 lakh in 2003. About 10.8% of this consisted of heavy vehicles that consume large quantity of diesel, the pollution potential of which is higher than that of petrol. Two and three wheelers, which also emit high amount of pollution, formed 68%. In the absence of any regulation that enforce the use of less polluting CNG, as in the case of Delhi, buses and other goods vehicles in Kerala run on diesel. Perhaps the larger part of the air pollution may be attributed to inadequate expansion in road net work. As against an estimated 2000 per cent rise in total number of vehicles on the roads, increase in road length was a paltry 44 per cent in the period 1975 to 2002.[42] On the one hand land is extremely scarce and costly; in the peculiar geographical condition of Kerala, road development is very expensive; added to these, the financial condition of the state was never comfortable for massive investment in roads. The BOT model, which the neighboring states adopted liberally in road development–which in turn necessitates collection of toll-does not find favor with the left parties. It is a well accepted fact that traffic under congested condition lets out multiple times emission than otherwise. No wonder that all the tree major cities-Thiruvananthapuram, Kochi and Kozhikode have severe air and noise pollution from automobiles.

The second major cause of air pollution is industrial activity. Absence of substantial number of large industries has inadvertently helped Kerala to keep air pollution down. But a more equitable distribution of industries would have been ideal. No serious study has been done on indoor air pollution, specific to Kerala as a whole, so that exact account of this component of air pollution is not available. Yet there are some facts that suggest the presence of the problem in considerable magnitude. Fuel wood is the widely used medium for cooking. While the ratio of fuel wood- user households to LPG-user ones is three for the nation as a whole, it is higher at 4.37 for Kerala[43] indicating higher levels of indoor air pollution from cooking.

Studies on ambient air quality have been conducted in selected locations of Kerala, the results of which do not suggest an alarming state. Highlights of one study conducted in the three largest cities of the state are available in table 1.3. Presence of Sulphur Dioxide (SO2), Oxides of Nitrogen (NOx) and Suspended Particulate Matter (SPM) and Respirable Particulate Matter (RSPM) in the air (μg/m3) was studied for the period August 2003 to March, 2004. Minimum and maximum values for 24 hour periods were noted. We show below the percentage of *maximum values* to permissible 24 hour limit, for each of the above mentioned items.

Table 4
Maximum Value of Pollutants to Permissible Limits (Per cent)

Pollutant	*Thiruvananthapuram*	*Kochi*	*Kozhikode*
SO2	18.2%	34.1%	05.9%
NOX	41.6%	35.2%	46.3%
RSPM	197%	122%	119.3%
SPM	103%	93%	84.0%

Source: KCSTE (2005), Tab. 6.5, p. 329, (adapted).

Of the four pollutants, RSPM, at maximum points, is excessive in all three cities. Its value is in danger zone in state capital. On 58 occasions in the survey period, RSPM value was found at higher levels than that prescribed. SPM value also was above norms in the city.

POLLUTION FROM WASTE

Kerala has certain unique features leading to large scale generation of waste. Urban population increased 18 times in the last 100 years.[44]There are hundreds of small towns. Over 10 lakh migrant labor work in Kerala, most of whom do not posses proper housing facility. They generally spend night in makeshift facilities or simply sleep on premises of business establishments. Lacking publicly provided sanitation facilities they defecate in the open. Another significant factor is the spread of consumerism, which, in Kerala's case, is not limited to the rich alone. Propped up by remittances from family members working abroad, households are accumulating consumer durables and non durables in large quantities. Kerala which accounts for 3.1 per cent of India's population has over 10 per cent share in the country's aggregate consumption. Last three decades saw phenomenal growth in consumption. Kerala was ranked 8th in aggregate consumption, among all states in 1972-73; her rank 'improved' to *one* in 1999-2000.[45]Throw-away consumption culture has taken root, something which can be gauged by a cursory look in the premises of conference halls and eateries. While traditionally food in Kerala households, on auspicious occasions, was served on pieces of plantain leaves, it is now served in disposable paper plates or sometimes in *'plastic plantain leaves'*! In spite of several rounds of banning plastic carry bags, the waste piles of cities and towns contain huge quantities of the stuff. The new found enthusiasm to promote tourism, under present dispensation can only aggravate waste pollution. "The proportion of tourist arrivals in Kerala to total tourist arrivals in India increased from 2.7 per cent in 1980 to nearly 10% in 2002"[46]. Last few years witnessed further 'gains', which may turn out to be a loss in environmental terms if proper monitoring of the process is not ensured.

In addition to waste generated by routine civilian life, more dangerous wastes from industry and numerous hospitals in the state are also often carelessly thrown around. About 423 industrial units are generating and handling hazardous waste and the total quantity of hazardous waste involved was about 82724 ton in 2005.[47] The coir industry generates about 500 tons/day of waste, 29% of which is of hazardous nature as production involves dyeing and bleaching.[48] Waste disposal facilities in hundreds of small industrial units are inadequate. There are a number of units producing electrical and electronic items which generate highly poisonous waste. The large net work of hospitals in the state (28% of all India total) is poised for further expansion under the banner of medical tourism. Total waste presently generated per bed is estimated to be 1.3-2 kg/day, which makes an aggregate load of 1.5 lakh Kg every day. 15 to 20% of such waste is highly dangerous type of biomedical waste.[49] Even government run medical colleges lack sufficient number of incinerators, which are vital for safe disposal of biomedical waste. Condition in the rest of government sector is deplorable.

The record of local government bodies on waste collection as well as its safe disposal is not enviable. There are 5 municipal corporations, 53 municipal towns and 991 grama panchayaths in Kerala. They together face the challenge of safely disposing 60000 tons/d of municipal solid garbage. Chronically in financial trouble, local bodies do not succeed in removing a sizable part of garbage. What is collected is typically dumped in land fill sites, often close to residential areas. This is followed by contamination of land and water in the vicinity- and acrimony between people and local body. In a bid to improve waste collection and disposal, the govt of Kerala, has lately come forward with the *Clean Kerala Mission*. Emphasis is given to imparting technical training to the staff of local bodies in modern methods of waste disposal. Services of the members of the Kudumbasree are enlisted in house to house collection and transportation of waste.

The degree of mortality and morbidity is widely used as a proxy of environmental quality in the sense that, should the quality deteriorate both of them shall rise. Though Kerala has the minimum mortality in India, morbidity rate is the highest among states. Number of persons per thousand reporting ill in rural Kerala is 118 while the average for the four least developed BIMARU states is only 41.5; for urban areas the respective figures are 88 and 46.[50] Increased literacy and resultant health awareness may explain part of the gap, but the other part of the problem has to be explained in terms of unhealthy environment. Per capita spending on health care (outpatient-rural) in Kerala is 3.2 times that of national average.[51]

We may conclude that the environmental problems of Kerala are, on the whole, within manageable limits. However there is the absence of an efficient environmental management system. Perhaps more serious issue is the absence of urgency on the part of the government to deal with environmental issues in a proactive way. There is a dearth of relevant information on critical aspects. This, perhaps explains why, none of the currently available volumes on Kerala economy, have an exclusive chapter devoted to environment. One may explain away this lacuna by saying that environment is everywhere so that there is no need of a special chapter. But that would amount to repudiating well accepted principles of sustainable development and going against the current trend in Development Economics. When environment is made a mere appendix of production and consumption system, no one will seriously take into account the repercussions of his action on environment. It is very important to place environment at the proper place–the very center.

NOTES AND REFERENCES

1. Baumol, W.J. and W.E. Oates (1979), Environmental Policy and Quality of Life, Prentice Hall, New Jercy.
2. *www.economistview.typepad.com/economistview*
3. Meier G. M. and Rauch (2000), Leading Issues in Economic Development(ed.7), Oxford University Press, New York.
4. Richmond, Amy *et. al.* (undated), "Environmental Kuznets Curve", in, *www.eoearth.org/article/Environmental* Kuznets curve.

5. Naduthotty, Jose (1998), "Cost of Environmental Controls: Evidence from the Past", IASSI Quarterly, July-September, pp. 1-11.
6. *www.economistview, opp.cit*
7. Sreedharan, K. (1996), "Environmental conscience in Kerala", in. Institute of Social Sciences, Abstract of the International Conference on Kerala Development Experience, ISS, N. Delhi, p. 125.
8. *www.travellerskerala.com/newsletter/ethnic/june2003*
9. Planning Commission (2008), Kerala Development Report, GoI, New Delhi, p. 173.
10. *Ibid*, p. 178.
11. KSCSTE (Kerala State Council for Science, Technology and Environment), (2007): State of Environment Report-2007, Volume III, KSCSTE, Trivandrum, p. 9.
12. Planning Commission, *opp. cit.*, Table 6.16, p. 181.
13. *Ibid*, p. 37.
14. Sreedharan, K., *opp.cit*, p. 124.
15. *www.indiatogether.org/2006/jan/env-cokesaga.htm*
16. *www.vakindia.org/Kerala.htm*
17. KSCSTE (2007), *opp.cit*, Volume I, p. 29.
18. *Ibid*, p. 34.
19. KSCSTE (2007), *opp.cit*, Volume I, p. 17.
20. *Ibid*, p. 44.
21. *Ibid*, p. 44.
22. *Ibid*, p. 18.
23. World Bank (2007), World Development Report-2008, WB, Washington DC.
24. Jeromi, P. D. (2007), "What Ails Kerala Economy-A Sectoral Exploration", in, R. Sathyamoorthy (ed.), Kerala Economy-Achievements and Challenges, ICFAI University Press, Hydrabad, Table 4, p. 28.
25. KSCSTE (2005), State of Environment Report-Kerala 2005, KSCSTE, Trivandrum, p. 221.
26. *www.indiatogether.org/2008/feb/rlf.endosulf*
27. KSCSTE (2007), *opp.cit*, Volume I, p. 70.
28. D. Narasimha Reddy (2008), "Crisis in Agriculture and Rural Distress in Post Reform India", in. R. Radhakrishna (ed.), India

Development Report-2008, Oxford University Press, New Delhi, pp. 47-49

29. KSCSTE (2007) *opp.cit*, Volume IV, p. 7.
30. KSCSTE (2005), *opp.cit.*, p. 233.
31. M. Mohandas (2005), "Agricultural Development in Kerala", in, Rajasenan, D. & G. D. Groot (eds.), Kerala Economy, CUSAT, Kochi, P.
32. Nandakumar, Quoted in , KSCSTE (2005), *opp.cit.*, p. 237.
33. Satheesh Chandra, Quoted in, KSCSTE (2007), Volume I, p. 19.
34. *www.indiatogether.org/july/2004*
35. *www.thehindubusinessline.com/2005/3/08/stories.*
36. KSCSTE (2005), *opp.cit.*, pp. 17-19.
37. Planning Commission, *opp.cit.*, p. 50.
38. Chattopadhyay (1996), "Land and Water Management in Kerala", in. Institute of Social Science (ed.), Abstract of the International Conference on Kerala Development Experience, ISS, New Delhi, p. 128.
39. KSCSTE (2007), Volume I, p. 70.
40. *Ibid.*, p. 25.
41. Planning Commission, *opp.cit.*, p. 50.
42. KSCSTE (2007), *opp.cit*, Volume I, p. 70.
43. KSCSTE (2005), *opp.cit.*, 322.
44. *www.censusindia.gov.in/Census-Data-2001/*
45. KSCSTE (2007), *opp.cit.*, Volume I, p. 18.
46. Oommen, M. A. (2006), "Is Kerala Changing from Crisis to Turn Around", in. R. Sathyamoorthy (ed.), Kerala Economy-Achievements and Challenges, ICFAI University Press, Hydrabad, p. 375.
47. Planning Commission, *opp.cit.*, p. 46.
48. KSCSTE (2005), *opp.cit.*, 335-336.
49. *Ibid.*, p. 340.
50. *Ibid.*, p. 337.
51. Planning Commission, *opp.cit.*, p. 302.
52. *Ibid.*, p. 317.

INDEX

F

Q & R

T